PRAISE FOR *WORDS OF WITNESS*

It is certainly regrettable that the great writer Elie Wiesel was awarded the Nobel Peace Prize instead of the Nobel Prize for Literature. But even if the writer is perhaps better known for his struggle to preserve the memory of the Holocaust than for his works, this Nobel Peace Prize also testifies to the ability of literature to have an impact on our world.

Léonard Rosmarin's book pays tribute to the power of this work, inviting us to discover or rediscover it with a new perspective. This work is the first to consider all of Wiesel's fictional texts, examining them in the light of his very first text, *Night*, a testimony to his experience in the Auschwitz camp, which led him to adopt French as the language of his writing and to become a writer.

In five short, hard-hitting chapters, Léonard Rosmarin takes the reader through this rich and dense body of work, in which Judaism, from the bible to the Talmud, plays a key role. He takes the reader from the darkness of the night of the camps to the light of a modern, secularized messianism that gives substance to the universalis ethic of a man nourished by Jewish culture.

Léonard Rosmarin is to be highly commended for his exceptional work, which combines discreet and skillful scholarship with great analytical insight. His text is brimming with intelligence and, because it is so easy to read, will appeal both to readers who know Wiesel's work and to those who wish to discover it.

> — Maxime Decout, Professor of Contemporary French Literature, Université de la Sorbonne, and author of *Faire trace: Les écritures de la Shoah* (Éditions Corti, 2023)

From the darkness of hell to the light of celebrity, Léonard Rosmarin invites the reader to embark on an extraordinary journey through the experiences of the eminent writer Elie Wiesel. Rosmarin deftly navigates Wiesel's texts, transforming them from fictional narratives into historical metaphors, and from lived experiences into whimsical tales. This intricate dance is intertwined with Wiesel's own life, marked by the curse of the Holocaust and his encounters with pivotal events of the twentieth century.

With great sensitivity, Rosmarin addresses the profound challenges Wiesel faced in his mission to convey both a vanished world and the horrors he survived. Rosmarin illuminates the depths of Wiesel's literary genius and the enduring impact of his experiences.

> — Sylvie Anne Goldberg, internationally recognized
> historian of Jewish civilization, former Director of the
> Center for Jewish Studies at the École des hautes études en
> sciences sociales, Paris, and Editor in Chief of the acclaimed
> *Histoire juive de la France* (Les Éditions Albin-Michel, 2023)

Léonard Rosmarin is today one of the finest connoisseurs of Elie Wiesel's oeuvre and, since the latter's death, one of the rare ones as well. His book is more than just important, it is indispensable since too few young adults, whether in North America or elsewhere, still read Elie Wiesel's texts. Now, with our own world tottering at the edge of the abyss, the vision of a scholar such as Léonard, equally at home in several languages and cultures, is urgent.

His critical assessment full of depth, gravity but also of a humor tinged with the irony inherited from the Yiddish language, offers us a new approach to Wiesel's novels.

He and I both share a special fondness for three among the most neglected of Elie's novels, *Day*, *Twilight*, and *The Time of the Uprooted*. In the latter, the heroine is a Christian, Ilonka, who risks everything by adopting a young Jewish boy whose family is about to be deported. Wiesel calls her a saint!

Thank you, Léonard Rosmarin, for reminding us that Elie Wiesel is far more than just the author of *Night*.

> — Michaël de Saint-Chéron, one of the foremost scholars of
> Elie Wiesel's works, and author of several books including
> *Evil and Exile*, written with Elie Wiesel (University of Notre Dame
> Press, 2000) and *Dialogues avec Élie Wiesel* (Parole et Silence, 2017)

WORDS
OF
WITNESS

WORDS
OF
WITNESS

THE FICTION OF
ELIE WIESEL

LÉONARD ROSMARIN

Library and Archives Canada Cataloguing in Publication

Title: Words of witness : the fiction of Elie Wiesel / Léonard Rosmarin.

Names: Rosmarin, Léonard A., author.

Description: Includes bibliographical references and index

Identifiers: Canadiana (print) 20240406745 |
                 Canadiana (ebook) 20240406753 |

ISBN 9781771617567 (softcover) | ISBN 9781771617574 (PDF) |
ISBN 9781771617581 (EPUB) | ISBN 9781771617598 (Kindle)

Subjects: LCSH: Wiesel, Elie, 1928-2016—Criticism and interpretation. |
LCSH: Holocaust, Jewish (1939-1945), in literature. | LCGFT: Literary criticism.
Classification: LCC PQ2683.I33 Z852 2024 | DDC 843/.914—dc23

Published by Mosaic Press, Oakville, Ontario, Canada, 2024.
MOSAIC PRESS, Publishers
www.Mosaic-Press.com
Copyright © Léonard Rosmarin 2024
Cover Design: Amy Land

Printed and bound in Canada.

 ONTARIO ARTS COUNCIL
CONSEIL DES ARTS DE L'ONTARIO
an Ontario government agency
un organisme du gouvernement de l'Ontario

Funded by the Government of Canada
Financé par le gouvernement du Canada

 Canadä

 ONTARIO CREATES

MOSAIC PRESS
1252 Speers Road, Units 1 & 2, Oakville, Ontario, L6L 2X4
(905) 825-2130 • info@mosaic-press.com • www.mosaic-press.com

For Beatrice, Chantal, Nicole and Danielle, Bruce, Andy and Éric,
William, Jared, Léah and Brooke, Keith, Virginia and Michelle.
Warmest thanks to Howard for believing in this project.

TABLE OF CONTENTS

PREFACE

lie Wiesel received the Nobel Prize for Peace in 1986 and it was fully deserved. For many years he had circled the globe bringing succor and hope to the oppressed, from the former Soviet Union where he helped Jewish "Refuseniks" emigrate to Israel, Cambodia where he strove to comfort victims of the murderous Pol Pot regime, to Nicaragua where he showed solidarity with the persecuted Indian tribes. But he should have been awarded the Nobel Prize for Literature instead. Humanitarian activities are often inscribed in water whereas great works of art remain as a legacy for future generations. And it is especially in his works of fiction that Elie Wiesel expresses most eloquently his life-affirming philosophy. The author informed me back in 1999 that had he not endured the nightmarish experience of the Nazi concentration camps in all probability he would never have entertained the notion of becoming a novelist. After traversing the night of flames and horror that was the Shoah, however, he felt he absolutely had to create imaginary destinies to see more clearly within himself. Paradoxically, it is in his novels far more than in his essays that he truly bares his soul.

This study, then, charts Elie Wiesel's spiritual trajectory as reflected in his novels. His journey takes him from the darkest, most overwhelming despair to a heart-warming celebration of life. This book is the only one that encompasses all his works of fiction, from *Dawn* (1961) to *Hostage* (2010) which was published six years before his death. After exploring them it will be obvious that this wise and caring man sought to celebrate the triumph of the human spirit over the forces of degradation and death.

My exploration of Elie Wiesel's novels first appeared in French as an e-book. Even though the author acquired American citizenship in 1956, he composed most of his oeuvre in the French language which he assimilated with almost lightning speed as a young refugee allowed to enter France after the Second World War. Consequently, I have based my study on his original French texts, and the footnotes here refer to them. Also, all the English translations provided in this book are my own. Let my readers not feel that they will be at a disadvantage, however. Elie Wiesel's major themes, ideas and mastery of the narrative are magnificent regardless of the language in which they appear, provided, of course, that the translation has been scrupulously faithful to the spirit of the original.

We will begin tracing his itinerary with his first great work, and undoubtedly his most famous, *Night*, even though it is not a novel but rather a narrative evoking the day-to-day hell of the Nazi death camps. The author himself justified this decision. In the preface he wrote for the new English translation of *Night* published in 2006, he declared that if he had been destined to write only one book, it would have been that one. Just as the past survives in the present, all his texts, including his novels, have been marked indelibly by that very first one, and cannot be fully understood unless one has read it. As we follow Elie Wiesel on his momentous journey from darkness to light, we will understand why.

CHAPTER 1
DARKNESS AND DESPAIR

I n 1944 Elie Wiesel, a 15-year-old adolescent along with his family and the whole Jewish community of the Hungarian city of Sighet, crashed into the realm of night. Even up until the end of the previous year when the Second World war was raging, the Jews of Hungary still felt reasonably safe. The idealistic youngster had an unshakeable faith in the coming of the Messiah. He and two other comrades were giving themselves over to kabbalistic experiences[1] under the tutelage of their teacher, Rabbi Kalmen. Their goal? To take by storm God's very fortress. To succeed, they practiced a most rigorous spiritual asceticism including thoughts and prayers pushed to their very limits. Through these mental exercises they hoped not only to pierce the mystery of creation and its ultimate purpose but also to resolve the previously unsolvable problem of the coexistence of Good and Evil. In other words, they were striving to reach absolute knowledge. Armed with this superhuman wisdom, they were going to free the Savior whose tardiness was trying their patience. Young Elie and his friends were thus attempting to force the Messiah's hand so that he would hasten to finally bring lasting peace and love to an unhappy universe.

The three lads accepted with joy the deprivations they had to suffer because these were indispensable for realizing their dream of liberating the cosmos. After living through the nightmare of the concentration camps, it was no longer possible for Elie to safeguard his religious convictions.

---

[1] The Kabbala is the age-old Jewish tradition of interpreting the Old Testament in a mystical and symbolic fashion.

Contrary to what certain commentators, including the great Catholic novelist, François Mauriac, thought, Wiesel never lost completely his faith in the God of Israel. But his religious belief acquired the tragic resonances of the biblical character Job. In other words, the Messiah would probably never come. Undoubtedly, the author uses this story of a good man afflicted without justification to understand his own crisis. Indeed, Wiesel's texts ask again and again the same lacerating question: why did God not allow the Savior to liberate humanity? As the author's novels follow one another, the answer wells up with a resounding force. If men and women want the Messiah to appear, they will have to become God's envoy themselves.

Night, then, and the fifteen novels that follow chart the spiritual itinerary of a man who sinks to the nadir of despair before being able to reach out for hope. This journey from darkness to light does not always move in an ascending curve. Some of the author's novels published well after the Holocaust reveal a very pessimist tendency. Nevertheless, even in his texts where a somber atmosphere prevails, there appear now and then individuals whose generosity embody, or rather, reembody, for a short yet dazzling moment, the Messiah during our time on earth. Thanks to them, the Savior is temporarily liberated. When the latter appears in the form of a courageous and compassionate human being, his fellow creatures forget their despair for one blessed moment. Consequently, when one follows Elie Wiesel's spiritual trajectory through his novels, one perceives, implicitly orchestrated, a meditation on the presence of the Messiah at the very heart of human destiny. The author has obviously not lived through all the experiences that he has created for his various heroes. Nevertheless, it remains true that these touch off a metaphysical reflection on the possibility for man and woman to transcend their limits and confer upon their acts an exemplary moral value. Inasmuch as his protagonists think of the cosmic repercussions of their earthly actions, they become transfigured and illumine the lives of those around them. In *Night, Dawn, and Day*, Wiesel's first three major texts, he questions the reality of the Messiah. The latter is not categorically negated but, in a world that God seems to have abandoned to its despair and reduced to its most elemental impulses, His ambassador to humanity also appears to have slipped away.

Night

Night is far more a journalistic account than a work of pure literary creation. Gripping in its very starkness, it reflects the author's determination to bear witness, in his own way, to the industrialized slaughter of innocent human beings in the Nazi death camps. *Night* represents the starting point of his novelistic production as well as its full-blown flowering. Everything the author wrote afterwards was inspired directly or indirectly by the one-year period of his internment beginning in April 1944 when he had to face the possibility that the God of Israel had abandoned his people. One can even maintain without exaggerating that during his career as a novelist Elie Wiesel continued rewriting this first book, because he was so traumatized by the unspeakably hellish experience he had endured. All the novels written after *Night* are impregnated with the same obsessive fear of demonic cruelty exploding within the heart of our human condition. They all express the same heartrending pity for the victims of History's injustices.

The account the author gives us in the first person is linear to the extent that he relates the successive stages of the calvary that he, as an adolescent, and his family endured between April 1944 when they could not decipher the signs of the disaster to come and April 1945, when, a living cadaver and a soul even more cadaverous, he was liberated from the Buchenwald camp by the Americans. But the events of his narrative unfold in a way that suggests a descending spiral movement. Before tragedy struck, life for the Wiesel family resembled a very large circle. They did not travel a great deal, but they enjoyed a considerable measure of personal freedom within their community that was quite reassuring. The young and carefree Elie was being initiated into the mysteries of the Kabbala and was getting ready to venture forth with his confidant, Moché the Beadle, into the domain of the eternal. Suddenly, sinister news jolted them as well as their fellow Jews back into reality: the expulsion from the city of Sighet of all the foreign Jews of which Moché was a member. Since the Hungarian Jews of the city were not affected by this unjust decree, they took it easily in their stride. It did not occur to them that they would be part of the next batch of deportees. And so, without yet being conscious of it, they were descending from the first circular space into one that was a bit smaller. Two years of their life went by in a state of heedlessness bordering on blindness because in the spring of 1944 the winds of defeat were blowing stronger and stronger against the Germans. The Jews of Sighet were becoming so confident about their future that they even convinced themselves that Hitler's plan to exterminate all of Europe's Jewish population was a myth.

Then, suddenly, in rapid succession, two news bulletins reach them, which for the first time concern them directly, they, the Hungarian citizens who thought they were sheltered from all danger; and for the first time they become conscious of the fact that they are being dragged down from a reduced space to one even more constricted. The Fascist Pary takes control of the government, and German troops enter the country. Three days later the SS are walking about the streets of Sighet. From that moment on, the circular spaces of the Jewish community shrink more and more as the decrees affecting them become more and more draconian. Then, the circles closing in on them become more and more stifling and they are fully aware of tumbling down faster and faster despite their attempts to reassure one another: the deportation order, the sealed train cars, their arrival at the death camp, the separation of families, and the revelation that the crematory ovens do indeed exist. They finally notice that they have fallen to the very bottom of the infernal spiral. The Sighet deportees now begin intoning for themselves the prayer for the dead that Jews would normally recite only for the deceased.

All through the first two chapters that underscore each stage of this spiraling descent into hell, the reader occupies a position resembling that of a spectator watching the performance of a Greek tragedy. Like a member of the audience, we know in advance how the tragic mechanism is going to function. We know that these victims of the Nazis' racial hatred will be crushed. But the essential lies elsewhere. What counts in the first two chapters of *Night* is the feeling of terror and pity that we experience when reflecting on the ineluctability of their doom. This feeling stems from the gap that exists between what we already know and what the deportees still don't. We also feel furious exasperation when we remember that the world knew what was happening yet chose to let it happen. When the deportees of *Night* finally gain the knowledge that we readers have had for well over a half-century, they join us in an anguished awareness of the murderous brutality of which so-called "civilized" people are capable. And again, just as in a Greek tragedy, messengers warn the victims of the fate that is in store for them.

The first one, Moché the Beadle, continuously entreats his coreligionists to flee while there is still time. Caught in a roundup against foreign Jews in 1942, he was able to escape his tormentors miraculously after witnessing horrible scenes: adults forced to dig their own graves before being shot, babies used as living targets by the Gestapo who threw them up in the air then gunned them down, a young woman whose mortal agony went on for three days, a father imploring the Nazi brutes to kill him before his own children. When he returns to Sighet, Moché seems profoundly changed. The sweet, timid clown who used to strive to go about without being noticed takes every opportunity to exhort the members of his community to listen to his account and believe it. Although the author never states this explicitly, Moché probably lost his religious faith after living through this hell. Neither God nor the Kabbala interest him any longer. Herein lies his tragedy. Having lost everything—his family and his belief in God—in this dress rehearsal of the Holocaust, he tries desperately to give a meaning to his existence by saving his coreligionists from disaster. But not only do the latter not believe him, they no longer listen to what he is saying. The unfortunate Moché has thus suffered in vain. His powerlessness to convince the Jews of Sighet simply throws into a more striking relief the gullibility and blindness that will drag them down into the abyss. When the German troops enter the city two years later, the distraught man rushes to the Wiesel's home and cries out to Elie's father: "I warned you."[2] He then disappears from the narrative. Having failed in his mission, his life is now devoid of meaning. He allows himself to be victimized by the Nazis in another roundup.

The second messenger is a woman, Mrs. Schacter, who loses her mind when the Germans ship off her husband and two older sons by mistake in the first trainload of deportees. The Jews of Sighet have no choice but to listen to this one. Reluctantly, no doubt, probably with dread, all the while wishing that her prophesies are nothing more than the ravings of an unbalanced person, because now they are locked up in sealed freight cars. They feel in the depths of their hearts that perhaps poor Moché was right. Very often during their voyage to hell Mrs. Schacter howls out words like the following: "Jews, listen to me: I see a fire! What flames! What an inferno! (N, 45). The words this woman utters terrify them because they exteriorize their own repressed anguish. At the outset, they explain away her howls by saying that her pain as a mother and wife have gotten the better of her, later they try to convince themselves that thirst is now torturing her. But as the trip to the far-off concentration camps continues, Mrs. Schacter's heartrending cries touch off unbearable reverberations within them. The madwoman's persistence prevents them from entertaining their last illusions about the fate that awaits them. She compels them to confront the fears they dare not confess to themselves. Hence the physical violence that they no longer hesitate to inflict on her to silence her. Nevertheless, like an inspired prophetess, she refuses to be silenced.

---

[2] *Nuit*, Paris: Les Éditions de Minuit, 1958, 22; referred to henceforth as *N*. All translations are mine.

Once the train reaches its destination, she howls out one last time: "Jews, look! Look at the fire! The flames, look at them!" (*N*, 49). This time, reality bears her out. When the others peer through the train window, they see flames coming out of a high chimney. When they disembark, there is an odor of burned flesh in the air. Having accomplished her mission, Mrs. Schacter lapses into indifference. But as soon as she becomes mute, the camp prisoners take over from her and confirm what the unhappy woman had uttered. They welcome the newly arrived inmates from Sighet with insults. They call the latter imbeciles for having let themselves be trapped without resisting.

This movement of tragic ineluctability that drags the young Elie, his family and the Jewish community of Sighet towards their death also resembles a hideous parody of the book *Exodus* from the *Old Testament*. In fact, it is the book of *Exodus* unfolding backwards. In the *Bible*, God frees the Hebrew tribes from slavery and designates Moses to lead them towards the Promised Land. In *Night*, God allows Hitler to tear His people away from a rather peaceful and reassuring existence and ship them off to a death factory. As soon as they arrive in Birkenau, the young narrator sees trucks dumping Jewish babies into the flames. He wants at all costs to believe that he is dreaming this horrible scene: "I pinched my face: was I still alive? I couldn't quite believe it. How was it possible that adults and children were being burned, and the world remained silent. No, all this could not be true. A nightmare... I would soon wake up with a start, with my heart beating and would find again my child's room, my books..." (*N*, 56). In *Exodus*, the Lord intervenes many times during the forty years that the Jews are wandering in the desert, bringing them succor and comfort. In *Night*, His tormented people offer up desperate prayers to Him to which he seems to remain oblivious. Or if God is nonetheless touched by His children's distress, He does not show it in their presence. What is even worse, the God of Israel is replaced by Hitler's false gods intoxicated by gratuitous cruelty and the myth of Aryan superiority. From the third chapter onward episodes follow one another that are almost literally unbearable: the infamous Dr. Mengele, holding a baton in his hand like an orchestral conductor possessed by Satan himself, pointing the prisoners to one or the other of two lines to follow, one for the healthy that leads to the work camp, the other, for the weak and elderly, that ends up at the crematory ovens; Corporal Idek's brutal and unpredictable flare-ups against Elie and his father; the execution of several inmates and the order given on pain of death to all the others to file past their hanged bodies so that they would register in their minds the punishment to be meted out to anyone tempted by the thought of revolt.

This daily cruelty that the sadistic guards practiced on their prisoners was part of a program of systematic degradation of the human person ending up in exhaustion and death. All the inmates, including young Elie Wiesel, were victims of all kinds of vicious acts, from pulling out gold crowns from their mouths to whippings that led to fainting. But what afflicts the adolescent even more than his own suffering, is the degradation he sees his father enduring. Of all the people he had known before entering the concentration camp, Shlomo Wiesel was the one for whom his son felt the most admiration. Indeed, Elie venerated him. Thus, to witness the collapse of a person that his imagination had transformed into a hero represented for the boy a traumatic shock as terrible as his other experiences as a prisoner. Naturally, it is normal and necessary for the child to discover the vulnerability of a parent behind the idealized image he creates of the latter. But for the future author of *Night*, something far more dreadful occurs. During the year he spent with his father as they traveled from Sighet to the death camps of Auschwitz then Buchenwald, he was forced to observe the whole infernal process through which Shlomo Wiesel would progressively lose his dignity as a human being and degenerate into a wreck.

First, the Germans uproot his father emotionally, spiritually and physically by expelling him from his home and his community. The narrator notices that his father weeps when leaving the family dwelling. "It was the first time I saw him cry," he writes, "I had never imagined that he could" (*N*, 35). Then his tormentors make it clear to Shlomo Wiesel that he and his coreligionists are totally subjugated and in their power. Once they arrive in Birkenau, young Elie sees him cry again when the new batch of deportees of which he and his son are part is convinced that they will all be burned alive in the flaming pits just like the babies. Shlomo Wiesel sheds tears of sorrow because at that very moment he has a stunning revelation. He realizes that his humanistic idealism has just been shattered into smithereens in the face of the unstoppable killing machine that functions day and night in this huge death camp. Now he knows that his profound optimism and confidence in humanity is an illusion. The world promises nothing except indifference and brutality. No one will come to rescue the Jews. But his greatest torment consists in his powerlessness as a father to protect his child. When Elie tells him that he prefers to throw himself against the electrified barbed wires rather than endure the slow death by fire, Shlomo Wiesel's whole body is "racked with trembling" (*N*, 57).

There follow acts of gratuitous sadistic cruelty of which Elie's father is the victim. The Gypsy deportee assigned to keep a close watch in the compound of the Jewish prisoners deals Shlomo Wiesel such a heavy blow that the latter is forced to crawl on his hands and knees to return to his place in line. All Shlomo had done to deserve this act of cruelty was to ask politely where the lavatories were located. Idek the Kapo went even further in wickedness. Living sadism in search of a victim, he swooped down on Elie's father for no apparent reason. He struck him with an iron bar. "My father gave way under the blows," his son notes, "then broke in two like a dehydrated tree struck by lightning, and crumbled to the ground" (N, 88). And this inhuman treatment reaches its climax when the SS evacuate the Auschwitz prisoners and send them to a camp within Germany. They impose on Shlomo Wiesel and the other detainees a forced march of several days in a glacial winter cold and snowstorms, then shove him with all the others into open freight cars of a train going to Buchenwald. Once they arrive in that death camp, Elie's father, prematurely aged, dies of dysentery in atrocious pain, crying like a helpless child and beseeching his son to come to his aid. The brutal blow that an SS inflicts on him to put an end to his moaning marks the final stage of the torture that had begun nine months earlier.

Shlomo Weisel's degradation affects young Elie all the more because it arouses within him a mixture of powerless rage, shame and guilt. The more father and son sink into the concentration camp hell, the more this knot of conflicting sentiments tightens. After the adolescent witnesses the first act of violence against the head of his family, he realizes, aghast, and remorsefully that he did not intervene to protect this man he venerated, whereas in normal life circumstances he would have rushed to help him immediately. Later on, when the sadistic Kapo Idek strikes his father, Elie doesn't even bother feeling any indignation. His anger is directed rather against Shlomo Wiesel for not having had enough good sense to get out of the way on time. And when his father dies, his son, exhausted by his own traumas and tormented by hunger, experiences a feeling of liberation that he does not have the courage to bring up to the surface of his consciousness.

His fellow-prisoners succumb to this same weakness as much if not more than does the adolescent. The author places his narrator's dilemma within the context of the other prisoners to emphasize that the lack of courage, generosity and compassion was a moral sickness engendered by the dreadful conditions in which they were all forced to function. Considering that they were constantly racked by physical fear and hunger, it was inevitable that their behavior was often no better than any animal's. Several episodes occurring during the narrative illustrate the dehumanization that overcomes the detainees in the death camp. The one involving the two cauldrons of soup is one of the most gripping. During an air alert, the prisoners are ordered to remain within their compounds or risk being shot. One famished inmate, more intrepid than the others, crawls towards these objects which seem to him more precious than all earthly riches. Instead of admiring his action, the other men are devoured by envy and jealousy: "Poor hero who would commit suicide for a soup ration. We were assassinating him mentally" (N, 95-96).

Other manifestations of moral weakness follow that are just as heartbreaking. One day the sinister Dr. Mengele presides over a medical examination to determine which prisoners are no longer capable of working. These will be dispatched to the gas chambers and then to the crematory ovens. A certain number of prisoners, including the narrator and his father, pass the test. Others are condemned. But those who escape death couldn't care less about the fate of the unlucky ones, so happy are they to remain alive. The survival instinct has turned them into ferocious egomaniacs. They don't even have a single drop of energy left in reserve to worry about others. The same holds true for a promise made to one of their comrades, Akiba Drumer. Having lost his will to live, that kind and pious man who was withering away perceptibly was selected for the gassing. He begged his fellow-inmates to say kaddish for him after his death. They promised him solemnly that they would do so. Despite their best intentions, however, they forgot to recite this prayer in his memory. Hunger was tormenting them to such an extent that it had erased from their conscience the promise they had made to the innocent victim.

They plunge rapidly into the nadir of degeneration during the forced march in the snowstorm and the trip by train in open cattle-cars to Buchenwald. With hunger and fatigue gnawing at them literally from within, the detainees are often reduced to being knots of elemental urges. During this infernal voyage, some lose all sentiment of humanity. The son of a rabbi universally venerated by the camp deliberately abandons his father to rid himself of a responsibility that weights on him. In the cattle-car where Elie and his father have been herded, a vicious fight breaks out between dozens of prisoners for a miserable bit of bread. A son kills his father before being trampled to death in turn by other starved men.

From time to time, however, surges of generosity, of compassion and courage temporarily light up the night of this interminable nightmare that the concentration camp represents. They provide proof that even at the very heart of this reign of industrialized barbarity, the word "humanity" still preserves its meaning. The narrator remembers the extreme kindness of the first leader of his compound, a young Pole who exhorted his co-detainees to practice unwavering solidarity, the indispensable condition for them to perhaps come out of this hell alive. He recalls with deep emotion the comforting words a woman prisoner in the same workshop spoke to him after the Kapo Idek had beaten him up. He notices the absence of fear among several prisoners condemned to hanging after being tortured. They had revolted against the tyranny of SS guards. One of them curses Nazi Germany until his last breath. All accept death without flinching. Even when the detainees are transferred to Buchenwald during the horrible blizzard there appear acts of genuine nobility. The narrator relates an incredibly moving moment. He thinks he is hallucinating. Then he realizes that his comrade, Juliek, an extremely talented violinist, is playing a fragment of Beethoven's violin concerto with an other-worldly purity before collapsing on a heap of cadavers and dying inmates in the Gleiwitz shed. All the way through the infernal voyage, Shlomo Wiesel and his son show an extraordinary solicitude towards one another. Each one watches over the other to prevent him from sinking into a sleep from which they would never wake up. They persist in wanting to live because they know they are necessary for each other's survival. If Elie experiences an ambivalent feeling of liberation after his father's death, it is only because he himself is on the verge of breaking down under the combined stresses of exhaustion and hunger.

This ability that certain individuals possess to transcend, if only temporarily, the degrading conditions prevailing in the concentration camp world throws into even more striking relief, in contrast, the apparent impassibility and injustice of the God of Israel. *Night* brings up a question that Elie Wiesel never phrases explicitly but that remains nevertheless perfectly expressible: if some of the detainees who are vulnerable and under the threat of death were courageous enough to oppose the cruelty reigning in the camps, why did God, supposedly all-powerful and eternal, not intervene? Could it be possible that some of His creatures are morally superior to Him? It suffices to re-read the unforgettable passage where the narrator offers us his thoughts after seeing the Nazis throw babies by the hundreds into the flames. On the one hand he evokes for us the monstrousness of the crime committed; on the other he shows the inertia and silence of the Creator of the universe. Even the unalterably azure blue of the sky into which smoke rises from the little incinerated bodies seems like a diabolic mockery of human suffering. Here the author's terse style uses the anaphor to hammer out his anger. The word "never" opens each one of the seven successive paragraphs or verses, thereby creating an incantatory effect, and returns in the form of an elliptic phrase as though to howl out, indeed smash out his revolt one last time:

> Never will I forget this night, the first night in the camp that turned my life into a night both long and locked up seven times.

> Never will I forget this smoke.

> Never will I forget the little faces of the children whose bodies I saw transformed into volutes under the mute azure blue.

> Never will I forget these flames that consumed my Faith forever.

> Never will I forget this nocturnal silence that deprived me for all eternity of any desire to live.

> Never will I forget these instants that assassinated my God and my soul, and my dreams that took on the face of a desert.

> Never will I forget this, even if I were condemned to live as long as God himself.

> Never (*N*, 58-59).

In another heartbreaking passage in Chapter V, Elie Wiesel describes the religious ceremony to celebrate Rosh Hashanah, the New Year in the Jewish calendar, in which all his coreligionists are participating. He established a contrast between the submissive reverence of all those poor bodies and innocent spirits tortured by deprivations and fear and an all-powerful God who allows satanic punishments to be inflicted repeatedly on His faithful people. Because the narrator is capable of revolting against this monstrous injustice, he considers himself superior to the God who could put an end to it. Inasmuch as He does absolutely nothing to alleviate the suffering of His people, He is unworthy of their praise: "Today, I was no longer imploring. I was no longer capable of groaning. On the contrary, I felt very strong. I was the accuser. And the accused: God. My eyes had opened up and I was alone, terribly alone in the world, without God, without men. Without love or pity. I was nothing but ashes, but I felt I was stronger than the All-Powerful to whom I had linked my life for so long. In the midst of this prayer session, I was like a foreign observer" (*N*, 107). Ten days later the Jewish prisoners were celebrating their most solemn day of the year, Yom Kippur or the Day of Atonement. In Sighet, the narrator would have fasted to ask forgiveness of God for offenses committed during the year gone by. This time, however, nothing like this happens. He refuses to fast. Why humiliate himself before the Lord when He is the one responsible for the undeserved punishment that His servant is presently enduring?

Certain commentators have seen in such passages where revolt borders on blasphemy proof that the author was renouncing the God of Israël. Even the great François Mauriac who wrote an eloquent preface for *Night* to honor his young Jewish friend, misinterpreted it when he spoke of "the death of God in the soul of a child who suddenly discovers absolute evil (*N*, 7). But Elie Wiesel never renounced the God of his people despite being overwhelmed with anger and raising his fist against Him. After all, to revolt against the Creator is to continue believing in His existence. If the author really thought that God was dead, he would never have felt the need to address Him with such vehemence. He would have treated the Lord of Creation with the cold politeness and indifference of an Alfred de Vigny, the 19th century French aristocratic poet or an Albert Camus, the Nobel Prize-winning literary great of the mid-twentieth century.

An impression of unfathomable mystery emerges from this book. When a ten-year-old child is hanged and is subjected to a slow, atrocious death, a prisoner asks: "Where then is God?" And a voice within the narrator replies: "Where is He? Here he is – hanging here from these gallows…" (*N*, 103). For young Elie, then, divine majesty is sullied and scorned whenever men commit crimes against any one of His creatures. Obviously, the narrator never answers this question about the nature of God that he implicitly brings up, either in his first great text or in any of the novels that follow. His childhood faith, so radiant, so enthusiastic, has been shaken to its very foundations—and forever—by his experience of absolute evil in the death camps. But he will continue clinging to the God of his ancestors, because in the holy books this God embodies the highest moral and spiritual values to which every Jew endeavors to aspire. To lose one's faith would be the equivalent, for Wiesel, of losing one's soul. Unlike Akiba Drumer and Meir Katz, the narrator will survive because he will never succumb entirely to despair. The first co-detainee, a sweet, compassionate mystic, breaks down when he measures the abyss that exists between his conception of divine mercy and the baseness of His creatures. The second, a robust and generous man, allows himself to slide into death once he has lost his son. Elie Wiesel hangs on to the helm, as though propelled by an irrepressible instinct. After being liberated he looks at himself in the mirror and sees a cadaver. But at least the cadaver has remained alive and will eventually find life worth living.

Dawn

Elie Wiesel managed to escape—literally and figuratively—from the endless night of despair. He was able to welcome the light of the sun. The horror of the hell he traversed never impelled him to embrace violence as a solution. The same is not true for the hero of his first real work of fiction, a novel published in 1960 and dedicated to François Mauriac, his benefactor. One might say that Elisha, the tormented eighteen-year-old man represents a destiny that might have been the author's but that he rejected outright as being unworthy of the Jew he was determined to be. Thus, between the author and his protagonist there exist profound similarities as well as differences. Before the Holocaust both had an ardent religious faith and embraced the mission of freeing the Messiah in order to put an end to the unhappiness of their fellow man and woman. Both were traumatized by their experience in the death camps. Both were racked by seemingly unalterable sorrow during the year that followed their freedom from captivity. As students living in Paris, they both were striving to understand the meaning of our human condition.

From this point onwards, however, the roads they travelled on diverged. The novelist would become a guardian of the memory of the Shoah and favor non-violence, whereas his hero would engage in terrorism. Yet never, during the course of this sober and powerful narrative, does the author condemn the choice made by his protagonist. This is not necessary because Elisha, while relating his story in the first person, ends up condemning himself. The Judaism he continues to revere is founded on the principle of the sacredness of human life. By killing, he commits inexpiable acts, and he knows it. But he remains convinced that the conquest of freedom and dignity for his people in Palestine demands the sacrifice of his moral purity. Unable either to appease his conscience or renounce the murderous actions that he deems indispensable, Elisha faces an insoluble dilemma. He feels drawn and quartered. Yet another torture is added to this one: doubt over the motives that have attracted him to the terrorist movement. Was his decision made freely and lucidly, or did Elisha fall into a fatal trap while deluding himself into believing that he was exercising his free will?

The structure of the narrative plays skillfully on these two registers of anguish. We meet Elisha twelve hours before he is obliged to commit an assassination. The organization to which he belongs has ordered him to kill the British colonel John Dawson, taken hostage in reprisal for the death sentence by hanging meted out to one of its fighters, David Ben Moshe. If the British authorities refuse to defer to world opinion and to spare the life of the young Jew, the soldier will die. Between dusk that is falling and dawn that will finally break, Elisha attempts desperately to reassure himself about the necessity and free choice of his act as well as the sacredness of the nationalist cause he has espoused. His anguish increases as he switches back and forth between the past and the present. He returns through memory to the period immediately after the war when, as a student in Paris, he was approached by a charismatic man, Gad, sent to France by the secret organization to recruit new fighters for the cause of Jewish independence. Did Gad personify his ineluctable destiny? He also remembers the first terrorist action he committed that was supposed to help harden him against pity. The result was a feeling of utter disgust. Then, during that interminable night of waiting, he recalls another very upsetting one from the time he spent in France. He was walking in the forest with Catherine, a beautiful and fragile woman of twenty-six who had tried to seduce him. She was on the verge of succeeding when she let slip a phrase: "poor little one," in a burst of compassion that made him panic and run away. Now Elisha fully understands the meaning of these words several hours before committing the murder, and his anguish intensifies. Finally, when he encounters just before dawn the man he will execute, Elisha conjures up the image of a non-Jewish comrade who had been imprisoned in the same concentration camp, the German sculptor, Stéphane. The latter had participated in a resistance movement against the Nazis. As though to inflame his anger against the tyranny that the military man John Dawson represents, the protagonist remembers that the courageous Stéphane was punished by having the five fingers of his right hand amputated for refusing to divulge the names of his accomplices.

Two other temporal dimensions are added to this oscillation between the present and the past: an imaginary present and a mythical past that encroach upon his existence in real time. During this night of anguish, Elisha has recourse to his imagination to project himself into David Ben Moshe's final hours on earth. This mortal countdown unfolds at the very same time as the one that draws him ever closer to the moment when he will have to assassinate the English colonel. Elisha imagines the rabbi visiting the condemned man in his cell to bring him comfort and strengthen his courage. He conjures up in his mind the proud intrepidity of the young Israeli fighter who advances in the prison corridor towards the execution chamber, and the national hymn that the other prisoners intone to accompany the condemned man. Even though Elisha has never met David, he strives to identify with him totally to be able to kill John Dawson in cold blood.

The hero's mythical past is composed of the people who had left an indelible imprint on his consciousness during his childhood, before his existence had plummeted into the concentration camp nightmare: his father, his mother, his Kabbala teacher, his friend Yerachmiel with whom he had tried to force the Messiah's hand, the beggar and the innocent boy he once was. All these had disappeared during the Holocaust. They represent the ethical values of Judaism that are hard-wired into the deepest recesses of his soul. They may be dead physically, but they are omnipresent in the spiritual sense and accompany him everywhere. They invade the room where he waits for the shadows of the night to be dispelled. They go downstairs with him to the cell to witness the assassination of the hostage. Through their omnipresence, the young man's spiritual patrimony transmutes itself into an immutable present. Elisha cannot content himself with living in a time frame composed of instants that follow one another in rapid succession and then disappear. He must take this eternal dimension of his Jewish heritage into account. Although it enriches his life, it turns out to be a source of anguish as well because of the multiple moral exigencies that it imposes on him. The hero may very well pay a heavy price for this freedom to act as a terrorist which he deems necessary. Ambiguity is an integral part, then, of Elisha's freedom, of his inability to fulfill himself completely in terrorist activity. He may take pride in playing the role of the avenger of his people, but there will always be afterthoughts and anguished doubts concerning the nature and validity of his choices.

In the first place, how can he be sure that the trajectory taking him from his room in Paris to Palestine has been knowingly chosen and planned from one end to the other? Could it not have been influenced by the traumatisms of his past as well as by an encounter that seemed at the time ordained by destiny? To answer these questions, we must go back to his relationship with Catherine and his meeting with Gad. During their first evening walk in the forest, Elisha related to the young woman a story that his teacher had passed on to him. It was about a little boy whose father was dying. According to the teacher, there are nights when the skies open to allow the prayers of unhappy children to ascend.[3] Not knowing how to pray, the boy told God that he would become a prayer to save his father. The night when he called out to the Lord, the skies were open. God cured the dying man but transported the latter's son up to the heavens in the form of a prayer for all eternity. Ever since that event took place, the teacher explained, God sometimes manifests Himself at night, when the skies open, in the guise of a child. But Elisha never succeeded in perceiving the image. When he showed the empty sky to Catherine, this sensitive and intelligent woman suddenly realized that the adolescent carried within him an incurable wound and let slip the words, "Poor little one! ... My poor little one" (A, 52). As I remarked, Catherine repeats the same words just before she and Elisha are going to make love. He grasps their meaning immediately. He recalls that she had uttered them the time before. Through this discrete and heartrending allusion to the absence of God in his life, the narrator makes us understand that the concentration camps have killed the mystical fervor that he used to carry within him. He was able to save himself from physical destruction, but an essential part of his nature went up in smoke as though it had passed through the crematory ovens along with the other prisoners condemned to die. Having lost his religious faith or, at least, his unlimited confidence in an infinitely merciful God, Elisha will become an easy prey to a form of nationalism based on terror. Since the Messiah will never come willingly, it will be necessary to act in his place.

From the chronological viewpoint, the episode of his relationship with Catherine unfolds before his meeting with Gad. But it is significant that the narrator informs us of this only when his distress at the thought of executing the hostage becomes visible to one of the members of the movement, Ilana. Like Catherine, she feels pity for him and, with tears in her eyes, pronounces the very same words: "Poor little one." Only then does this fragment of his past link up with his present to underscore even more his spiritual disarray. Even though he has renounced (or thinks he has renounced) the mystical dimension of his faith, the nostalgia he still feels continues to haunt him.

---

[3] Elie Wiesel, *L'Aube*, Paris: les Éditions du Seuil, 1960, 51. Referred to henceforth as *A*.

A vacuum had opened within Elisha's soul during the Holocaust, and so he was searching for a new ideal to give a transcendent meaning to his existence. After his liberation from the death camp, he hoped studies in philosophy would fill his spiritual void. This was before Gad came upon the scene. The irresistible recruiter erupted in Elisha's life, tore him away definitively from his books and conquered him by conjuring up an exalting adventure: the creation of a country for their people that had been oppressed for too long. As soon as he entered the young man's room, Gad dominated him completely. To what could this power be attributed? The recruiter had utmost confidence in himself and an unshakeable, indeed contagious belief in the cause he was serving. These traits of character were sorely lacking in the young student at that stage of his life. Also, Elisha saw a kind of Meshulah in this unexpected visitor who seemed to know everything about his past. Like the legendary personage of Hassidic stories, Gad appeared as the mysterious messenger of destiny, invested with the all-powerfulness of God, since he had a mission to accomplish that went way beyond himself and his interlocutor. Finally, with his fiery enthusiasm and the vision he had for the future of his fellow Jews, the recruiter seemed to embody the mystical hopes of a several thousand-year-old people and its determination to never again be humiliated. After so many centuries of persecutions, the Jews would be able to define their own time and space on this ancient land of which they had been despoiled. Miracles could happen, but it would be up to the people of Israel to make them materialize by having the courage to fight for the reconquest of their country. Elisha found himself exalted by this dream that Gad's eloquence rendered almost palpable, yet he could not repress in himself a premonition of doom. Recalling this first meeting in Paris, he said to himself: "I believe that, already, at that moment, something inside of me knew that at the end of the road I was taking side by side with Gad, a man would be waiting for me, a man who would look like me, a man who would be called on to kill another man who, perhaps, would look like him?" (A, 25). Thus, the so-called freedom Elisha exerts by agreeing to join the terrorist movement may be partly an illusion.

Gad does not compel him either physically or mentally to espouse the nationalist cause. The young concentration camp survivor makes his own decision with full knowledge of the facts. Nevertheless, without the mesmerizing influence of this Meshulah, would Elisha have embarked on this path of violence at the end of which he would hate himself? He will never be able to give a clear answer to this question. As soon as he says

"I accept" to his interlocutor, his destiny as a murderer is inevitable. A powerful symbol underscores the fatality to which he has allowed himself to be subjugated in Palestine. At the beginning of his narrative, the young man talks about a mysterious beggar with whom he struck up a friendship. The latter taught him how to determine when dusk and dawn arrive. It suffices to look at a windowpane. If one detects on it a face made of shadows, it is proof that night has already arrived or has not yet disappeared. As dusk falls, about twelve hours before he is supposed to shoot John Dawson, Elisha sees his own face when looking at a window. His life is already enveloped in night.

After killing the hostage at dawn, he looks at the window once more, and once more he finds his own image. Dawn has an ironic connotation for him. It matters little that day has arrived, his soul will be plunged forever in darkness. Moreover, it plummets into darkness during his first terrorist mission: the successful ambush of a convoy of British soldiers on a road near Tel Aviv. Gad, who supervises the operation, is jubilant. Elisha is overcome by a feeling of anguish and shame. For him, to kill men through an act of treachery is to cheapen them, to dehumanize them and, as a result, to devalue the whole human condition. While remembering that attack, he has recourse to a gripping image to describe how these human beings riddled with bullets have been reduced to the state of crazed animals: "They were running like squirrels, squirrels that had become drunk, looking for a tree or a branch in the shade. One would have said that they had neither heads nor hands: all they had were legs. And these legs, they were running, they were running like drunken squirrels that had been drenched in wine and pain" (A,34). Once he returned to the headquarters, his disgust increased. The experience of felling men as though one were pulverizing objects unleashes in him the memory of the cold cruelty of SS guards in the Polish ghettos. Just like the Jewish terrorists in Palestine, the German soldiers used machine guns as though they were fiery sickles, and Elisha's helpless coreligionists were, they too, running like "squirrels drenched in wine and pain" (A, 34).

The young man's self-loathing reaches its peak during the hours that separate him from the instant when he will become the executioner and put his hostage to death. Killing people in an ambush is relatively easy for an idealist who believes in his mission. He does not have any direct contact with them and is not the only one who sets the murder machine in motion. Destroying another human being with whom you establish a victim-executioner relationship compels you to assume a crushing personal responsibility. Here anonymity is no longer possible. The hostage exists as an individual and you are forced to recognize him as such. In Elisha's case, the dilemma is further complicated by the fact that his deceased family members and friends will never let him forget his act. The role he plays as an executioner will stick to his spiritual flesh like a tunic of Nessus, no matter how large or small will be the number of hostages he kills during his life as a terrorist. It is enough to murder one solitary victim for him to be sullied for the remainder of his days on earth. "This is the problem," he observes, "The durable influence of the décor on the subject" (A, 70).

While having their individual personalities, the other members of the terrorist movement serve as foils for Elisha for the purpose of emphasizing his dilemma even more strongly. The young man resigns himself sorrowfully to committing murders, and at the end of the novel one wonders whether his guilt complex will drive him to despair. The others accept killing enemies as an unavoidable necessity. Not that his comrades are monsters. They do not take pleasure in acting as killers. When Elisha tells Ilana: "I don't want to be an executioner," she replies: "Who would want to be one?" (A, 70). Even Gad who exults each time his pupils pull off a mission of murder is not a dehumanized brute. He does not rejoice in destroying human beings but in removing obstacles that stand in the way of independence for his future country. It is nonetheless true that the narrator's comrades do not go through his moral hell. They have decided once and for all that the ends justify the means. Nothing is more significant in this respect than the speech Ilana pronounces on the movement's clandestine radio station on the eve of John Dawson's execution. She expresses sentiments of compassion for the British soldier and for his mother who will soon mourn his death. She acknowledges the fact that in other circumstances the terrorists could have welcomed him as a brother. But she denies categorically the accusation that her group of nationalists are assassins. For her and her comrades, the assassin is the British government that forces them to kill Colonel Dawson by refusing to pardon David ben Moshe. The enemy is the army of Her Majesty that refuses to leave of its own volition, thereby preventing the Israelis from realizing their dream of an independent country.

Hence the phrase the terrorists repeat like a mantra to justify their acts of violence: "This is war." The British refuse to go home, so the Israelis have no choice but to sow panic within their ranks to compel them to leave with all deliberate speed. The members of the movement know very well that behind their idealistic rhetoric lies the primitive reality of murder.

LÉONARD ROSMARIN

They are fully aware that the freedom of their people in this Holy Land already saturated with blood will be bought with many crimes. But they are ready to pay this price and so refrain from calling into question the laws of war. To do so would mean to paralyze them at the very moment when it would be necessary to act. It would mean renouncing the spiritual infinity that gives a meaning to their existence.

Unlike his comrades, Elisha cannot allow himself to be mesmerized by the mantra of the movement to the point of anesthetizing his anguish. As I have emphasized, he is torn between the terrorist logic and his Jewish spiritual patrimony that rejects it. According to the terrorists, violence remains the indispensable condition for creating a country of free individuals where peace and brotherhood will finally reign. According to Judaism's ethical principles, however, violence constitutes a sacrilege committed against life. The law that forbids killing weighs all the more heavily on the young man's conscience because his several thousand years memory as a Jew takes on the tangible form in his imaginary world of all the people who had shaped his personality and inculcated their values into him. We have seen how they accompany him right into the hostage's cell. Now his father, mother, Kabbala teacher, Yerachmiel, the beggar and the little boy that he once was represent the metaphor of his moral conscience illuminated by the sacred principles he had inherited from his ancestors. This moral conscience multiplies to the infinite his feeling of remorse despite his will to adhere to the terrorist logic. No wonder he speaks to these deceased people as though they were still alive, and, in a sense, they are for him far more alive than many mortals. He is trying desperately to explain himself and vindicate himself in their eyes.

When addressing his father, he has recourse to the metaphysical argument: God's abandonment of man and the aborted nature of His creation. In the imperfect universe where human beings are condemned to live out their lives, Evil reveals itself as indispensable for the presence of Good. It is impossible to fight for a new country where justice and compassion will reign without committing innumerable injustices and acts of destruction. "If we conduct ourselves in an evil manner towards our fellow man, it is because God did not leave us any choice. He never taught us how to create happiness on this earth without spreading unhappiness. The Master of the cosmos is the one who must be judged, because He rigged it in such a way that a nation's freedom just like the freedom of citizens is a statue erected over the bodies of people condemned to death" (A, 72). When speaking to his mother, the narrator's sorrow becomes heavy with emotion and reaches a paroxysm. He no longer exhorts her to accuse God of having created in Man a creature riddled with imperfections. His defense is no longer metaphysical. It is moral, even visceral. Far from being a killer, he maintains that he is an idealist, a fighter in the cause of freedom who sacrifices his peace of mind, and consents to his spiritual death so that his coreligionists may finally find joy and live in the sun.

When facing the others, his anguish softens, and he uses a line of reasoning instead. For his Kabbala teacher he invokes the same argument the former would use, namely, that it is necessary to give priority to the living. If he had refused to obey the order to kill the hostage, he would have endangered the lives of his comrades. Quoting the Bible that says: "And you will choose life," Elisha intends to justify the murder he is going to commit. But not being sustained by the same emotional intensity, his speech appears less convincing. The narrator chooses only one aspect of life by showing solidarity with the members of his organization. As concerns the fate of John Dawson, he deliberately opts for death. Now, is not the life of this soldier as precious in its way as that of his comrades? Does a Jew really have the right to affirm that the existence of a non-Jew possesses a lesser value? He approaches his dilemma from another angle by speaking to his beloved fellow-student, Yerachmiel. Elisha insists that his comrades in the nationalist movement are trying to force God's hand. But can one accelerate the reign of the Messiah through bloodshed? If the Savior represents justice and love, does one not sully Him irremediably by killing in his name? Do Elisha's coreligionists deserve the Messiah more than others? Is that why they have the right, in certain circumstances, to shed blood?

When the narrator turns to the little boy he had been, he reminds the latter that death had been a blessing for him. By dying on the spiritual level in the concentration camp, the child had been able to safeguard his innocence. But then a new element presents itself in this moral struggle. The little boy orders him to fully assume his responsibilities in the face of the murder he is going to commit. Elisha's assassination of John Dawson will leave an indelible imprint not only on his own existence but on his whole past, because if the deceased have contributed to shaping the destinies of the living, it is the living who have, in turn, left a permanent impression on the memory of the deceased. There exists an organic link between the destinies of the departed and those of the guardians who still venerate their memories. The eternal present in which the deceased continue living coincides with the future that the survivors are creating for themselves and is affected by the latter's actions. As the little boy Elisha once was tells him, "When you raise your eyes towards the sky, you make us see it; when you caress the hair of a small child who is hungry, thousands of hands place themselves on his head; when you give bread to a poor man, we give him this delicious taste of paradise that only the poor can appreciate" (*A*, 75). The deceased, then, are content simply to bear witness in silence without pronouncing judgement. Nevertheless, being the sum of all of Elisha's acts, the silence of the dead that he reveres carries with it a very heavy significance. According to how the young man acts, this silence will be soothing or incriminating. "We are not the ones who are judging you," the child explains, "it is the silence within you" (*A*, 76).

This face to face between Elisha and the dead people he still cherishes emphasizes the tragic dimension of his condition and, by analogy, of our own. In certain harrowing situations we are forced to play the role of God without having the omniscience and omnipotence that alone would justify the exercise of such power. Having only finite intelligence and strength, whatever the young man decides to do, it will be wrong. If he refuses to gun down John Dawson, he will endanger the dream of an independent country for his coreligionists; at least that is what he thinks. If he executes the British soldier, he will dishonor himself as well as the dead people he loves who remain inseparable from his being. The decision to commit the murder can thus appear totally justified or totally reprehensible according to the angle from which one envisages it. An element of arbitrariness inevitably comes into play in all the important acts of our life. But this arbitrariness also reveals itself in the whims of fate that can determine one's life or death. Hence the acute awareness in all of Elisha's comrades of the extreme fragility of their destinies. Without the sudden emergence of an event or a reaction on which they depended, they would all have been dead by now. As they wait for dawn to break, they relate episodes from their past during which they succeeded, almost by a miracle, in escaping death.

Elisha remembers the brutal Kapo who nearly strangled him. The sadistic guard suddenly released his grip when he noticed that his victim's head had swollen like a balloon on the verge of bursting. Overcome by uncontrollable laughter, the brute left him alone. Ilona informs the group that it was a cold that saved her from being executed. The British were looking for the mysterious voice on the clandestine radio station that was inciting Jews to commit acts of violence. On the day she was arrested, she was completely hoarse, so it was impossible for her captors to identify her. Another terrorist, Joav, managed to cheat death by convincing the police through his behavior that he was mentally ill. Gidon, his friend, resisted torture by imagining that God was watching him. Because he admitted nothing, there was no evidence against him, and the police let him go. But if all these people whom the terrorists had to deal with had made different decisions, they would not have avoided the fate that was hounding them.

The arbitrariness reappears when Elish gets to know John Dawson better before killing him and takes on the form of cruel irony. The young terrorist would have so wished that the British soldier had been a monster. It would have been so easy for him to hate the man and to summarily execute him. But as though destiny was determined to flout him, the narrator soon discovers that the hostage he is supposed to kill inspires in him an immense empathy. Endowed with an unostentatious courage, John Dawson seems to possess the inalterable serenity of someone who is already residing in a realm beyond death. He can thus allow himself to feel real compassion for his executioner who is the same age as his son. He senses the torments that will overcome his assassin. He is even able to keep his sense of humor, because he tells Elisha that what he finds so funny in his situation is that he doesn't know why he is going to die. Moreover, Elisha realizes that it is precisely the victim-executioner relationship imposed on them by circumstances that allows a friendship to develop between the two. Since the time they must spend together is literally short, they go straight to the essential and, as a result, again become agonizingly aware of the tragic dimension inherent in their fragile existences. They know they are prisoners of events beyond their control. And fate derides the narrator even more through the name his parents had bestowed on him. In Hebrew "Elisha" means "saved by God," and now Elisha will make a sacrilegious parody of the Messiah's raison d'être by killing one of His creatures.

Given the fallibility of terrorists like Elisha who agree to become criminals in the hope of creating a better world, one wonders how a humanist like Elie Wiesel could sympathize with this kind of warped idealism. As concerns terrorism itself, no doubt is possible. The author denounced it vehemently on many occasions. For him, to see one's fellow man or woman as objects to be crushed is to dehumanize the human condition. On the other hand, he approves Elisha and his comrades' refusal to conform to the stereotype of the helpless Jew victimized by a cruel destiny and enduring his suffering with resignation and sweetness. He always believed that it was natural for his coreligionists in Israel to retaliate vigorously when attacked. He always maintained that they had every right to act like any "normal" people, reacting forcefully against aggression, even at the risk of displeasing some of their so-called non-Jewish "friends" who would have preferred to see them nailed back again on their crosses to enjoy the selfish and hypocritical pleasure of shedding tears of pity on their misfortune.

The tragedy facing Elisha and his friends lies in having understood the problem but in having chosen the wrong solution. The hero of the next novel will paint himself into a similar corner. Elisha had wandered into a one-way street by adhering to a terrorist movement. The protagonist of *Day* will find himself in another kind of dead-end: illusory escape.

Day

There exist several striking similarities between the narrator of the novel *Day* and the hero of *Dawn*. Both are survivors of the death camps. Consequently, both suffer from incurable moral wounds. Both carry the weight of an eternal present symbolized by their relatives who disappeared during the interminable night of flames. From this point onwards, however, the roads they take lead them in different directions. Elisha uses his concentration camp experience to legitimize terrorist action as a means of creating a beautiful future. The narrator of *Day* invokes the horrors of the past to justify worshipping the memory of his deceased family. His guilt complex as a survivor of the Shoah engenders within him a death wish. Hence the irony of the title of the novel. Although the young man has come out of that nightmare alive, his mind adamantly refuses to emerge from the darkness. This may explain why Elie Wiesel chose not to give his hero either a first name or a surname. Since he is obsessed by the past and the void, it is not of primordial importance for him to define himself as an individual who enjoys the present and looks forward to the future. The nature of this narrator, however, remains far too complex to be reduced to a death wish. In agreement on this point with the young woman, Kathleen, who is desperately in love with him, he does not believe, unlike Hamlet, that the dilemma of human existence can be limited to the Shakespearian question "to be or not to be." For him one must express it in this way: "To be and not to be."

While maintaining his career as a journalist that appears completely normal, the narrator nevertheless embodies a yearning for an end to his existence that he expresses openly both to himself and the people who know him best. This constitutes his tragedy, and the narrative will be its illustration. At the beginning of the novel occurs the capital event, the accident that puts his life in danger. When the hero is run over by a taxi as he is crossing Times Square on an asphyxiating summer night, the reader takes it for granted that he was simply the victim of his own carelessness and never intended to commit suicide; but thanks to the extreme skill with which Elie Wiesel structures the narrative, he progressively raises doubts about the real motives behind his character's behavior. The narrator will not have the courage to confess these motives to his best friend until close to the end of the novel. It unfolds on two levels. On the one hand, the hero describes in a linear fashion the ten weeks he spends at the hospital from the first days when he hovers between life and death until the eve of his return home. On the other, the novel goes backwards and forwards between the present and the past, thereby enabling us to become progressively aware of the curse that has never let go of him from his time in the death camp and, as a result, the hell he has created without consciously intending to, in the life of the woman who loves him. We can then fully understand the redoubtable power he wields over all those who need to latch on to absolute certitudes.

The narrator's terrible drama crystallizes around Kathleen and the desperate love she feels for him. By going backwards and forwards between their present relationship and the one they had well before the accident, the novel accentuates the radical change that has taken place in the young woman's soul. It thus provides the reader with the key to open a door that the protagonist is anxious to keep rigorously shut. We meet Kathleen at the very beginning of the novel, several hours before the accident. She appears anxious, on the verge of breaking down. She clings to her love for the narrator the way a drowning person hangs on to a life buoy. She needs to hear him repeat again and again that he loves her. She practically begs him to do so. But their relationship did not always function in that manner. Through a series of flashbacks, the hero, lying immobile in his plaster cast on his hospital bed, remembers the young woman at the beginning of their affair in Paris. She cut a fine figure then. She demanded total independence in her dealings with men. In fact, she had dropped an admirer one evening at the theatre to go off with the narrator, simply because she felt like it. She acted like a conqueror; she possessed an unlimited self-confidence that bordered on arrogance with more than a touch of naiveness. Kathleen became passionately interested in the hero because he represented a challenge she could not resist. Yet he had warned her in advance: "You risk hating me." Being intrepid, she replied: "I accept this risk"[4]

---

[4] Elie Wiesel, *Le Jour*, Paris: Les Éditions du Seuil, 1961, 92; henceforth referred to as *J*.

At that precise moment there is a brief recollection of an event that took place in a more remote past. Although it does not seem to have any connection with what has just preceded, it nevertheless prefigures the nefarious influence the narrator will have on this very proud woman. The narrator remembers a voyage on an ocean liner going to South America. While standing on the deck he was fascinated by the sea's mysterious depths, so fascinated in fact that he was on the verge of succumbing to a death wish and letting himself be engulfed by the waves. A compassionate stranger who had already gone through the same experience hastened to neutralize the narrator's dangerous obsession by starting up a conversation with him. The latter was not generally inclined to bare his soul, but this time he opened the floodgates of his heart, described the hell to which he had been subjected in the concentration camp, and revealed the diabolical baseness into which so-called "civilized" people could sink. The stranger reacted in horror and disgust as though he had just seen death facing him. "I think I am going to hate you," he repeated several times before running away (*J*, 54).

To maintain her mental balance and emotional robustness, Kathleen should have undoubtedly run away like the unknown person. Instead of fleeing, she cockily fixed her gaze on the hell that the narrator was about to uncover for her. He related to her the death of his family, father, mother and little sister in the crematory ovens. He told her about the shame the survivors experienced, their feeling of guilt towards the dead. He revealed to her details about the behavior of human beings in the realm of death horrible enough to make one's hair stand on end. Far from recoiling in dread, Kathleen asked him to go on. Fascinated by the story and the young man's wild personality, she believed she was perfectly capable of fighting boldly to secure his happiness. She withstood his snickering laughter and anger after provoking him inadvertently by suggesting that his suffering had perhaps made him a saint. She did not suffer failure at that moment. It was much more a fight to a draw. They agreed to leave one another after a year. But the poison of doubt and despair that the Jewish journalist had inoculated into her made its way through her emotional and intellectual bloodstream during the five years that they remained separated from one another. The effectiveness of this poison became obvious in her chronic anxiety, her compulsive need to be reassured, and to hear again and again that she was loved, especially now that she is at her lover's bedside in the hospital.

The novelist suspends this return to the past regarding the narrator's relationship with Kathleen and begins another within the context of a long discussion that the young man has with Dr. Russel, the surgeon who snatched him from the jaws of death. This new flashback focusing on other aspects of the Jewish journalist's life will shed more light on his tormented attitude towards the woman who loves him. A fervent idealist, the doctor reproaches his patient for not having helped him repulse death during the long hours of surgery that ultimately saved him. He maintains that unlike other sick people whose organisms were doggedly determined to survive, the journalist seemed ready to let himself be vanquished without making any effort to resist. The latter is then gripped by dread. He wonders whether he had revealed anything under anesthesia. He is afraid that the doctor might know... But what? Nothing is divulged yet. Instead of disclosing what he really thinks about his doctor's idealism, the narrator remembers at this point a certain number of nightmarish episodes that traumatized him for good when he was trapped in the realm of night, in a place where his faith in man and God sank without a trace. The dialogue between the two men comes temporarily to a halt. Like a counterpoint to Dr. Russel's idealistic convictions, it is followed by a series of proofs that negate them. Shmuel appears, a detainee who strangled a several-months-old baby because his wailing might draw the S.S. guards into the bunker where a group of Jews were hiding. Then there was Moishe, his former fellow-student who was dreaming of becoming a rabbi. He turned himself into a smuggler wanted by all the police of Europe after having seen a religious Jew exchange his bread rations for a prayer book and die less than one month later.

When the narrative returns to linear time, the Jewish journalist realizes the futility of baring his soul to the doctor. He pours out instead noble abstract platitudes about the necessity of making a commitment to humanity and wins over his confidence completely by having recourse to the argument that sweeps away all doubts: love. As the narrator remarks, it was easy to dupe the doctor because he really wanted to be duped. With Kathleen, the task had been more difficult since she knew him far better. There occur two more flashbacks dealing with the evolving relationship between the hero and the woman who would have so wished to vanquish him. These frame the recollection of a traumatic event which had taken place long before: his encounter with a prostitute called Sarah, also Jewish and a survivor of the death camps, too. These three events shed light on one another, complete one another and end up by giving away the narrator's repressed secret.

When he and Kathleen rediscovered one another after an absence of five years she looked like a beaten down woman. As though to punish herself for not having succeeded in forcibly bringing joy to her lover, she had married a man far older than herself for whom she did not feel any real tenderness. The marriage ended in divorce. Disoriented, in desperate straits, she beseeched the journalist to rescue her. He agreed to help Kathleen the way a doctor would take responsibility for a patient, all the while wondering whether it would have been better to categorically refuse to burden himself with this task. After this flashback evoking the resumption of their relationship in New York, the narrative returns briefly to the present. We now understand better Kathleen's torment because we know that she will have to do battle against all the deceased people in the journalist's life and that she will never be able to fight them on an equal footing. Hence the quiver of anguish that passes through her body when she hears her lover pronouncing the name "Sarah" shortly after the accident, while he was still in a coma. She speaks to him about it four weeks later. To calm her, he asserts that in his delirium he called out for his mother who bore the same name. In reality, he uttered the name of the prostitute who had invited him to sleep with her in a Paris hotel.

The narrative returns abruptly to the past to conjure up this young girl whom he met one afternoon and who disappeared without a trace. She both fascinated and terrified the journalist by telling him how at twelve years old an SS officer initiated her forcibly into sex, and how she became the erotic plaything of all the German soldiers in the camp. Overcome with emotion, he maintained that she was a saint. Was this why he unleashed his fury against Kathleen when she told him the same thing? Was this an ironic symmetrical effect arranged by a cruel destiny to mock him? But Sarah vehemently denied this idealization of her nature by howling out her anger. A saint, she insisted, did not take a bestial pleasure in sleeping with torturers while being overwhelmed with disgust against them. She shook up the narrator even more by asking him if he too would have enjoyed making love to a twelve-year-old girl. Horrified, he fled the room.

The last flashback concerning the relationship between Kathleen and the journalist unfolds immediately after the recall of the episode with Sarah and brings us back definitively to linear time. Out of compassion for the woman who loved him desperately, and to give her a reason to live, the hero finally promised to try to free himself from his sorrowful past and from the grip that the dead still exerted on him. And the next day the accident occurred. As soon as the reader learns this detail, there is no longer any doubt possible. We are practically convinced that the hero has tried to commit suicide. Having made himself believe that he had betrayed the deceased people he loved by opting for the living, nauseated when he remembers the vileness of his fellow man, tormented by his awareness of the potential for evil within himself, the narrator seems to welcome death as a deliverance. The final episode of the novel that describes his friendship with the painter, Gyula, simply confirms our conviction. During the narrator's stay at the hospital, his friend comes to paint his portrait. Thanks to his art, Gyula manages to capture the obsession with the martyrdom that the journalist's family had endured. When the latter scrutinizes the portrait too intensely, however, the painter decides suddenly to set it on fire. Understanding implicitly why his friend wanted to put an end to his life, Gyula inflicts on him a kind of mental electroshock to force him once and for all to flush out the malediction of the concentration camp world. The journalist's cries of despair prove to the painter that his interpretation of his friend's state of mind was the correct one. At the end of the novel, the Holocaust survivor who has just had a brush with death will have to make an irreversible decision either for, or against life. Which one will it be? On leaving the hospital room abruptly, Gyula forgot to remove the cinders of the burned picture. Will the narrator have the courage to do this in the metaphysical as well as in the physical sense?

This note of anguished uncertainty emphasizes one last time and in a startling manner the hero's agonizing struggle, both mental and emotional, which the novel's structure has uncovered. We know that he has been living with the constant fear and shame of betraying the dead. But why does the Jewish journalist choose to worship the martyrs of the Shoah, with all the nefarious consequences this choice implies, to the detriment of a commitment to life? The explanation that immediately comes to mind is the traumatism he suffered in the concentration camp hell. The young man believes that he cannot act in any other way. On several occasions, he maintains that the survivors of the Shoah are discarded human objects or psychological cripples unable to lead a normal existence despite signs that seem to demonstrate the opposite. During his long discussion with the doctor, he says in an interior monologue: these people have been amputated, not in the physical sense, but in the sense that their will to live has been destroyed. One day or another, things they saw will re-emerge at the surface. And when it does the world will be struck with fear and will not dare look into the eyes of these spiritually mutilated people (*J*, 89-90). When Kathleen exhorts him to bury his past in the name of the love that

29

he supposedly feels for her, the narrator replies that the horrible images are an integral part of his being and will never cease haunting him: "Our sojourn down there planted time-bombs in us. Now and then, one of them explodes. When this occurs, we are a mass of suffering, shame and guilt. We feel ashamed and guilty to be alive, to eat as much bread as we want, to wear good warm socks in the winter. One of these bombs, Kathleen, will bring on madness. It is inevitable. Whoever has been down there has carried off with him a bit of the madness of humanity. One day or other, it will come up to the surface" (*J*, 126).

On studying this explanation closely, one realizes that it is merely the symptom of a deeper cause, namely, the fury the young man harbors against God for having messed up His creation and abandoned His creature. A thought he expresses within himself on the fifth day following his operation illustrates his attitude of revolt: "For a long time now I have failed to understand what He, the good God, could have done to deserve man" (*J*, 24). Thus, he takes the opposing view of his venerated teacher, Kalmen. The latter affirmed that God had endowed man with extraordinary spiritual powers thanks to which they form an inseparable couple. The human creature is the necessary ally of his Creator, since both are embarked on an enterprise to restore the primordial unity of the universe and, consequently, to hasten the Messiah's liberation. The journalist rejects this exalting vision of the God-man relationship and substitutes another that is grotesque and caricatural. Far from cherishing His creature and seeing in him a carrier of divine sparks indispensable to the consolidation of His unity, the Master of the universe views him as a toy. Like some cruel spectator. He takes delight in observing how this poor, laughable mechanism functions.

The narrator's encounter with Sarah, the prostitute, provides the most terrifying illustration of his conception of God's nature. As though her gaze was piercing the wall of the hotel room where she had invited the young man to make love, the poor tormented woman was reliving in a kind of hallucination her descent into hell in the special compound of the concentration camp. In this accursed place were assembled the women prisoners earmarked for the Nazi officers' sexual pleasures. Not sparing any detail for the horrified journalist, Sarah told him about the loss of her innocence at the hands of a brute greedy for fresh human flesh. How could God have allowed such horrors to be perpetrated against innocent, helpless victims? Was it possible that God Himself enjoyed sleeping with twelve-year-old little girls through the human garbage he engendered?

It was then that the narrator understood in a blinding intuition the meaning of the Bible's solemn warning against the temptation of looking straight into God's face. In the past he considered it incomprehensible that the Lord of the universe would kill anyone who dared look at Him. After hearing Sarah's story, everything became clear: God was ashamed. He liked sleeping with twelve-year-old little girls. And He didn't want anyone to find out. Whoever sees this or figures it out must die so as not to divulge His secret. Death is simply the guardian who protects God, the concierge in the immense house of prostitution called the universe. "I am going to die," I thought. "And my fingers, tightening around my neck, were involuntarily squeezing, squeezing, squeezing" (*J*, 111). So it is not God's majesty that risks killing mortals, but their earth-shaking awareness that He can embody injustice, sadism and crime. And it is this knowledge of the nature of God that devastates the narrator. As he declares, the believer would rather burden himself with every imaginable sin than acknowledge the evidence that hurts him so much (*J*, 48).

Having lost his faith in a God who, in his eyes, had botched up the creation of the human condition, it was inevitable that the journalist would lose confidence in his fellow man as well. His experience in the kingdom of night led him to this sorrowful conclusion. In the grip of physical suffering, prisoners would inevitably tumble down into bestiality. There came a moment when they would cross the line of demarcation separating civilized man from primitive brute. When he forces himself to eat a meat sandwich to please Kathleen shortly before the accident, he remembers an episode of his life in the concentration camp hell. A prisoner was devouring a slice of meat without bread. Tormented by hunger, the narrator would have wanted the latter to throw him a piece of it. The next day, he found the man's body swinging at the end of a rope in the lavatory shack. His fellow detainees had hung him for cannibalism despite his having protested, to vindicate himself, that the flesh had been taken from a cadaver. And what if the man had seen the narrator and had thrown him a piece of that cadaver? Hence the fear that overcame survivors at the idea of looking at themselves in a mirror. They might find the reflection of the evil they harbored in the abyssal depths of their beings. They might discover in it their inner self: "the one that laughs at unfortunate women and dead saints …" (*J*, 57).

This is why these very same survivors arouse the hatred of those who have not taken this trip into the depths of night. The latter have never ventured into the tortuous labyrinths of their hearts, and so will never forgive the survivors for having demolished the flattering mental image they entertained about themselves and the human condition in general. It suffices to recall the reaction of the stranger who had finally been repelled after listening to the narrator reveal thoughts that would make even Hell blush. Thus, if the narrator repudiates God and despairs of man, what is left for him to respect? The martyrs, because these people were lucky enough to die before degenerating into brutes and sullying themselves irremediably. The journalist safeguards their memory with religious piety. The dead represent for him the only unsullied part left of his idealism.

This worship of the dead manifests itself in two principal forms: the grandmother and the train. Sweet, generous, lavishing her compassion unconditionally, the hero's grandmother remained for him a living sanctuary where he was always sure of being loved and understood. (She resembles in many ways the one Elie Wiesel lost during the Holocaust.) The burning tears she would shed when she held him on her lap and commiserated with his sorrows, her clear eyes radiating kindness, the black kerchief she always wore on her head constitute essential elements of his mythical childhood universe. This saintly old lady is omnipresent even when he is not thinking consciously of her. The duty the narrator imposes on himself of never forgetting her is all the more sacred because she has no grave. Having died in the gas chamber, her body was burned, and her ashes scattered to the winds. Hence his cries of despair when Gyula sets fire to the painting. It is as though his grandmother was being incinerated for the second time.

The symbol of the train is organically linked to the smoke emanating from the bodies of family members consumed by fire. Before the people he cherished went up in smoke—literally—they had to take the train to get to the accursed places where stood the crematory ovens. In the young man's imaginary world, this train carries away his parents and soars into the sky. Being alive, he will never be able to go up there with them; he will remain forever on the station's quay. And the train will never be able to move into reverse to pick him up. The train thus symbolizes the insurmountable distance that death has created between the camp survivors and the beloved people who lost their lives there. No matter what he does, the narrator will never be able to join them. He will not even be able to meditate at their gravesites because they don't have any. Therein lies his shame. What right does he have to continue living when these relatives who were far more worthy of remaining alive have perished in the night of flames and horror?

In this context we can understand his pessimism tinged with exasperation as he faces Kathleen's and Dr. Russel's combativeness. They belong to a category of individuals who have never descended to the bottom of the abyss, and so it is difficult for them to comprehend that for certain survivors of the Holocaust the spiritual itinerary leads to a dead end: "Whoever has seen what they have seen cannot act like all the others, he cannot laugh, love, pray, bargain, suffer, have fun or forget. Like all the others. One must observe them carefully as they pass in front of a harmless factory chimney, or when they bring a piece of bread to their mouths. Something within them shudders and makes others turn away" (*J*, 89).

Having fought duels on many occasions against the dead who haunt her lover's memory, Kathleen, at least, knows the strength of her adversaries. She writhed in pain like a victim undergoing torture when he spoke to her about his mother after his operation. But she refuses categorically to admit that the deceased are invincible. This is why she proposes a deal: let him allow her to help him tear himself away from the kingdom of night and she will agree to let him help her take pleasure in living again. The doctor, on the other hand, is walled up alive in a simplistic and immutable system of values. Not that he is antipathetic. In many respects, he is an admirable man. He has devoted himself to the mission of fighting death to the finish while knowing that one can win battles and lose the war. But he cannot imagine how a traumatized death-camp survivor like the narrator can yield to suicidal impulses. For the doctor, life will always remain the supreme value, whatever be the circumstances that might legitimize a contrary form of behavior. For him existence consists in a Manichean struggle between Good and Evil, the first being synonymous with life, the second with death. To refuse this vision is to incur the accusation of sacrilege. Dr. Russel feels so much sympathy for the Jewish journalist that he believes the latter as soon as he assures the doctor that he loves Kathleen and is hanging on to life for that very reason.

The narrator uses this argument to put an end to their dialogue of the deaf and to avoid wounding a man whom he really respects. But when one fathoms the young man's personality, does one not discern deep forces capable of impelling him to make a definitive commitment to life? In the first place, the journalist would never have succeeded in persuading Kathleen after his operation that he loved her unless he did feel a genuine affection for her.

Moreover, the shame that overcomes him at the thought of being the only one among his relatives to have escaped destruction and to be able to enjoy the elementary pleasures the earth has to offer implies an instinctive attachment to life despite its tragic potential. Finally, his friendship with Gyula testifies eloquently to his will to live. That man represents a force of nature. He has lead a stormy existence, has known poverty, had a brush with death, but always managed to triumph over a cruel destiny thanks to an emotional and spiritual resilience that never failed. He can penetrate the heart and mind of his unhappy friend like a laser beam, and orders him to drive away the dead with a whip if necessary. According to Gyula, the dead are no longer free, so they cannot suffer any longer. Only the living can suffer. They, therefore, are the ones who deserve priority. We recall that he compels the narrator to choose life by destroying the painting that the latter's family is haunting. The fact that ashes remain on the floor of his hospital room at the end of the novel signifies, perhaps, that no one except the narrator can save him. We know that his creator, Elie Wiesel, nearly succumbed, if only very briefly, to the temptation of suicide during the years following his liberation from the death camps. The reader would like to imagine that the hero of *Day* will, like the author, draw from his reservoir of spiritual energy the strength necessary to put an end to his self-imposed exile from life, return to the kingdom of the living and rediscover joy.

CHAPTER 2
GLIMMERS OF LIGHT

In *Night*, *Dawn*, and *Day* the atmosphere prevailing is extremely somber. Having ventured into the heart of the Nazi hell, none of the three narrators are able to combat the shadows to emerge into the light. Even though they are survivors of the Holocaust, they regain their freedom in the physical sense alone. From the spiritual point of view, they remain prisoners of the concentration camps. Their vision of the world is centered on themselves. As proof of this, we need simply remember that all three express themselves in the first person. At the end of *Night*, Elie Wiesel considers himself a living cadaver. The hero of his first novel, *Dawn*, loses his soul in terrorist activity, thereby reproducing the brutality of the very experience he is striving to transcend. The unnamed protagonist of the second novel, *Day*, feels crushed under the weight of guilt. What right does he have to enjoy life when the people he loved most were exterminated by the barbaric Nazis? The reader would like to believe that the journalist will reconnect with life, as his friend Gyula orders him to do, even at the risk of forgetting his deceased relatives, but nothing is less certain. Starting with *The Town Beyond the Wall*, however, one notices a significant change. After slipping away, the Messiah reappears in the most singular and unexpected manner through human relations. This tendency is confirmed even more strongly in the following novel, *The Gates of the Forest*. Light begins henceforth to prevail over darkness.

The Town Beyond the Wall

What a strange road the hero of Elie Wiesel's third novel takes to bring meaning to his life! Like Elisha and the narrator of *Day*, Michael was traumatized by his experience in the concentration camp hell. Like them as well, he saw loved ones suffer degradation and death in the Nazis' extermination factories. But whereas the protagonists of the first two novels sought out false solutions to resolve their dilemmas, the main character of *The Town Beyond the Wall* succeeds in making a breakthrough as salutary for him as for his fellow man. He returns to the place where, as a child, his life plummeted into tragedy: the town of Szerencsevàros, which means in Hungarian, "the City of Chance." Without yet knowing why, he is convinced it contains the answer to questions that obsess him. Contrary to what happens in *Dawn* and *Day*, the title of this third novel is only in part ironic. Certainly, his return to his place of birth draws him into a tragedy almost as terrible as the one he lived through during the Second World War. By the most notable of paradoxes, however, the new dangerous situation in which Michael finds himself trapped will enable him to accept himself fully as a human being linked to his fellow man in a relationship of brotherly responsibility.

When the novel begins, Michael is already in the clutches of the ruthless Hungarian secret police several years after the end of the war. Having crossed communist Hungary's border illegally, he is apprehended and subjected to a form of torture, half-physical, half-mental, that is particularly diabolical called "the prayer." Michael is forced to stand, immobile, for eight hours straight in a cell called "the temple." The police is waiting for him to break down at any moment and divulge the identity of the person who helped him enter the country clandestinely. He is determined not to give in. He wants at all costs to hide the escape of Pedro, the friend for whom he feels a fraternal affection. During these four "prayer" sessions corresponding to the four parts of the novel, the hero reassembles the whole chain of events of his life and relives the episodes that left an imprint on him as a way of keeping his physical pain at bay and preventing his mind from disintegrating into madness. These recollections are interspersed with brutal reminders in the present: the guards interrogate Michael, demanding that he confess what he knows, warn him that his personality may very well collapse if he persists in his stubbornness. But the hero is comforted in his solitude whenever he remembers his best friend who, beyond time and space, brings him courage and solace.

After reliving the episode leading to his arrest, Michael functions henceforth in the present. He resisted long enough to save his friend. But an ordeal just as dangerous as the previous one awaits him. How will he resist succumbing to nervous depression in a cell in which he is shut up with three other detainees? Once again, the spiritual glow cast by the image of his friend comes to his rescue. The hero picks up the challenge, overcomes his despair, and in the very heart of this physical hell reaffirms the nobility of the human condition. His impressive combativeness and his devotion to his unfortunate fellow prisoners bring the Messiah to life among them.

Michael is obsessed with the issue of insanity because he has been around people during his youth who suffered from mental illness in their respective ways. The first was Marthe, the village drunk. A living reminder of original chaos, an earth mother sent from all the devils in hell, an urgent invitation to lechery in its most repugnant form, this woman fascinates as much as she repels him. Having become aware of the irreducible ugliness of life as much on the moral as on the physical levels, Marthe yells out her revolt against an absurd order by preaching sexual anarchy and the violation of all tabus. She had exhorted the ten-year-old Michael to unite his body with hers. Many years later, during one of the torture sessions, Michael imagines that this woman has returned to renew her offer of hideous sex. Is he a victim of a cruel destiny? Let him show his contempt, then, towards these inhuman forces by systematically going in for immoral overkill. Herein lies the meaning of her invitation to lustfulness: "Come on!" The drunken woman joyously exhorts him. "Vomit to your heart's content but come to me. Become a god and act like one: be the ally of ugliness, of the inhuman. Come into me, give me your disgust and your love. This is the only kind of love that life deserves." [5]

This unleashed insanity is in sharp contrast to a form of madness that inspires veneration in the young Michael: that of Moishe the beadle. The latter uses the mind's breakdown as a mask to protect his interlocutors. As Michael's father affirms, Moishe has the gift of clairvoyance. The gaze of his mind penetrates way beyond the visible world to foresee events that have not yet occurred. If he didn't pretend to be crazy, he would without a doubt arouse terror in other people. He knows in advance what his fellow man and woman don't even want to imagine. Is that why Moishe appears sad so often? Can he predict the fate that will befall his coreligionists? Does he already see the flames of the Nazi hell in which he and the other Jews of Szerencsevàros will plunge? It is not farfetched to think this. On the eve of the Shoah, the beadle praises madness in a way that suggests it is the only attitude possible in the face of a universe that is spinning off its

---

[5] Elie Wiesel, *La Ville de la chance*, Paris : Les Éditions du Seuil, 1962, 102; henceforth referred to as *V*.

axis. Indeed, why bother being guided by reason and logic when existence seems to be drifting into sheer insanity? A diabolical destiny that is hounding man relentlessly does not deserve to be taken seriously by human intelligence: "The others!" Moshe called out while banging his fist against the table. "The others! Why shouldn't they be crazy? Given the times we live in, decent people should do only one thing: become crazy! Spit on logic, intelligence, sacrosanct reason! This is what we must do, this is how we can remain human and keep our integrity" (V, 25). Even though Moishe's and Marthe's temperaments are at opposite extremes, one detects in both of their words the same metaphysical revolt against a universe in which injustice reigns.

All things considered, Moishe never loses contact with reality. His so-called madness reflects his disdainful rejection of an existence given over to evil. In this respect, Michael remembers the anguish the beadle felt the day when some children made him drink urine while persuading him that it was wine. On the other hand, the hero's Kabbala teacher tumbled straight into insanity and dragged down two of his disciples in his wake. Kalman is not content to disdain earthly existence. He is doggedly determined to cut off all ties to it in order to catapult himself, freed from the weight of matter, into the infinite spiritual space where God resides. Kalman's goal is to liberate the Messiah imprisoned by Time so that the latter will finally come, bringing with him joy and consolation to all the poor earthly mortals, and put an end to the murderous vicissitudes of history. Exalted by this project, the teacher and his disciples disconnect themselves from reality at the very moment when their coreligionists are snatched by the tens of thousands and crushed in Hitler's killing machines. Much later, Michael, who was considered one of Kalman's preferred students, will realize how wise his father was to entreat him not to break his body in order to liberate his soul. Our body, his father maintained, is the hyphen linking us to our fellow man. Annihilating it is as serious as killing life; "He who does not live for his fellow man right now, for the one who walks next to you and whom you can see, touch, love and hate, creates for himself an unjust image of God" (V, 55).

Deaf to his father's entreaties, Michael nearly sank into madness like his two other comrades. He was saved (just like Elie Wiesel) by the arrival of the Nazis in his town. And yet, the adolescent's father was not the only person to warn him against the dangers of mystical trances. A somewhat bizarre centenary neighbor, Varady, also gave Michael a solemn warning. During his youth Varady had been pious, everyone saw in him a future chief rabbi. But obsessed as he was by his vision of man's super-power, he pronounced a blasphemous sermon in the synagogue and was ostracized by the Jewish community. Michael struck up a friendship with the old man despite being forbidden to do so by his parents and told him that to please them he was going to study both religion and philosophy. Varady's reaction led the adolescent to believe that a long time ago the religious pariah had almost lost his reason because of his attempt to follow these two contradictory paths of knowledge As he said: "Man is too weak, his imagination is too poor to penetrate the garden and remain at the same time on the other side of the fence" (*V*, 36).

Having entered the realm of mysticism of which the garden was the metaphor, the centenarian's experience left indelible traces on his mind. As an intrepid young man, he had ventured well beyond the known frontiers of the spirit. Now, in the shadow of death, he persists in believing that the grandeur of man consists in deploying his energy to impose his will on the universe rather than submit to its law. Without going so far as to jeer at God's creation, at the end of the novel Michael will also draw from his reservoir of spiritual energy to dispel his own despair and save another human consciousness from darkness.

After having brushed against the madness of others, the hero almost succumbs to it himself after the war, during the accident and death of his friend Yankel in Paris. A prisoner like Michael in the same concentration camp, Yankel enjoyed exceptional privileges. He became the "pilpel," or spoiled child of the SS guards, so was saved from the inhuman regime to which the other detainees were subjugated. In fact, Yankel called the shots there. If he interceded with the police a coreligionist would avoid punishment. If he didn't the Jewish prisoner could be treated sadistically. Because he was very young and most often inclined to feel pity for his co-detainees, the latter tended to forgive this little prince's whims. Michael's feelings towards him remained ambiguous. He liked and hated him at the same time. This ambiguity could not be explained by solid reasons. Michael never had it in for Yankel for exerting the power of life or death over the other inmates. But the hero could not forgive the spoiled child for having noticed his absence of emotion when his father was dying in the concentration camp. The little prince was weeping in silence whereas Michael, the son who sincerely loved his father, remained impassive because of his moral and physical exhaustion.

This explains why fury overcame Michael when Yankel himself lay dying after being struck by a truck. While feeling deep compassion for his unfortunate friend, the hero persisted in seeing in him the witness of his secret shame. Had the doctor not entered the room on time, Michael would not have gotten hold of himself and released his grip on the dying man's neck. But madness tempts the hero once again after the little prince is deceased. Yankel's death exemplifies the cruelty of destiny towards the whole human condition. It has a symbolic value. It prefigures the fate to which we are all subjugated sooner or later. Michael holds God responsible for this injustice. To revolt, then, against this power the Creator of the universe possesses to destroy life unfairly, to protest against His bungled creation, the hero contemplates taking refuge in another form of insanity, this one being a world constructed by his imagination. What prevents him from falling into the abyss is his awareness that his decision to go mad would deprive him forever of the freedom to cry out his revolt against God, and as a result, would take away from him the superiority he enjoys in his relationship with the Father of Creation: "Choosing madness is an act of courage than cannot be multiplied. It is an end in itself. It is a free act that destroys freedom. Freedom is given to men exclusively. God is not free" (V, 11-112).

To soften somewhat the anguish of being alive, all he had to do was respond to the love offered to him by a beautiful young woman, sweet and welcoming, called Milika. He met her at Varady's place where she had a job as his guardian. He remembers that as an adolescent his senses were extremely aroused in her presence. He would have given himself to her in the garden if he had not suspected the old man, an impenitent joker, of having prepared this erotic setting to make fun of him. He finds her again in Paris. They are both poor and alone. They could love one another. And this emotion nearly comes alive again in their hearts. Michael is astonished by what is happening within him: "A woman appears, and the world is no longer the same. Suddenly, everything is filled with her presence. Everything becomes simple, true, possible. I am, you are. That is enough. It means that man is not alone, that his dispersed energy is reassembled somewhere" (V, 95). But he fights against his inclination, convinced as he is that their relationship has no future. Their attraction to one another was born in Szerencsevàros and this town for him resembles a cemetery now. Even when he becomes gravely ill, subject to a terrible fever, he refuses to give the young woman's name to his landlady even though he was on the verge of pronouncing it. Despite the comfort that Milika seemed to send him via remote control through her name, the hero categorically refuses to go backwards.

He will never see Milika again. On the other hand, Michael will not avoid being fascinated by Pedro, a man who will become his best friend, indeed his spiritual brother and guardian angel, the one who will always manage to stay close to him, even when the two of them will be separated physically. Sent on a mission as a journalist to Tangiers by a boyhood chum, Meir who, after the war, transformed himself from a pious Jew into a smuggler, Michael encounters there yet another smuggler named Pedro. He had agreed, reluctantly, to make the latter's acquaintance to please Meir. Once the meeting takes place, Michael knows that his destiny is at a crossroads. He is even convinced that he had traveled the distance from Paris to Tangiers for the sole purpose of establishing an exalting brotherly relationship with that man.

Incomparable Pedro! The ideal friend of whom Elie Wiesel dreamed, the meeting place and living synthesis of the most ruthless pessimism and the most joyous generosity, a hydroelectric power station in the figurative sense to which lost and tormented individuals like Michael can connect to revitalize themselves on the moral level. As soon as the hero approaches this singular smuggler, he becomes conscious of the powerful influence that this man exerts on everyone around him. When the young Jewish journalist enters the Black Cat Café, he finds Pedro surrounded by a band of marginals who are drinking the smuggler's words without fully understanding their meaning. There is nothing surprising here. Pedro possesses a depth of intelligence worthy of a great philosopher combined with a gift of compassion that would honor an exemplary religious believer. In addition, there is his voice, the sonorous mirror of his soul: mesmerizing, moving. Describing the special quality of this voice, Michael says: "His voice was nostalgic, vibrant, it opened up a shadowy path within the shadows. It suggested infinite fields, dark forests, immense solitudes. To some it brought disquiet, to others, peace. It was the dagger that opened wounds and the balm that healed them" (*V*, 128).

Through this voice, Pedro deploys his clairvoyance that allows him to get to the core of the stories his new friend tells him and so helps him to better understand his past. Michael does not take offense in the least when some of them provoke the smuggler's laughter, even though they are impregnated with sadness. Nor is he surprised that this perspicacious man uncovers the anguished side of people who, on the surface, do not carry within them any reason to feel anxiety. The young man knows that Pedro's prodigious mind functions through intuitive leaps. It grasps in one fell swoop the far-reaching consequences of certain actions that bear no resemblance to their beginnings. Thus, having full confidence in this exceptional friend, convinced that he is understood and loved for himself, Michael shares with him progressively all the significant episodes of his past involving the people who made them happen: his relationship with Moishe, Varady and Kalman, the horrors his family had suffered in the death camp, and his attraction to Milika. And by sharing this past with such a friend, Michael can finally free himself from it.

In fact, the young man's liberation begins from their very first encounter at the Black Cat café. Urged by the other guests to tell a story, the survivor of the Nazi hell frees himself from a traumatic experience deeply rooted in his being by relating to them the tragedy of Mendele. This courageous little Jewish boy did not let out the slightest groan of pain when Hungarian fascist soldiers pierced his body with the thrusts of their swords while he lay, covered by straw, at the bottom of a cart driven by a compassionate peasant who was taking him along with his mother to a less dangerous place. Having promised her to remain silent no matter what happened in order not to betray their presence, Mendele kept his word till the very end.

The story of the little boy, like the others Michael shares with the smuggler, arouses in the latter the same surge of sympathy enabling him to espouse the destiny of all who suffer. Now the compassion Pedro lavishes unconditionally on all victims of the insane cataclysms of history explains his pugnacity towards God. More so than Michael, he raises his fist against the Creator of the universe and does not hesitate to demand that the latter explain His misdeeds. The young Jewish man, at least, revolted against the injustices of the Divine order within the context of his faith. He remarked that giving vent to one's anger against God was still a way of acknowledging His existence and glorifying Him. Naturally, Michael unleashed his fury against the insensitivity of the Master of the universe who had allowed the Nazis to throw Kalman and two of his former Talmudic classmates into the crematory ovens. Despite knowing that their bodies had been born aloft by the flames and their ashes scattered in the sky, Michael never considered renouncing God definitively. He had taken as his own the following prayer: "Oh, God! Stay by me when I need you, but above all do not leave me when I renounce you" (*V*,56). Pedro, on the other hand, does not hesitate to go beyond blasphemy. He takes pleasure in belittling the Creator by unmasking his fallibility. He replaces his Jewish friend's fervent prayer with another, both aggressive and denigrating: "I, too, have a prayer that belongs to me, made to measure. Here it is: "God! Give me the strength to sin against you, to oppose your will. Give me the strength to renounce you, to reject you, to imprison you, to ridicule you! That is my prayer" (V, 60). And yet, while denigrating God, Pedro does not at all exclude Him from his existence. The Creator comes back into it through His most moving work: the human being. It is by loving His creature that Pedro finally returns to this God he so despises. "Endeavor to help others. Many others," he urges his young friend (V, 143).

An adept of Emmanuel Lévinas' philosophy without being aware of it, Pedro affirms in his way, just like the great Franco-Jewish thinker, that the ethical relationship with one's fellow man or woman remains insepa-rable from the knowledge of God.[6] It is through the Other that one has the best chance to glimpse the trace of the infinite. The Other's vulnerability deeply moves the subject and arouses within him/her the desire to elu-cidate the mystery of the former. During one of their evening conversa-tions, Pedro reproaches Michael for letting himself get too obsessed by the problem of God to the detriment of the human condition: "He who thinks of God while forgetting man risks missing his objective: God may be the next-door neighbor" (V, 134). Thus, instead of placing God at the centre of his preoccupations, Pedro incorporates Him into his own humanistic phi-losophy which reverberates with echoes of Albert Camus. Moreover, Elie Wiesel pays homage to the illustrious writer through his personage. One evening the two friends approach the subject of love. Pedro unburdens his heart and reveals to Michael an extremely painful secret. He had loved a woman during the Spanish Civil War. He called her Félicità to evoke the immense joy she awakened in him. An impassioned revolutionary, Félicità was captured by Franco supporters and raped thirty-seven times. She was already dead before the soldiers had finished their ugly deed. Shattered by this appalling account, Michael once again is overcome by the temptation of madness. If he had been in Pedro's place, he declares, he would have made the universe tremble. He would have unearthed all the cadavers in Spain to find Félicità's body and would have made love to it. But for Pedro this is a false, illusory and juvenile solution. One does not eliminate suf-

---

[6] An important French thinker of the twentieth century, Emmanuel Lévinas (1905-1995) founded his metaphysics on the relationship with the Other as being infinitely other and irreducible to the subject relating to this Other. For Lévinas, the ethical dimension was inseparable from philosophical thought. He thus opposes the totalitarian tendency of western philosophy that consists in devaluing the individual and incorporating him into the Whole. His most significant works are *Totalité et Infini* (Totality and Infinity), *Autrement qu'être* (Otherwise than Being), and *Humanisme de l'autre homme* (Humanism of the Other Man).

fering by pushing it to a paroxysm, because one ends up drowning in one's own sorrow and, consequently, one feels an aversion for one's fellow man. The suffering he experiences must make man become conscious of that of the whole human condition. It must incite him to denounce a cruel cosmic order and proclaim his moral superiority to it by striving to bring happiness to people around him: "Camus said somewhere that it is necessary to create happiness as a way of protesting against a universe where unhappiness rules. It is an arrow indicating the road to follow. It leads to the other and not through the absurd" (*V*, 138).

In the context of this compassionate and heroic humanism, friendship occupies a place of choice. As a communion of hearts and minds, it melts the walls of solitude that imprisons two consciousnesses and doubles their ability to think and feel. Since each one expands towards the other, each one becomes the other. As Pedro explains to Michael, "Henceforth you can say I am Pedro, and I in turn can say I am Michael" (*V*, 143). According to this spiritual mathematical operation touched by divine grace, one plus one equals one. But this fusion of two beings does not imply in the least a loss of individual identity. The two friends will keep their personalities and personal histories, the indispensable condition for their mutual enrichment. Nevertheless, the strength and idealism of the one will watch over the other like guardian angels. Wherever they may be in the world, they will never again be alone.

To show his devotion towards Michael, Pedro, through his many international contacts, can fulfill a wish that the former inhabitant of Szerencsevàros thought unrealizable: to see one last time the town where he was born. Before arriving there and walking around the streets of the town, the young man could not put his finger on the exact reason for wanting to return. As soon as he passes in front of the space where stood the Great Synagogue destroyed by the Nazis, something clicks in his memory. Michael recalls the dreadful summer day when the Hungarian police, the Nazis' servile lackeys, rounded up the Jews of the town in that holy building before shoving them into cattle cars. Then the hero remembers that a man was watching through his window. His face did not betray any emotion. It expressed indifference. At that shattering instant Michael knows why he has come back to Szerencsevàros. It is to understand how so-called civilized human beings were able to watch abominable acts being committed against their fellow men without reacting. Michael understood the Nazi logic while detesting it. Impelled by ugly racial hatred, the executioners existed to exterminate their Jewish victims. But the adolescent Michael was at the time flabbergasted by the indifference of the spectator watching from his window. The presence of this witness was a form of absence, and the unfortunate Jews were for him nothing more than actors in a play who were going to return to the wings once the performance was over. Remembering this spectator, Michael said: "He is there, but he carries on as though he wasn't there. Even worse: he carries on as though we were not there" (*V*, 175).

Michael goes up to the man's apartment and throws two glasses of wine in the latter's face to humiliate him. The former spectator remains impassive. The day when the Jews of the town were rounded up, he had not felt anything. Today, he does not feel anything either. The former anonymous observer tries to justify his impassiveness on that day by maintaining that the Jews being far more numerous than the Hungarian police, it would have been easy for them to attack the enemy and win. But Michael insists that such an argument is irrelevant. What counts is that the victims came from the Jewish community. The spectator, on the contrary, as a member of the unthreatened majority should have intervened to help them. Repressing his hatred, Michael makes his interlocutor understand that what he feels for the latter is the deepest contempt. Hatred implies a human relationship. Contempt devalues the person and reduces him to the state of inert object. In the face of this negation of his person, the spectator is disconcerted, gets desperate and almost demands to be hated. When Michael refuses, the non-Jew denounces him to the police, convinced that this cowardly act will at last provoke the hatred he so longs for and restore his self-image. But Michael does not react the way the spectator expected him to. It matters little that the young Jewish man is now in the hands of the police. By smiling at the former spectator who denounced him instead of hating him, by playing the merciful God as he describes the scene in his imaginary dialogue with Pedro, Michael continues crushing his interlocutor under his scorn.

Pedro's fraternal presence that has constantly sustained the young Jewish man during the torture sessions will not fail him once he is thrown into a cell with three other inmates. Armed with the spiritual strength and exalting humanistic ideal that his best friend has bestowed upon him, Michael will overcome his worst ordeal since the death camp. He will stop his slide into madness by embodying the Messiah for two of the detainees. And herein lies the moving paradox: by opening his heart and mind to them, they, in turn, will help him save himself.

The first with whom Michael empathizes is Menachem, a very handsome Jewish man with an affecting face that resembles a Byzantine Christ.

The name the latter bears is very significant. It means in Hebrew "he who brings comfort." Menachem expresses his admiration for the courage Michael showed in resisting his tormentors long enough for Pedro to flee Hungary. He is also enduring a dreadful ordeal. He was imprisoned for wanting to give clandestine religious courses to combat the virulent antisemitic propaganda propagated by the communist regime. An unconditional believer, he nevertheless asks himself some anguished questions about God's secret intentions. Why does God insist on making us take the hardest path to come to Him? These questions are often accompanied by tears. At the beginning of their relationship, Michael has a rather disdainful attitude towards the unconditional faith of his coreligionist. He considers it incongruous that Menachem refuses to renounce his belief that God will never abandon him and will protect him from madness. But the hero's disdain is transformed into deep emotion when one of the inmates, nicknamed the Impatient one, is on the verge of strangling the pious Jew. Michael frees Menachem in the nick of time from the clutches of the madman and Menachem expresses through his gaze immense affection and gratitude. The hero weeps for the first time in years. Far from being a sign of weakness, these tears represent the indispensable opening up towards the Other thanks to which a wave of spiritual oxygen penetrates his inner prison.

Unfortunately, Menahem is transferred to another part of the jail. His departure seems to signal the disappearance of the Messiah whose spirit had brought to life a brotherly relationship founded on the reciprocal gift of the self. Having only the company of two madmen, the Impatient with violent tendencies, and the Silent one, an adolescent enclosed in an apparently impenetrable mutism, Michael again fears that his personality may disintegrate. It nearly does, in fact, get swallowed up in the shadows. This fear is reinforced when he is tempted to strangle the Impatient after the latter nearly killed the Silent one. At that very moment Pedro comes to the rescue. Speaking once more to his Jewish friend in the form of an imaginary conversation, the charismatic smuggler exhorts him to save the mute boy to reconquer his spiritual strength. Is the universe in a mess? It doesn't matter! Let Michael reconstruct it. By committing himself to this herculean task, his energy will surge upwards even more powerfully: "This is precisely what I want you to do: recreate the universe. Give the boy back his sanity. Cure him. He will save you." (*V*, 197).

Once the Impatient one is removed from the cell, Michael remains alone with the young mute and throws himself with wild enthusiasm into the mission of wresting a human consciousness from the night where it had allowed itself to be enclosed. He knows that by effecting the spiritual resurrection of the Silent one, he will participate in the healing of the whole of humanity and, at the same time, will win a magnificent victory over his own despair. The cry of exasperation emanating from his mouth when confronting the impassiveness of the mute illustrates his awareness of how important the stakes are: "Wake up, in the name of God! This is our only chance! One of us will win! If I don't, we are both lost! Do you understand me?" (*V*, 200). At first, Michael feels powerless to overcome this barrier of silence. Nevertheless, through gestures, movements, frenzied pantomimes, words indefinitely repeated, the hero finally succeeds in reaching the boy. Just then the miracle takes place. The Messiah appears in this fraternal relationship where two beings know that they exist for one another. Speaking to himself as well as to the Silent one, he summarizes eloquently the spiritual inheritance that his best friend, Pedro, bequeathed to him. The meaning of life does not reside in indifference towards the Other, because in that case human existence in general and our own in particular sink into the void. Each one of us, as individuals, is alive only to the extent that he is attuned to his fellow beings to bring them succor. In this way he sanctifies the whole of humanity of which he is an integral part. "Real heights are like true depths," he declares. "We find them at our level, in simple and pure dialogue, in a gaze charged with human density" (*V*, 203).

Michael is now certain that he will finally cure the Silent one. On that day, he will transfer to the boy the wisdom that Pedro had bestowed on him as a gift. Michael will become Pedro for the boy, and the latter, eventually, will acquire the name of his benefactor. In this brotherly solidarity that transcends time and space the Messiah will continue living. Knowing that he has been saved by the boy whose mind he was heroically determined to bring back into the light, Michael feels a profound gratitude towards this young person. Through the Silent one, Michael's belief in man and in God has been revitalized, and this God remains inseparable from the ethical relationship. It is significant that the boy's name, which the reader does not learn until the last paragraph of the narrative, is the biblical Eliezar, meaning "God has answered my prayer." Thus, the novel ends on an optimistic note. If night has not completely disappeared, at least it is receding.

In the second-to-last paragraph of *The Town Beyond the Wall*, Wiesel writes: "Michael was reaching the limits of his strength. In front of him, night, like a mountain before dawn, was backing away" (*V*, 204). Not only does the hero begin to hope again, but so does the author who created him.

The Gates of the Forest

The novel *The Gates of the Forest* (1964) contains two principal charac-
teristics that distinguish it from the preceding one. In the first place, the
title is not ironic. It signifies the choice the hero, Grégor/Gavriel will have
to make towards the end of his spiritual journey between the return to
solitude that the forest symbolizes or his reconciliation with his wife and,
beyond the marital context, with the community at large. In second place,
even before embarking on his inner itinerary, Grégor is one length ahead
of Michael in the novel *The Town Beyond the Wall*. As we have seen, traumatized by his experience of Hitler's final solution, the uprooted Michael
was not really able to connect with anyone other than Pedro until the last
stage of his journey through life. Grégor, on the other hand, never had any
difficulty entertaining relationships with his fellow man since he was not
a Holocaust survivor even though he lost all his family in that catastrophe.
Indeed, his spiritual trajectory consists in enlarging his circle of relationships until he rediscovers his religious faith.

Named for the successive seasons of the year, the four major parts that
make up the novel, Spring, Summer, Autumn and Winter, correspond to
the four main stages of his existence. Each one is laden with ambiguities.
In the spring, Grégor seeks refuge in a grotto in the heart of the forest to
avoid being pursued by the Nazis after his whole family has been victimized during a raid, but he discovers Gavriel there, the friend of a lifetime.
The latter will breathe into him the spiritual energy necessary to confront
the terrible ordeals that await him. In the summer the hero descends into
the moral sewer of a whole village that proudly calls itself Christian. He is
even on the verge of being stoned by a crowd thirsting for Jewish blood.
Nevertheless, his experiences enable him to confirm the effectiveness of
the gifts of courage and compassion that his friend had bequeathed to him.
In autumn, Grégor suffers horribly when the leader of the Partisans, Leib,
is captured by the fascists. Feeling responsible for this tragedy, he is desperate. Yet, this is the period of his life when he becomes aware of his love
for Clara. The final season, winter, takes possession of New York City,
immobilizes it under heavy snowfalls, and seems to reflect the hero's profound sadness. But in the heart of his depression and of winter that creates
an atmosphere of desolation he finds the moral strength necessary to fight
his way back again and return to the faith of his childhood.

Grégor begins to plumb the depths of his being when he meets an
enigmatic man of about thirty years old, a Jew like himself, but who has

witnessed the horrors of the enflamed night. The reader is never absolutely certain about the character's identity. Does he really exist? Or is he Grégor's alter ego, the idealized fantasy of his imagination? In the long run this does not matter very much. The essential to remember is that whether he is real or imagined, this mysterious person helps the hero discover the spiritual power within himself.

This strange man fascinates Grégor for several reasons. He has lost his name, or rather, his name has left him. At first glance, such an allegation appears entirely absurd, since this survivor is extremely lucid. This loss of his name can be explained, however, on the symbolic level. Having witnessed the destruction of his family and his community, having seen the world he thought he knew plummet into insanity, his identity which was based on this emotional and spiritual foundation collapsed along with it. "It can happen that a name becomes old, falls ill and dies before the person who identifies with it," he declares to Grégor, "Well, mine has deserted me. Is it clear now?"[7] The hero had chosen the name of Grégor to hide his Jewish identity and consequently escape persecution. Since he does not need the Hebrew name that his parents had given him, namely, Gavriel, he offers it to this mysterious man with whom he creates a symbiotic relationship.

There exists yet another reason for Grégor's fascination with the enigmatic Gavriel: his laughter. For Grégor, it symbolizes a ruthless Manichean struggle between the forces of Good and Evil. Anger and love express themselves through it, as though both were emerging victorious from this combat while losing their lives. His laughter rises above the bodies of both fighters. "It is not only the soul of [their] conflict but its conclusion as well" (*P*, 11). It reflects Gavriel's sorrowful awareness that the human condition is condemned to wage perpetual intestinal warfare. But it also testifies to his heroic will to triumph over his sorrow. This categorical refusal to succumb to despair, this courageous lucidity with which man confronts his tragic situation, proclaim his nobility. Through laughter, they also proclaim his superiority vis-à-vis God. According to Gavriel, the Creator of the universe committed a grave error by giving His creature the ability to laugh. By doing this, the Master of creation placed an instrument of vengeance in the latter's hands. Although the world is no doubt irremediably sullied, at least man still has the possibility of making fun of God's

---

[7] Elie Wiesel, *Les Portes de la forêt*, Paris : Éditions du Seuil/Points, 1964, 17; referred to henceforth as *P*.

mistake by laughing uproariously. And against this human reaction, He can do nothing, no matter how powerful He is. Speaking of God's attempts to silence this insolent laughter, Gavriel asserts: "He chased him out of paradise, invented just for him an infinite variety of sins and punishments, made him aware of his own nothingness for the sole purpose of preventing him from laughing. Too late, I tell you. God's error preceded man's: they have this in common that they are irreparable" (*P*, 29). Endowed with this laughter that defies the whole cosmos, Gavriel is now situated beyond fear.

Grégor is shaken up as much or even more by his friend's tragic yet exalting conception of the Messiah. According to Jewish orthodoxy, the liberator of mankind will come at the end of Time and establish the reign of brotherhood and justice. For Gavriel, this is not the case. The Messiah will never come. He has already made an appearance on earth without anyone being able to recognize him. He has a name, a face and a destiny to fulfill. As soon as these three aspects are combined in the same individual, the Messiah will turn up on earth. From whom does Gavriel get this information? From a conversation with Elie, God's messenger. Should one believe him? It matters little whether he did or did not have a discussion with the biblical prophet when he freed himself from the order of time. What is essential is that this Jewish idealist expresses on the imaginary level his conviction, which is also Elie Wiesel's, that the Savior of humanity reveals himself whenever two individuals are engaged in a relationship based on justice and compassion.

As Gavriel relates the story to Grégor, he was sure he had met the Messiah embodied in the person of the beadle of the synagogue in his city, a bizarre personage called Moshe whom the children used to hound. Him again! A rather taciturn man about whom the community knew nothing, he would spend his nights in prayer in the synagogue. The tears he shed on the misfortunes of Israel seemed to Gavriel to contain all the ones that would flow from the beginning till the end of time. The young idealist entreated Moshe to reveal his identity even if it meant disobeying God, disobedience being saintly when it was necessary to put an end to all the suffering that was tearing the earth apart. As soon as the Nazis launched their campaign to exterminate the Jews, an angry Gavriel ordered the beadle to revolt against the Almighty. Moshe did not comply. On the contrary, Moshe adopted a middle-class outlook by marrying the daughter of a pawnbroker and became completely indifferent to his redemptive mission. The day the Germans rounded up the Jews of the city to massacre them all at once, Gavriel, frothing with rage, made one last attempt to incite

Moshe to act. The latter, "while smiling humbly, sketched out a gesture of powerlessness, of weariness" (*P*, 57), as though resigned to divine will and crushed under its weight.

How should one interpret this episode? Is Gavriel deluding himself into thinking that this humble beadle carried within himself the divine potential of the Messiah and missed his appointment with destiny? Or do we have here, just like his supposed conversation with the messenger Elie, a fable he has imagined for the purpose of illustrating in another manner this very same conception both moving and tragic of the Messiah that we have already pointed out? The Savior will come forward only when all men will view one another with respect and compassion. Whenever some consider their fellow creatures as mere objects to be crushed, they kill the Messiah in themselves just as they annihilate him physically in other living consciousnesses. Grégor is too puzzled when he hears this story to interpret it on the symbolic level. But, as the reader will notice, he will grasp its meaning on the day he will have to confront a crazed antisemitic crowd.

If Grégor has trouble grasping at that very moment the meaning of Gavriel's words concerning the Messiah, he understands right away the lofty ideal of friendship that his friend proposes. In fact, the two conceptions are organically linked, because in the fraternal relationship that develops between two friends one can glimpse the presence of the Savior. For Gavriel, friendship remains far superior to love. It has the intensity of that sentiment while being sheltered from the emotional chaos passion can engender. I have used the term "symbiosis" apropos of this commitment that Elie Wiesel exalts at various times as much in his novels as in his non-fictional works. But through the most marvelous of paradoxes, this fusion of hearts and minds constitutes the best protection for the independence of the two partners. Gavriel breathes into Grégor his immense spiritual energy so that the latter can, later on, embark on his own trajectory. Their friendship illustrates, then, the miracle, in the etymological sense of the word, of two parallel destinies that crisscross while pursuing their individual paths. Their profound fraternal affection establishes a bridge between their two solitudes, indeed, eliminates them. Once this bridge has been constructed, total confidence reigns between the two friends. Consequently, each one can become the resonance chamber of the other thanks to which the thoughts, aspirations and questions of the two are elucidated by flowing freely and being amplified.

According to Gavriel, when many philosophers hold forth, metaphysical and moral issues can sound false. This does not happen when one friend discusses them with another. Since friendship is synonymous with sharing, all these abstract problems become astonishingly concrete and immediate. They acquire an intensely human expression. Let us listen to Gavriel's words that arouse Grégor's admiration: "In the mouth of the philosopher, these questions often ring hollow, but asked during adolescence and in a spirit of friendship, they bring about a change in one's being. One's gaze becomes fiery, daily gestures go beyond themselves. You want to know what a friend is? It is the person who, for the first time, makes you aware of your solitude and of his, and helps you overcome it so that, in turn, you help him overcome his own. Thanks to him you can remain silent without feeling ashamed, you can open your heart without feeling diminished" (*P*, 35). Gavriel proves his indefectible loyalty towards his friend through his self-sacrifice. The Hungarian police was scouring the forest, searching for a young Jew who had escaped the raid. He offers himself in place of Grégor. He disappears physically. His messianic presence, however, will leave an indelible imprint on his friend. In the future, Grégor will go through periods of anguish and torturing doubts but will never sink to the bottom.

After Gavriel is captured, the hero flees from the grotto and seeks refuge in a far-off village at the home of the former non-Jewish servant of his family, Maria. She personifies devotion and generosity. She takes him in without the slightest hesitation. In order to protect his identity, she passes Grégor off as the deaf mute son of her young sister, Iléana who had left the village a long time ago. Iléana had been quite a vamp. She could have damned all the saints in paradise. All the village men had known her in the biblical sense or slobbered with concupiscence in her presence. But this woman was infinitely more than a brazen tramp with insatiable sexual appetites. As proud as a goddess whose physical splendor and charisma she embodied, she challenged death through every man who sought to conquer her. Since she had never encountered any lover courageous enough to tame her, she despised them all. Only one man in the whole village, Mihai could perhaps have found favor in her eyes if, as he confessed to Grégor, he had become angry enough to want to kill her. Simply by hearing the villagers' reactions to his so-called mother, Grégor felt boundless admiration for her. At the very moment when he will confront the furious antisemitic mob, he will strive through his courage to make her proud.

As much as Grégor pays homage to Maria and Iléana, he is nauseated by the hypocrisy of the so-called "Christians" in the village. Protected by his fictitious identity as the illegitimate and deaf son of Iléana, he receives the most intimate and vile secrets which people would be ashamed to reveal in the confessional. Especially in the confessional, since the priest is an impenitent gossip monger. The villagers pamper him and enjoy pouring out their hearts to him because they know, or think they know, that Grégor does not understand a single word of what they are saying. Thus, the hero discovers very quickly that the Christian faith for them is nothing more than a façade behind which they conceal from the others and even from themselves all their primitive impulses. The priest is even more unforgiveable than his parishioners. Plagued by remorse, he confesses to the mute that he had denounced a Jewish fugitive to the police because the Jew refused to accept Christ, thereby denying the man of God the victory of having converted an infidel. This hypocrisy will reach its climax during the performance of the Passion in which Grégor will play the role of Judas. During that episode the villagers prove that their antisemitism, and antisemitism in general, is nothing more than a pretext for giving full vent to the ugly delight of hatred if not of sadism without feeling in the least monstrous.

Robert M. Brown was right to point out in this novel a real ambivalence on the part of Elie Wiesel towards Christianity[8]. Naturally, through his hero the author does not fail to pay homage to Christians whose conduct during the Second World War had been exemplary. In addition to the courageous Maria, there is the taciturn mayor, Petruskanu, who will save Grégor's life. Nevertheless, one discerns in some of the hero's reactions the exasperation and anger of the author against well intentioned Christians who invoke Christ without realizing that their coreligionists have already sullied and killed Him many times by hounding ruthlessly the Jewish people from whom He had never dissociated Himself. When Maria murmurs the prayer "Sweet Jesus," Grégor hastens to inform her that Jesus was also transformed into a cloud in the crematory ovens like the other Jews: "He, too, is exhausted; he let himself be killed one day and since then the killing has just gone on" (P, 68).

It is Grégor's turn to become the target of the village's antisemitic hatred at the end of the school year. But supported by the intrepid courage that Gavriel bequeathed to him as well as by the pride he feels in assuming the identity of Iléana's presumed son, he transfigures himself and, reaching a level of almost superhuman serenity, transcends the murderous rage of the mob. Despite Maria's vehement objections and premotions of danger,

---

[8] Robert McAfee Brown, *Elie Wiesel: Messenger to All Humanity*, Notre Dame, Indiana: University of Notre Dame Press, 1983, 91.

Grégor's services are requisitioned by the schoolteacher, the pretentious Constantin Stefan, to play the silent role of the traitor Judas in a particularly antisemitic version of the Passion of Christ. In this way, the schoolmaster expects to achieve glory. But like a car that swerves and then skids more and more, the play suddenly changes direction under the influence of unexpected events, unleashing in the actors as well as in the spectators a kind of insanity where the most primitive cruelty alternates with the most superstitious of fears.

The disciples of Jesus, played by the pupils of the school, are out to punish Judas for the death of their master. So, the actors start to beat Grégor, whipped up by a paroxysm of two thousand years of antisemitism transmitted from one generation to the next. The adult members of the audience feast on this show with such a bestial joy that they are not just content to encourage the actors, they throw themselves into the dramatic action by raining blows on the body of poor Judas. Grégor's face is bloodied but he maintains his sang-froid. He communicates with the mayor, Petruskanu, seated in the first row, by almost imperceptible signs, makes him understand tacitly that he knows he is under the man's protection, but will ask for help only if he really feels he will faint. With a masterful flair for timing, Grégor, the so-called mute, cries out at the top of his lungs: "Men and women of this village, listen to me." As though struck by lightning, the sadistic brutes are transformed into superstitious believers transfixed in terror. They are convinced they are witnessing a miracle. They beseech Grégor to forgive them. They had it in only for Judas. Grégor is a saint.

But the villagers have even more surprises in store for them. First, Grégor stuns them by announcing that forgiveness cannot come from him. Only Judas can forgive them. "He is the victim, not Jesus; he is the crucified one: not Christ. Have you understood that?" (*V*, 120). Overcome with remorse and fearing the divine thunderbolt, the villagers acknowledge the saintliness of Judas. Even the priest, half-dead with shame, is forced to humiliate himself like the others. But barely have they recovered from this first traumatic shock when Grégor deals them yet another crushing blow: He confesses that he is not the son of Iléana. Disarray reigns among the spectators. As master of the situation, Grégor realizes that there are two paths before him: either he denounces these hypocrites or he forgives them. For an ordinary human being, the temptation of wrecking vengeance on them would be irresistible. Does he not know the most shameful secrets of all the people there? He could tell them which person acted as a spy and betrayed his best friend, which man covets his sister-in-law. At that very instant, his gaze meets that of Petruskanu, and Grégor decides to honor this decent man by telling the truth. He will make his confession. So he deals them the third lethal blow: the hero announces to the crowd that his name is Gavriel and that he is a Jew. Dumbfounded just a second before, the crowd becomes bloodthirsty. Since a Jew holds within his hands enough secrets to destroy them all, he must be annihilated right away.

Egged on by their wives, the male spectators rush towards Grégor to kill him. This episode remains among the most dramatic and painful that the author has ever conceived. The reader would prefer to minimize its impact by saying that this crescendo of religious and murderous insanity is too implausible. But as though he was anxious to compel us not to switch off, the author ties this scene, through discrete allusions, to so many other examples of antisemitic persecution that are unfolding at the very same time that we end up wishing we could deny reality. It is too frightening to contemplate. Just when Grégor is convinced he is going to die under the blows of the savage mob, Wiesel reminds the reader that, unknown to the hero, many other victims of antisemitic hatred are about to die, too: "The executioners are moving towards the stage, they are going to invade it and their honor will be avenged in blood. Grégor remains immobile: at this very moment, in the red fields of Galicia, elegant, distinguished looking officers shout out orders: fire, fire, fire! And one hundred Jews, ten thousand Jews tumble into the ditch: and so, one does not die alone" (*P*, 123).

When Petruskanu sees that Grégor is really in danger of dying, he jumps up on the stage, whisks him off into his vehicle, and drives him off into the forest where the young man will be able to meet up with a band of partisans. When the hero links up with the partisans, however, another form of torture awaits him, this one being essentially moral in nature and just as excruciating in its way as the preceding one. He finds again a childhood comrade, Leib the Lion, who is the leader of the band. A great friendship could have developed between the two if circumstances had not separated them. Grégor remembers that even as a child, Leib had the makings of a hero. In the first part of the novel, he described how the Lion helped him overcome his fear of the young antisemitic rowdies of their village who set up ambushes for him on his way to school. Between the two of them, they succeeded in chasing away their assailants because Leib's courage was so contagious. The renewal of their ties now unfolds in a climate of sorrow. Grégor informs his comrade of the tragic fate their coreligionists have been enduring. Hidden as they were in the depths of the forest, the partisans were not aware of the crimes the Nazis were perpetrating:

rounding up whole Jewish communities, then shipping them off to concentration camps, death camps, gas chambers and crematory ovens. He tells Leib about the capture of Gavriel. Leib is determined to free him if he is still alive. To that end he organizes with his customary boldness an action designed to gather information on the place where the prisoner is being held. He asks his lover, Clara and Grégor to participate in it. The project fails, Leib is captured, tortured and sent off to a death camp.

Grégor feels doubly guilty. In the first place, he was the one who had informed the leader of the partisans about Gavriel's existence. But there is another reason, one he almost doesn't dare to admit. It explains his torment. He and Clara had pretended to be young lovers as a means of worming their way into the favor of a prison guard, Jànos. By dint of pretending to be in love, Grégor fell genuinely in love with her. Consequently, shame at having committed an act of betrayal intensified his feeling of guilt. The other partisans are convinced that he is indeed guilty and subject him to a frightening cross-interrogation. If Clara had not intervened in extremis, he would have probably been executed. On hearing his defense in the face of his accusers, she alone understands the depth of anguish the young man is experiencing. She alone grasps that the ironic, self-accusation overkill Grégor is practicing during his trial betrays a distress without limits.

From then on, Grégor lives in the same kind of moral hell in which the narrator of *Day* was imprisoned. Since he has not joined the ranks of the victims, he considers himself now in the camp of the executioners. The mere fact of continuing to live seems to him a betrayal of the dead. He sees himself as responsible for the death of Leib and remains totally powerless to rid himself of this sense of responsibility. There occurs at times in Elie Wiesel's novels an encounter that suddenly reorients an individual's destiny. Grégor gets into a conversation with a young man of twenty, Yehuda, who possesses the wisdom of many centuries. He happens to be on duty that night. He has the intuitive certitude that his death is imminent. He hastens, then, to bring succor to his comrade whose suffering he senses, and what is more important, he understands the repressed love Grégor feels for Clara. At first glance, nothing appears to be more incongruous than to talk of love at a time when innocents are being killed every day by the tens of thousands. But this is precisely why one must have the courage to love. To love means giving life a vote of confidence, it means preventing life from sinking entirely into the absurd.

Just as in friendship, love, according to Yehuda, establishes a bridge between two abysses of solitude. Since this passion exalts life, it would be almost a crime to be ashamed of its presence. Armed with the freedom to speak that the imminence of his own death gives him, Yehuda exhorts his comrade to accept as a divine grace the possibility of loving another human being: "You love Clara. From where I find myself, I see everything, I have the right to say everything. I tell you, then, that you are wrong to love her in shame, you should be proud of it. In this bloodstained, inhuman world love is the greatest of rewards and conquests" (*P*, 190). But Yehuda does not stop there. He reproaches Gavriel for misusing suffering. Worse than misusing it, Gavriel is committing an act of sacrilege against life. Suffering has a meaning only to the extent that it engenders in us a surge of sympathy that draws us closer to another person. When it leads us to shrivel up, to wallow in a morose delectation, it turns us into spiritual cripples. In full flow, Yehuda quotes the Talmud to corroborate his thought. According to this sacred book, even God sees in suffering the opportunity to draw closer to man, to enter with him into an alliance of mutual understanding. Grégor is doing the exact opposite: "Now you, you seek out suffering for yourself. This suffering shrinks you, diminishes you, it verges on cruelty". (*P*, 190). Yehuda does indeed die, stabbed by a peasant during a village mission shortly after compelling his comrade to see clearly within himself. But his death is avenged and Grégor declares his love to Clara.

After the war, Clara and Grégor meet again by chance in Paris. They get married and settle in the city of New York. Their marriage turns out to be a catastrophe. Clara refuses to free herself from a universe filled with her fantasies. She pretends that Leib is still alive and that he remains her lover. She can love Grégor only if he agrees to assume the identity of his deceased friend. Gavriel knew he was taking a risk by persuading Clara to marry him. He used the same argument as Yehuda to incite her to choose life. It is normal to feel suffering, he told her. But this pain is legitimate only to the extent that it does not drag us down into a kind of spiritual sclerosis: " I often feel hurt as you do," he admits to her. "But I endeavor to tame my suffering, to disarm it. You, on the other hand, endure it and you often call for it. The two attitudes are human, of course. Except that one connects you to life, to strength; the other to resignation, to death" (*P*, 224). Grégor entreats Clara to leave the cemetery of the past and to place her confidence entirely in human love that can create, during this terrestrial existence, a celestial kingdom all the more desirable because it is real: "There is more eternity in the instant that unites two beings than in the memory of God; there is more peace in the gaze that reaches into a heart that is loved than in the whole kingdom of heaven" (*P*, 226).

Clara remains deaf to her husband's exhortations. No more than his new friend, Mendel who had lost a son, she refuses to combat the night. Instead of taking a risk and betting on the future, she digs deeper into her memories of the past. Since all his efforts have failed, Grégor does not see any other solution possible except separation. The horizon seems definitively blocked. But in some of Elie Wiesel's novels a spiritual unblocking occurs at the very moment when the hero is convinced that he has lost his way forever and is trapped in a blind alley. I have already pointed this out in the final pages of *The Town Beyond the Wall*. We will also notice the same tendency in several of his other works as well. The hero returns to the religious roots of his childhood by frequenting a Hassidic congregation in the Williamsburg neighborhood of Brooklyn.[9] He goes there to have a theological fight with the "Rebbe" or spiritual leader of the synagogue. Grégor considers it aberrant to offer praise to the Almighty after He closed His eyes to the massacre of six million of his faithful. To rejoice, as the Hassidim do, when there is no objective reason to rejoice, seems to Grégor a completely futile exercise.

The Rebbe, however, does not let himself be nonplussed. Not that he has a blind religious faith. Neither deaf nor blind to the horrors recently perpetrated against his coreligionists, he, too, knows where he stands vis-à-vis the Creator of the universe. He, too, considers God unforgivable for having allowed this murderous insanity to be unleashed. Nevertheless, the Rebbe is a Hassid and a Hassid he will remain. A member of a Jewish religious movement born in central Europe in the 18th century, he persists with his disciples, in the middle of the 20th century, just like his predecessors two hundred years before, in making joy triumph over despair, despite God's apparent indifference, indeed against His apparent indifference. Engendering joy when there is no logical reason to be joyous represents for him and all the Hassidim the best way to defy the Master of the universe. The act of rejoicing turns out to be even more effective than raising

---

[9] Hassidism is a movement of Jewish religious renewal born in the 18th century in Poland under the influence of a master (the "rebbe") Baal Shem Tov. Like all movements of religious renewal, Hassidism is a more spontaneous form of expression, mixing mystic and Kabbalistic influences, the supernatural and traditions, in which one can reach God in a personal relationship through music, song and dance, far more than through study, asceticism or the rigor that dominates the ritual in synagogues. Elie Wiesel devoted two texts to the Hassidic movement, in which he saw an expression of profound joy coexisting with an acute awareness of despair: *Célébration hassidique* (Hassidic Celebration) and *Contre la mélancolie* (Against Melancholy).

one's fist against Him. It testifies to our determination to transcend divine inadequacies and to demonstrate our triumph over destiny. A Hassid who sings and dances in a world rife with cruelty is obviously superior to it, because he refuses to let himself be crushed under its weight. Let us listen to the Rebbe: "The Hassid dances with fury, with joy as well, of course. In this way he proclaims: You do not want me to dance, so much the worse, I will dance; you take away from me every reason to sing, well! Lend an ear, I will sing about the day that lies and the night that tells the truth and the twilight that remains silent, yes, I will sing about that, too; You don't expect me to be joyous, it surprises you, well! My joy is here, it rises and will not cease rising; let it be and it will submerge you" (*P*, 210).

At that very moment a miracle occurs in the etymological sense of the term. Grégor participates in a service. The Hassidim's unbreakable determination to engender joy whatever the cost is such that this exaltation takes flight and transports them all infinitely beyond all terrestrial anguish. Their collective joy acquires a superhuman plenitude, and in this plenitude can be glimpsed the trace of God. Once again, the divine presence remains inseparable from the fraternal relationship that exists between people. Describing the song that soars from the throats of the members of the community, the author states: "The song is now carried aloft on its own wings and it is this very song that swells all chests, illuminates all faces, and calls for ecstasy so that all hearts have faith in eternity" (*P*, 215). Gavriel enters the synagogue at the very instant when Grégor is on the verge of allowing himself to be borne aloft by this sublime human whirlwind. Is he really the same Gavriel the hero had met, as an adolescent, in the forest grotto? It matters little. The presence of this enigmatic personage acts on him like a catalyst. As a result of pouring out his heart until daybreak, Grégor discovers who he is and what he really wants to do with his existence. He makes two decisions of primordial importance for himself. He realizes that he cannot leave Clara, and he asks Gavriel to give him back his Hebrew name. Now, to take back his name means to reclaim his whole past as well and to integrate it into his present and future.

Grégor emphasizes his reconciliation with his past and with the faith of his ancestors by agreeing to recite the Kaddish in the morning with nine other believers. Before he starts chanting with the others this most solemn prayer in the Jewish liturgy, he promises himself to return to Clara and to invite her to help him combat the phantoms that continue haunting them. When he begins reciting this prayer, he concentrates on each sentence, each word, each syllable. At first glance, reciting the Kaddish might appear to be a strange way of confirming his return to the Judaism of his childhood, because it is the prayer for the dead. This text, however, has nothing to do with the dead. It celebrates the living God. As the author explains, the Kaddish is the solemn affirmation tinged with grandeur and serenity through which man hands over to God His crown and scepter (*P*, 236).

Reciting this prayer means agreeing to commit oneself to a spiritual partnership with God to create a better world. It means striving to fulfill the potential for nobility that man possesses within himself. It means paying fervent homage to the dead without however neglecting one's responsibilities towards the living. When Grégor, who has become Gavriel again, recites the Kaddish, he frees himself at last from his feeling of guilt towards Leib. He honors in his deceased friend the grandeur that represents the portion of immortality within man. He is certain that his friend will bless his union with Clara. And because they will love one another, the Messiah will reappear among them, since the Messiah is not just one man or woman, but all men and women. And "as long as there will be men, there will be Messiahs."

CHAPTER 3
MYSTIC SOLIDARITY
AND
TRANSMISSION OF MEMORY

The two heroes of the novels *The Town Beyond the Wall* and *The Gates of the Forest* win personal victories. Michael frees himself from his isolation through the grace of friendship and moves towards his fellow man in a surge of fraternal solicitude. Embracing compassion more and more, Grégor embodies the messianic ideal and returns through it to the faith of his childhood. In the end he fully accepts a kind of spiritual solidarity with the people around him that transcends time and space. This tendence appearing in the last part of *The Gates of the Forest* is reinforced in Elie Wiesel's next three novels: *A Beggar in Jerusalem* (1968), *The Oath* (1973), and *The Testament* (1980. In these books the three heroes become aware that they are situated in a spatial and temporal continuum that transcends normal time and believe they have been invested with a sacred mission: to transmit the several-thousand-year memory of their people.

A Beggar in Jerusalem

Elie Wiesel did not intend to write *A Beggar in Jerusalem* immediately after the *Gates of the Forest*. He was thinking rather of devoting a novel to the dilemma of the Jews in the Soviet Union following his visit there in 1965 and which he described in a report titled *The Jews of Silence* (1966). But then cataclysmic historical events occurred beyond his control as a writer. In 1967 the Six Day War broke out. Like many Jews, the author was grieving inwardly during the weeks that preceded the conflict.

He feared a new version of the Holocaust. The Arab armies enjoyed a crushing numerical superiority. The western nations maintained their customary passivity. But for once the worst did not happen. The Israelis' astonishing bravery, and the unconditional support given to them by Jewish communities around the world guaranteed the survival of the Hebrew state. Inspired by the marvelous turnaround of a situation of which the tragic consequences seemed unavoidable, Elie Wiesel composed *A Beggar in Jerusalem* at lightning speed.

By the author's own admission, of all the novels he wrote this is the most difficult one to decipher. He speaks about it in the second volume of his memoirs titled *And the Sea is Never Full*: "More than one reader has let me know that it was not easy for him to sink his teeth into it. Of all my novels, this is the least accessible. It requires explanations that I feel incapable of providing".[10] It is neither a novel nor an anti-novel, neither a work of fiction nor an autobiography, neither a poem nor a work of prose, but the novelist shuttles between all these forms without sticking to any one of them. Narratives, lyrical outbursts, aphorisms, conversations, news reports and parables follow one another at a dizzying pace. But let us not make the mistake of thinking that the novel is disorganized. Under the chaotic surface *A Beggar in Jerusalem* reveals an organic unity. It is founded on two principal themes. The first one encompasses the text itself: the mystic solidarity that connects Jews as individuals and collectivities through time, space and legends. Hence the need to break open the frame of the conventional novel to suggest a continuum of several thousands of years that takes root not only in the realm of imagination but in history. The second theme is orchestrated within the first. It describes how a survivor of the Holocaust sheds his tragic past and allows it to die so that he can rediscover himself, thereby recommitting himself to life.

If the novel is built on these two themes, they, in turn, draw their raison d'être from the city of Jerusalem itself. The centre of spiritual gravity for religious Jews from time immemorial, the fabulous realm where history and legend mingle, this holy city enjoys an extra-temporal prestige. No matter where a Jew prays, he knows he is addressing his prayers in front of this sanctuary. For him, the city transcends its geographic space, is situated everywhere and has been in existence for all time. Fighting in 1967 for the liberation of the Western Wall signifies joining the Maccabees who had, several thousands of years before, achieved a brilliant victory

---

[10] *Et la mer n'est pas remplie*, Paris : Éditions du Seuil, 1996, 27.

over tyranny. To evoke the Six Day War is to remember simultaneously a venerable history marked by tragedies as well as triumphs. For the hero of this novel as well as for its creator, to think of Jerusalem or to go there is to return to the country of the soul where one draws strength, comfort, peace and humility: "Jerusalem: the visible and secret face, the blood and sap of what makes us live or renounce life. The spark that shoots up from the darkness, the murmur that crosses through clamors of light-heartedness, of happiness. For those in exile, it is a prayer. For the others, a promise. Jerusalem: a city that miraculously transforms every man into a pilgrim; no one can visit it and leave unchanged."[11]

As an adolescent the hero, David, dreamed of the holy city long before he contemplated it. As a Maguid, or ambulating preacher in the Hungarian town of his birth taught him, all you had to do was immerse yourself in Jerusalem's stories and legends to feel that you were there spiritually. The Maguid had never set foot physically in this city of all dreams, but he claimed never to have left it either. David, on the other hand, yearned to emigrate there as soon as the Jewish communities of central Europe were threatened by the Nazi scourge. Supported by his mother, he would exhort his father to take the whole family to the Holy Land before they were victims of Hitler's Final Solution. As a humanist with unbeatable optimism, his father refused to believe that men, even Nazis, could act with such an implausible barbarity. David was the only one to remain alive after the Second Word War and able to make that trip.

According to the hero, all Jews come to Jerusalem as beggars. They are seeking a spiritual plenitude or an illumination necessary to fill the void in their existences. Some among them don't even have to look far to find what they need. Since they inhabit the holy city, they have the unshakeable certainty of being connected to the fourth dimension, that of legend encompassing Time in its entirety. From the point of view of common sense, these beggars belong to the category of the mentally ill. They gorge themselves on illusions the way a dope addict consumes drugs. They sail on the sea of fantasies with mind-blowing ease. On the poetic level, however, the behavior of these screwballs is not devoid of meaning, and David feels a deep sympathy for them. By believing literally that they have an intimate relationship with the great biblical figures, by proudly proclaiming that they have lived at every era in the history of their coreligionists,

---

[11] Elie Wiesel, *Le Mendiant de Jérusalem*, Paris : Éditions du Seuil/Points, 1968, 19; henceforth referred to as *M*.

these lovable crazies show unwavering solidarity towards them. Their lives vibrate to all the historical and spiritual resonances of Israel. They lead an earthly existence at a precise moment in time, but they transcend this particular period by accepting in its totality their Jewish heritage. Poor in the material sense only, they are lords of an immaterial kingdom infinitely more significant than all earthly possessions.

Thus, Zalmen the beggar leaves a young Israeli aviator speechless by asserting that he had discussed military strategy with two legendary biblical heroes, Yehuda, the leader of the Maccabees, and Bar-Kochba, the fearless warrior who "raised the standard of revolt against Rome" (*M*, 52). One of his cronies, Shlomo, just as crazy, relates a conversation he had with Yeshua, namely, Jesus, warning him against the monstrous perversion that future Christians were going to make of his message of love, predicting, to the latter's horror, that his crucifixion would cause the affliction of his coreligionists. Dan, another beggar with an aristocratic demeanor, tells David about his incredible journey into the fabulous realm of the ten lost tribes of Israel. While showing a strange kind of wisdom in his madness, this visionary describes the moral transformation he underwent during his contact with these Jews who led exemplary lives. He decided to renounce all the honors bestowed upon him as a great intellectual by his country of origin and seek refuge in Jerusalem to show his contempt for a world given over to murderous insanity. Finally, Moshe—yes, him again—completely at ease in this universe of visionary nutbars, proudly describes how he heaped ridicule on illustrious theologians during a great debate on religion in a cathedral, in the Middle Ages, before the king and his court. Tipsy and overflowing with self-confidence, Moshe sowed confusion within the ranks of his adversaries and made the king laugh so heartily that His Majesty declared him the winner.

The connection that all the beggars and Jews of the diaspora have with the city of Jerusalem is greatly reinforced on the eve of the Six Day War. Their anxiety for the survival of the state of Israel intensifies all the more because they have long memories. They remember that only thirty years earlier, Hitler's irresistible rise to power was accompanied by a cowardly and hypocritical silence on the part of the western countries. They recall God's immobility during that period, His inability to defend his people in the hour of their need. They have not forgotten how many Jewish communities in Europe were annihilated when the Nazis decided to put the Final Solution into action. Hence the passages strewn throughout the narrative that evoke the horrors of the Shoah. On his return to the city of his birth after the war, the hero meets a young Jew locked up in a psychiatric ward. The latter's reason collapsed under the weight of the nightmare he had lived through. The deranged young man is convinced that his coreligionists are still alive, that their society is still flourishing. If he is incapable of finding them in the streets of the city, it is because his mind, he thinks, is possessed by a malevolent demon, or "dibbouk." According to him, his morbid imagination is depopulating a city from which the Jews have never been eliminated. His refusal to accept the reality of the Holocaust, his need to believe that the disappearance of the other Jews is an illusion created by his mental illness is expressed in his shattering words: "In the very depths of despair, on the very borderline of insanity, I rediscover the certitude that, in the end, it is just the work of the dibbouk; I am possessed. This is the explanation. Thus, I am the only one to suffer from my illness, since, in truth, my city still exists with its Jews and its myths, its songs and holidays, but without me, outside of me" (*M*, 30).

Next the hero resurrects through memory an episode of the Shoah in which the impenetrable silence of God rivals the barbarity of man. He remembers the words quivering with anguish and pride that the leader of a Hassidic community uttered to exhort his flock to confront death with such intrepidness that "the angels, overcome with shame, will lower their brows and no longer praise the Creator of the universe, never again" (*M*, 68-69). In this scene of mass murder, David underscores the monstrosity of the Nazi ideology that its followers conceal to themselves behind a so-called humanistic façade. To that end, he shows how the German lieutenant responsible for the village massacre conducted himself like a conscientious killer. As though he was getting ready to take a group photo of the people, he arranged them in tableaus before giving his soldiers the signal to shoot them. The German didn't lose his sang-froid until the Rabbi and his disciples confronted death as though they were in the process of celebrating the third meal of the Sabbath, by breaking into a Hassidic song in an ecstatic tone of voice and moving forward as though they were suspended between heaven and earth.

These reminders of the Nazi industry of systematic murder directed against the Jewish people in an atmosphere of indifference during the Second World War arouses a sinister foreboding about the security of the Hebrew state in the spring of 1967. They underline the analogy existing between the so-called "civilized" nations at that time and the febrile and futile agitation of world leaders on the eve of the conflict in which Israel will have to confront its Arab neighbors all alone. Through brief newspaper reports incorporated into the narrative, Wiesel demonstrates that the multiple appeals to Israel for caution and patience from the major powers simply cover up their hypocritical cynicism and their intention to let the Jews perish once again. Then, as soon as the tragedy is over, they will lament over the victims' cruel fate.

Fortunately, 1967 does not exactly resemble 1940. The author does not fail to emphasize that something essential has changed in the Jewish mentality over the past twenty-seven years. The new generation of Israelis will not allow themselves to be led to the slaughterhouse. Proof of this in the novel can be found in the altercation between the Sabra, Yoav, and Shimon, the former fighter in the ghettos during the Second World War. Shimon, a witness of the Shoah, entreats his young coreligionist not to insult the memory of the martyrs of the death camps who did not oppose their executioners. The scorn Yoav heaps on them is unfair but testifies to the Jewish people's new state of mind. The Jews in Israel will henceforth defend their right to live like any others: "If, to survive, I had to insult them, well, I would insult them! All they had to do was get angry, to revolt, even if it meant setting the rest of Europe on fire, the rest of the universe" (*M*, 102). Moreover, the Jews of the Diaspora are galvanized in favor of their brothers and sisters in danger. The novel describes the tidal wave of sympathy and solidarity that flows over the Hebrew state on the eve of the conflict, as though the Jewish communities dispersed throughout the world had suddenly become one, were speaking in a single voice, and sharing a unique identity: "Writers and artists, starving students and easy-going merchants, religious people and atheists, all found themselves in the same camp, borne aloft by the same wave. As a result, each one considered himself responsible for the collective survival of all, each one felt himself threatened, attacked" (*M*, 105).

This galvanization of the diaspora is accompanied by a surge of moral energy and hope in the hero himself. Parallel to the narrative of the victory that the state of Israel wins over enemies determined to destroy it, the novel describes how the young man frees himself from a past that was asphyxiating him and conquers a new being capable of welcoming the future and experiencing joy. Before the outbreak of the Six Day War, the death camp survivor views himself as a prisoner, like other Wiesel characters, of a traumatic past. At various times in the novel, he evokes episodes from that period which have left a permanent imprint on his consciousness. He remembers the day when his father, one of the leaders of the Jewish community in a Central European town, returned home looking afflicted after a meeting with the Nazi authorities, to announce the horrible news that the departure of the convoys was scheduled for the next day. He thinks also about Iléana, the non-Jewish woman who sacrificed her own life to save him during the Nazi occupation. Finally, after Jerusalem is liberated by the Israeli army, David sees, as though hallucinating, his mother and little sister tortured by thirst, just as they were on the day of their deportation thirty years earlier, file pas the Western Wall like thousands of other Holocaust victims. This sorrowful past he drags behind him explains his irreducible pessimism. If he has come back to Israel on the eve of the conflict with the Arab states, it is to die while fighting by his coreligionists' side, because he is persuaded that once again, the Jewish nation is condemned to disappear.

This epic event to which he intends to make a total commitment will shake up his existence from top to bottom. Embedded in the Israeli army without any precise rank or responsibility, David makes the acquaintance of a soldier named Katriel. The latter relates to him the strange parable the spiritual resonances of which will reverberate for a long time within his consciousness. At first it will arouse the hero's anger. Later, it will help him understand himself better. According to the story, a man leaves his home in search of adventures and a magical city. He sleeps at night in a forest, and to make sure he remains on the right path, places his shoes in the direction he will have to follow the next day. During the night a prankster turns his shoes in the opposite direction. Thus, when the traveler reaches the next day the city of his dreams, it bears an astonishing resemblance to the one he had left. He realizes that he knows the streets, the buildings and the gardens perfectly well. He wends his way towards a house identical to the one in which he used to live, he finds there his wife and children who seem the reincarnations of his own family. The lady serves him a meal and the smallest of the children climbs on his lap and begs him to remain with them. Very touched, the traveler finally promises them everything.

This story plagues David. Even though it seems familiar to him, he is incapable of deciphering its meaning with any clarity. He is angry with Katriel for having related it to him. He is worried about the implications it contains. The hero begins to understand the disarray the parable has touched off within him when he remembers what a beggar had once said to him during his childhood: "Be aware, little one, that the day someone tells you the story of your life, you will not have long to live "(*M*, 121). This warning will be repeated twice more in an elliptical form by two other beggars, the final repetition occurring just before the end of the novel.

His friend's story forces David to become aware of the fact that he himself is perhaps the traveler. Having traversed the interminable night of flames, he remains a prisoner of it. His tragic past is still an integral part of his present life. The David of 1967 does not have any existential density. He has never left the dead nor have they left him: "The living person that I was, that I thought I was, had been living a lie; I was nothing but an echo of voices that disappeared long ago. As a shadow, far removed from the other shadows, I was running into them day after day, they were the ones I was tricking, that I was betraying while going forward. I thought I was living my own life. All I was doing was inventing it. I thought I was escaping these phantoms. All I was doing was extending their power. And now, it was to late to turn around and go back" (*M*, 121). When he hears the third warning, at his wedding, David fully understands the meaning of the parable. The death in question is not of a physical order but of a spiritual one. The prisoner of the ghastly night dies at last in relation to his past without, however, forgetting it, and the new man thus liberated will be reborn to life and love.

To measure the interior seism that shakes up the hero and the spiritual distance he will have to travel before conquering an authentic identity, it will be necessary to dwell on the complex sentiments of friendship that link him to the soldier, Katriel whom he meets at the military camp. The latter whose name signifies "crown of God," is the son of a Rabbi in the holy city of Safed, and the husband of Malka, with whom David will fall in love. Is Katriel an autonomous personage or does he represent the hero's alter ego? It matters little, in the long run. He is as indispensable for our understanding of David's character as is Gavriel for Grégor's in *The Gates of the Forest*. One can interpret Katriel as a possibility of existence that the hero was never fortunate enough to realize. Indeed, David admits towards the end of the novel that he had been jealous of his Israeli friend's personal history and innocence. Katriel had been blessed with a childhood devoid of tragic upheavals. He had blossomed forth as a husband and father. Thus, Katriel had been a very fulfilled man. He had lived without obsessions or torments, and simply gave himself over spontaneously to the joy of loving his wife and son. He seemed blessed by God. Hence, perhaps, his name. This happy destiny, however, is destroyed overnight when his son dies following an accident. A heavy sadness and the torments of doubt then replace his fragile happiness. From the moment Katriel experiences unhappiness, he finds himself more enclosed in his past than is David. Since he despairs of ever knowing again the same depth of joy in the future, he really does not want to live any longer. He becomes a psychological cripple. What aggravates his existential situation even more is the necessity, as a soldier, to kill his adversaries as soon as the Six Day War breaks out. As a fervent idealist, he is filled with self-loathing after being forced to commit acts of violence that violate his most sacred principles. When he disappears after the liberation of Jerusalem—killed in action or reported missing, it is never determined—the reader is hardly surprised. His disappearance can be interpreted as a kind of suicide metaphor.

By the most remarkable of paradoxes, the war that was the psychological coup de grace for Katriel allows David to free himself, finally and definitively, from the prison of his past and renew his confidence in life. Having gone through the nightmare of the death camps, the hero knows that one must sometimes fight fire with fire. He realizes that to safeguard a portion of his idealism it is necessary in certain circumstances to commit acts that go against this idealism. In other words, he is infinitely better prepared than Katriel to confront the future. Thus, the liberation of the old city of Jerusalem in which he participates brings him immense joy, a crescendo of exaltation, and an awareness that he has reached an almost superhuman fulness of being. During those incredible hours when the Israeli army zeroes in on the Western Wall at lightning speed, David is convinced that a fusion is taking place between his personal destiny and that of the city which had always been for him a spiritual magnetic pole.

Shelving his pessimism, David now connects to a spatial-temporal continuum, that of the several-thousand year history of his people, composed of fabulous legends as well as actual facts. Hence the indescribable emotion that overcomes him once he reaches the Wall. These remains of the Temple symbolize the whole body of spiritual and ethical values of Judaism. As a result, the old stones of the legendary structure constitute an urgent invitation, indeed an exhortation, to every man and woman, to fulfill his/her potential for nobility and beauty of which the extrapolation to the infinite coincides with the very presence of God. Although David had never seen this object of his people's veneration, he has the singular impression of knowing it all his life. He feels, then, that he is floating between dreams and reality: "As though I was paralyzed, strangled by emotion, I was looking at the Wall the way one looks at a living human being from which one has been separated for a long time, or forever. I had never seen it before, yet I recognized it. The feeling that I was living a dream had not left me, however. On the contrary, it was growing. A part of my being did not dare believe it. I knew that this wall was the Wall of the Temple, but I could not entirely believe that I was there contemplating it. The triumphant victor within me seemed to me as strange as he was unreal" (*M*, 174).

Because of the legends, the thousands of years of history and the exalting aspirations that it symbolizes, the Wall transcends the present and encompasses the whole of time. Thus for David, who feels suspended between reality and a kind of hallucination, it is perfectly natural that in front of these venerable stones should walk all those people for whom the Jewish faith represented the battle fought incessantly to make humanity constantly more human: "The kings and prophets, the warriors and priests, the poets and thinkers, the rich and poor who, through the ages, have begged everywhere for a little tolerance, a little brotherhood: Here is where they came to deliver their message" (*M*, 176). But David's dazzling vision reaches a new threshold when he believes that he is witnessing the third big gathering together of the Jewish people. The first took place before Mount Sinai, when God granted the Ten Commandments to the tribes of Israel. The second occurred in the kingdom of night where the Jews contemplated the hidden face of their God and died as a result. The third unfolds in 1967, in the old city of Jerusalem, and in a climate of unbridled joy, because this time it is the image of man that is transmitted. But the greatest source of wonder is the certitude that the victims of the extermination camps who had never been laid to rest had now joined the living to celebrate the victory. Since their cemeteries are in the sky, they did not have to wait for the Messiah to be freed from his chains to come out of their tombs.

Far from heaping reproaches on the living and terrorizing them as they had done in *Dawn* and *Day*, the martyrs had come to the rescue and given their support to the defenders of the state of Israel. As the preacher who is part of David's vision explains, Israel was victorious because its army and people had six million more names. Thus, the breakthrough begun in *The Gates of the Forest* now get sufficiently enlarged to allow the Holocaust survivors to emerge definitively from the tunnel where they risked asphyxiation. The dead have become allies. Remembering them no longer imprisons the survivors in a tragic past. The act of safeguarding the memory of the deceased can henceforth give the living the courage to move on with their lives. To this end, David places a note in the interstices of the Wall. Written for the dead, it asks them to "take pity on a world that betrayed and denied them" (*M*, 186). David is now at peace with himself. He is convinced he possesses a future "the newness of which still causes dizziness"

(*M*, 187). This is because by showing solidarity with the Hebrew state at a time when its existence was threatened, he has succeeded in reconciling himself with his own past and has been able, when facing the Wall, to draw new strength by reconnecting himself to the people of Israel in its extratemporal dimension.

As he informs the reader: " A page is turned. The beasts in the hearts of men have ceased howling and losing their blood. The curse here has been revoked. Its reign has ended. One no longer attains glory or saintliness by killing or letting oneself be killed." This does not mean that evil has been definitively exorcised. It will continue ravaging our planet. But if the existence of good does not neutralize evil, the opposite remains no less true. As Elie Wiesel observes, only the human being can bring them together through memory (*M*, 187). Provided with this new wisdom that results from a lengthy process of reflection, David will be able to replace Katriel and marry Malka. Because he has succeeded in transforming his tyrannical past into an ally, the hero can now offer this woman who had been so unhappy the joy and will to live that was so sorely lacking in her first husband. Just like Grégor in *The Gates of the Forest*, a regenerated David will assume his responsibility as a Messiah for another human being.

The Oath

In its way, *The Oath* (1973) also relates the spiritual regeneration of a person through the solidarity he accepts with the history of his people that begins in biblical times and goes on into the twentieth century. As is so often the case in Elie Wiesel's novels, a fortuitous encounter occurs. It turns out to be a fruitful one that modifies significantly the destiny of several people. After meeting, their existences change for the better. This is fortunate, because otherwise the novel would be almost as implacably pessimistic as the author's first great text, *Night*.

The Oath has two narrators, a young man in his twenties with suicidal tendencies and an octogenarian by the name of Azriel, the sole survivor of a pogrom that took place at the beginning of the twentieth century in a little town situated between the Dnieper and the Carpathian Mountains in eastern Europe. Parallels exist between Azriel and the author. After being freed from the death camps, Weisel imposed on himself a ten-year period of silence because the events he had lived through seemed too horrible to be adequately evoked in words. It was François Mauriac who exhorted the young journalist to bear witness in favor of the deceased victims.

In *The Oath*, the elderly Azriel breaks a solemn vow of silence that has lasted more than half a century to save his young friend from death. The latter is the child of a Holocaust survivor. Having inherited his mother's nightmarish past, he has persuaded himself that he is devoid of a present and future. He is certain that his life counts for nothing. His despair impels him to reduce to zero the value of human existence in general and to want to commit suicide.

Without ever obeying this death wish, the elderly Azriel nevertheless carries a cemetery within his heart since the age of sixteen. In it are buried all the members of the Jewish community of the little town of Kolvillàg. Victims, all of them, of a destructive antisemitic fury. Thus, he remains the last witness of the history of his coreligionists that unfolded in the place where he was born. To tear the young man away from his obsession with suicide, the octogenarian begins telling his story, thereby freeing himself from the oath of silence he had pronounced in the Great Synagogue barely several days before tragedy struck. Azriel's listener is so fascinated by this narrative that he no longer thinks about putting an end to his life.

The story the old man tells is a typical illustration of the kind of odious and murderous religious fanaticism that have bedeviled Jews since the beginnings of their venerable history. A Christian adolescent called Yancsi, a sadistic little brute detested by all who know him, disappears without any trace. Scarcely several days after having disappeared, a rumor begins spreading that accuses the Jews of Kolvillàg of having committed a ritualistic murder against the youth. More and more people accredit this groundless accusation. A climate of madness settles over the city. The Christians seem to be waiting for the most appropriate moment to swoop down on their prey. Moshe, the most bizarre character in the Jewish community, a mixture of the mystic, the dreamer and the crazy, offers to sacrifice himself for his coreligionists by accusing himself of having killed the boy. But Moshe's sacrificial gesture is not enough to defuse this time bomb of fanatical hatred. Consequently, aware that the pogrom is ineluctable, the Jews of Kolvillàg assemble to determine what course of action to take. During this solemn meeting, Moshe pleads in favor of adopting an unusual method to confront the antisemitism which the Jews have always had to endure. Instead of transmitting to posterity all the episodes of their history when they have been used as scapegoats, they must now make silence reign. For centuries, the chosen people have always described in their chronicles the persecutions of which they have been the victims, and the persecutions have never stopped. This time, Moshe insists, let no one find out what happened. Instead of writing down their tragedy for future generations, let the Jewish community of Kolvillàg maintain an impenetrable silence. According to Moshe, the written word, in the end, engenders what it announces, perpetuates the horrors that it observes and deplores. If Jews renounce their tradition of historical witness, they will perhaps succeed in liberating themselves from another one that has marked them: that of martyr. Moreover, man's silence will perhaps be the best way of calling out to God and compelling him to explain His own silence in the face of His creatures' suffering. Moshe's speech convinces the community. Everyone who attends the meeting pronounces the oath of silence. Whoever survives will never speak of the final days and nights that the Jews of Kolvillàg have spent waiting for terror to strike. The pogrom does indeed swoop down on them and all perish except Azriel.

Carrying his silence like a kind of malediction, Azriel is compelled to travel the length and breadth of Europe for decades, in search of someone who might be able to free him from the oath he pronounced with his now-deceased coreligionists. At the end of his life, Azriel violates his vow to save the young suicidal man. In turn, the latter saves the octogenarian, since he gives Azriel a powerful enough reason to end his silence. The old man will, then, talk about the tragedy of the Jews of Kolvillàg to prevent death from winning an unjust victory over a living person.

To evoke this massacre of the innocents that prefigures the Shoah, the author gives his novel a tripartite structure. Each part corresponds to a decisive stage in the unfolding of the story of the city's destruction as well as of the relationship that develops between the two interlocutors. The first, titled "The Old man and the Child," describes the bonds of friendship that get woven between the young man tempted by suicide and the venerable Azriel. The octogenarian's train of thought is expressed in normal print characters whereas his interlocutor's reactions appear in italics. The survivor of Kolvillàg's mass murder does not relate right off the bat the tragedy that had annihilated the Jewish community. He talks about his years of wandering through Europe undertaken to anesthetize the affliction that is tormenting him. As though to remind Azriel of the imperious necessity of saving the young man from despair, there appear on three occasions short scenes where the latter's mother relives again and again the nightmare of the concentration camp that she has never been able to exorcize. She keeps seeing the dreadful moment when she let the Nazis thugs go off with her little child towards the gas chamber without making the slightest gesture to save him. Even though she did not know at that time what the Nazis did to him, she was never able to stop torturing herself retrospectively and heaping guilt on herself.

The second bears the title "The Child and the Madman." Here the child is Azriel when he was an adolescent and the madman is the crazy beadle, Moshe. While describing his friendship for the mature man, founded on an immense admiration and affection, the young narrator begins the tragic story of Kolvillàg itself, from the inexplicable disappearance of Yancsi till the terrible *hérem*, or curse that Moshe and the whole congregation in the synagogue pronounce against whoever among the survivors of the pogrom will dare reveal this irruption of antisemitism to the outside world. It is significant that the young man tempted by suicide does not intervene during this part of the novel. Thoughts that he shares with us at the beginning of the work explain his silence: "A sunlit, feverish period. My connection to Kolvillàg was increasing in depth, in intensity, turning into an obsession. I was hardly eating. I was sleeping badly. How can I explain his ascendancy over me? I could not explain it. Was I identifying Azriel with the prophet Elie whom the disinherited, the downtrodden dream about? With my grandfather perhaps, who died down there, during the upheaval? I couldn't say. Was he helping me to escape from myself? To accept myself? To fulfill myself? Possibly."[12] The young man is so fascinated by the evocation of the tragic destiny of Azriel's former community that he does not even think of interrupting him to make comments.

The final part of the novel, the shortest of the three, has as its title "The Madman and the Book" and conjures up the antisemitic explosion that destroys the whole population of the city, be it Jewish or Christian. The term "Madman" now refers to the elderly Azriel, who has become more and more of a screwball as a result of repressing in the depths of his being the terrible secret of his that is a half-century old. The book in question is the *pinkas* or chronicle of the Jewish community of Kolvillàg transcribed faithfully for hundreds of years. Azriel's father is the last person to have written down all the events concerning the life of his coreligionists until the moment when the pogrom was unleashed. He entrusts this precious document to his son when he orders him to flee the city in peril. The young man whom Azriel had rescued from suicide would have wanted to peruse it, but the *pinkas*, inseparable from the person to whom it had been entrusted, disappears at his death. Indeed, it is the young man torn

---

[12] Elie Wiesel, *Le Serment de Kolvillàg*, Paris : Les Éditions du Seuil, 1973, 20; referred to henceforth as *K*.

by Azriel from the fascination of death, who informs us of the passing of his octogenarian friend. In the last sentence of the novel, he declares: "Azriel had returned to Kolvillàg to die in my place" (*K*, 255). But, as we will notice, Azriel's death has far more significance than the one that had tempted the young man encountered by chance and saved by one of those human miracles that occur from time to time in Elie Wiesel's fiction. If Azriel was able to regain spiritual peace only on the threshold of death, it is because his Talmudic teacher, Moshe, had imprisoned him as well as all his coreligionists in Kolvillàg, in this terrible oath of silence I have pointed out. Azriel will call out to this bizarre and exalted mystic at various times, beyond the grave, to make him understand the need to break his vow to come to the rescue of a person crushed under the weight of despair.

The fifth and last avatar of the individual who first appeared in *Night*, Moshe takes on an importance he did not have in the previous texts. In *The Oath*, he sits enthroned majestically. All the Jews of the town agree that he is a madman. But the term as applied to this exalted personage must be accompanied by nuances and clarifications. The beadle's madness does not consist so much in being disconnected from reality as in being situated in an elsewhere to which ordinary mortals do not have access but which they would never have the slightest inclination to explore. The man who fascinates young Azriel and becomes his mentor knows exactly what is happening around him when he wants to. He can break into the sanctuaries of his coreligionists hearts, the places where they hide their most shameful secrets. He pierces through to their real motives like a laser beam. But, as a mystic determined to snatch essential truths from the shadows, he is only really interested in the universe of the mind. This determination can be perceived in his gaze. The beadle's eyes seem to penetrate beyond appearances and leap immediately towards the organic unity that transcends them all: "Strange eyes, red and black, uncommonly steady, with an unfathomable depth, eyes that see only the essential in everything, that shoot ahead, beyond the ramparts, pursuing reflections till their source, till the very first astonishment, till the first agreement and disagreement between the self and its conscience" (*K*, 115).

It is very difficult for the reader to track down the truths that Moshe pursues tirelessly, since religious experience is among the least likely to be targeted with precision. But judging from his own statements and the observations of his disciple, Azriel, it seems as though the mystic of Kolvillàg is striving to resolve the enigma of our human condition, namely, the inseparable link between Good and Evil in every individual. One would venture to conclude that he is endeavoring to understand why these two primordial forces function concomitantly and that he would willingly sacrifice himself if he could find a way to separate them. If only it were possible to isolate the Good, the powers man would have at his disposal to liberate the Messiah would be multiplied to the infinite. He could transform the universe. This is how one can interpret the objurgations Moshe directs at his coreligionists so that they will allow him to pursue his work without disturbing him. He is undertaking, he affirms, a heroic, indeed superhuman exploit: to seize the Absolute without having to pay the price that man's vulnerability entails. To break his connections to the real world, to abandon all his landmarks for the purpose of venturing into the limitless kingdom where God resides, is to run the risk of sinking forever into insanity: "When I explore my being, it is for you that I explore, for you that I walk on a tightrope suspended between dazzling light and oblivion, inebriation and damnation. Reaching this goal will mean total deliverance; if I fall, I and I alone, will fall into the abyss and the night. More than my own future depends on my success or failure; the powers I propose to defy do not forgive; no one flouts them with impunity" (*K*, 125).

Azriel's interpretation of Moshe's behavior during one of the latter's mystical meditations which he witnessed, confirms this. The danger involved in these magnificent spiritual flights is the necessity sooner or later of returning to ordinary reality with all the constraints this means: time, space, logic and the body's weakness. Through Herculean efforts, the exalted soul can temporarily wrest itself from the body that encloses it. The law of gravity to which this soul is subjected, just like the mediocre ones, will finally get the better of it and force it to come down to earth. The descent in the figurative sense will then be very painful: "[The soul] goes where it wants, comes down when it wants, and then, within one beat, man resembles the half-awake prophet whose burning and crazed eyes still contain the vision of sacred and luminous things: he tried to hold on to it, but his body thwarts him and reminds him of his human condition" (*K*, 133).

Terrible anguish continues to haunt Moshe following his mystical voyages. He is agonizingly aware of man's incapacity to seek out Good without simultaneously being subjected to the attraction of Evil. The kabbalist's awareness of the inseparable link between the two affects him all the more sorrowfully because he is compassionate and generous in nature. He agreed to marry Léah, a rather ugly and poor spinster whom no one wanted, and transformed her into a queen through the ardor of his love and conjugal devotion. He wasted no time accusing himself of the murder of Yancsi and offered himself as a holocaust to save his community from a pogrom. But his own goodness does not reassure him in the least about the human condition nor does it diminish his pessimism in the least. He remains distressed by the permanent weakness of the human creature who, according to him, will never succeed in enabling Good to reign to the exclusion of Evil. Before being brutally beaten by Sergent Pavel in prison, Moshe was able to entertain the illusion that such a triumph was possible. The tortures he endured after denouncing himself to the police seem to have uncovered a despair he had not known before. When young Azriel visits him in his cell, the mystic declares in heartbreaking accents that the extremities come together, and that by going towards one during one's spiritual journey, man never fails to reach the other. He cites the story of Abraham, whom God ordered to sacrifice Isaac: "Chosen by God, Abrahm nearly became a murderer on God's order. I'm afraid, because this means that evil also leads to God, that death also—misfortune on us—leads to God" (*K*, 176). In this perilous quest for the Absolute where abysses open up between mountain summits that one succeeds in reaching, the mystic walks on a tightrope. Even if he climbs up to the top, he can easily lose his balance and somersault into the void from one instant to the next.

The whole episode where Moshe in his cell converses with Azriel deserves a line-by-line commentary, because it evokes the helplessness of the Righteous who must face the irreducible presence of evil within the heart of the human condition and the ambiguity of the divine attitude. This obsession with the existence of omnipresent Evil within our human destiny, of an Evil capable of taking on the appearance of Good, explains Moshe's totally unexpected decision to demand of the whole Jewish community of Kolvillàg that it pronounce the solemn oath of silence on pain of being cursed for all time. As I have stated, according to the kabbalist, the act of transcribing and transmitting to posterity the persecutions that the Jews have suffered throughout history has done nothing to stop them. The beadle is almost ready to affirm the opposite. In the new metaphysical perspective within which he evaluates the events making up the history of his people, Moshe sees in the chroniclers' commitment yet another illustration of the pernicious link between Good and Evil. Wishing to testify in favor of their coreligionists, the chroniclers have done nothing except bring other misfortunes to them. It is imperative to reject this tradition. Far from waiting for the arrival of the Messiah with patience and joy, we must henceforth learn to do without his services. Through its silence, the Jewish community of Kolvillàg will defy a cruel fate. Through their silence, the Jews of the city will command God to explain why the universe is programed for hatred and why He forbids the Messiah from putting an end to the human tragedy.

Like the other members of the congregation, the adolescent Azriel, sixteen years old at the time, lets himself get carried away by Moshe's fieriness. He conserves, however, enough lucidity to realize that the beadle's argument is founded on a absolutely insane form of logic or absence of logic. He senses that the Jewish community of Kolvillàg will allow itself to be dragged into a blind alley. In the first place, not to bear witness is the equivalent of condemning one's coreligionists to death a second time. Secondly, pitting silence against antisemitic fury will not in the least prevent the enemies of Jewish people from perpetrating violence again. Hatred as irrational and murderous as this particular kind feeds on its own poison and renews itself constantly in other forms. Towards the end of the novel, when Azrael watches his city collapse under the flames, he has a sinister premonition. He is convinced that this infernal scene prefigures something even more frightening: " The asylum and the hospice, the inn and the synagogue were converging through a bridge of flames. The cemetery was burning, the police station was burning, the nurseries were burning, the libraries were burning. On that night the works of man were subjected to the power and judgement of fire. And suddenly I understood with all the fibers of my being why I was shuddering before this vision of horror: I had just glimpsed the future" (K, 254). We cannot help but imagine that what the adolescent glimpsed then was the Shoah to come sixty years later.

At the end of a long life of wanderings, at the time when he meets the desperate young man, Azriel the octogenarian finds an even more imperious reason to break his oath of silence. He contrasts it with the very human and exalting conception of the Messiah that the beadle had taught him before going insane. As his former disciple reminds Moshe by calling out to him in an imaginary face to face, the legendary liberator of humanity is none other than any solitary individual who transcends his solitude so that his fellow man will be less alone, but, what is even more important, each one of us has the sacred duty to save a human life in danger, since each one of them is infinitely precious: "To bring a person back to life, is to prevent the destruction of the world, says the Talmud" (K, 79). Good triumphs whenever a person, acting like the Messiah towards his fellow man, tears him away from death. In the evening of his existence, Azriel is anxious to vanquish death by relating to the young man the story of Kolvillàg so that the latter will be obliged to become a living witness of the vanished Jewish community. Thus, he entreats Moshe, while shouting at him, to revoke the terrible hérem, or curse: "Would you want me to end my life with a defeat? Are several decades of silence not enough for you? Release me from my oath, Moshe. Crazy friend, dead friend, give me back my freedom. I do not want to die defeated" (*K*, 79).

This Messiah that the elderly Azriel yearns to incarnate before dying is all the more moving because he remains so vulnerable. Contrary to the legendary and immortal personage who is supposed to bring peace to humanity at the end of time, this one knows he is mortal and fallible, and herein lies his eminent nobility. The courageous lucidity with which he confronts danger while knowing that he may very well fail, the energy he deploys to reach his goals in finite time as though he enjoyed immortality, confer upon him a dimension of tragic grandeur that makes him superior to the Messiah of legend. One perceives accents of Albert Camus in the definition Azriel gives of the attitude that man must assume towards existence: "The distinctiveness of man is to be combative, even though at each instant he may receive the confirmation that he will not win. The distinctiveness of man is to imagine himself as immortal" (*K*, 85). Now this existential and moral ideal based on an anthropocentric Messiah is very much like the myth of Sisyphus as Albert Camus interprets it. According to Camus, one must imagine Sisyphus happy despite knowing that the heavy stone he drags towards the mountain summit always ends up rolling down. Similarly, it is easy for us to agree that Elie Wiesel's Azriel draws from his determination to embody the Messiah enough spiritual energy to ward off despair and continue believing in man.

And so, the octogenarian becomes again the adolescent who, on the eve of the massacre of his coreligionists in Kolvillàg, already realized that it was useless to wait for the impossible legendary Messiah. Only man could come to the rescue of his fellow man. The young Azriel's skepticism concerning the Messiah of legend reveals itself in the episode of the festival to celebrate the inauguration of the new Torah. Despite the imminence of the pogrom, the Rabbi of the community insists that the celebration take place. Since people are afraid of congregating in the synagogue, he orders that the festivities unfold at the hospice, among the beggars. Unfortunately, the Jews are too heavy-hearted and disquieted to enjoy themselves. The drunk Kaizer is even bold enough to call into question this fundamental belief in Jewish orthodoxy according to which the Messiah will not fail to arrive one day to fulfill humanity's yearning. Having run out of convincing arguments, the Rabbi strives to persuade the beggar that we must be grateful for being able to yearn for the Messiah's coming, even if we despair of seeing him while we are alive. But the beggar refuses to yield. In a roaring voice he maintains that even the hour of waiting is now over. As a heartbroken witness of the scene, the adolescent Azriel, now a venerable old man, remembers it a half-century later: "I wanted to weep. Pity was rending my heart. I had aligned myself with Kaizer, this unknown man who looked like a beggar and acted like a drunk. He was right, not the Rabbi. I was sad and I was sixteen years old" (*K*, 209).

Given this purely human conception of the Messiah that Azriel had taken as his own even before becoming an adult, we can understand that he felt the moral obligation at the end of his own life to come to the rescue of the suicidal young man. Indeed, the reader is convinced that his temperament on the one hand, and the unfolding of his destiny on the other, made his decision to defy the *herem* inevitable. As a young adult, he is a tormented soul. He dreams of a great love with a woman that his chronic timidity renders impossible. Unable to live a great passion, he entertains a tender friendship with Rachel, an independent spirit, mocking yet compassionate, which lasts until her death. This ability to commit himself to others is revealed throughout his whole life as a wanderer. Having consulted a famous Rabbi, Zousia of Kolomey, about the possibility of breaking the vow of silence that is weighing heavily upon him, the latter orders him to travel ceaselessly around the earth as a Na-Venadnik, that is, a voyager condemned to never finding rest, until an intuition will lead him to understand that the curse has been lifted. On the surface, this existence of uninterrupted wandering resembles the kind of diversion that the French philosopher of the 17th century, Blaise Pascal describes when exploring the fundamental anguish at the core of our human condition that people spend all their energy trying to avoid contemplating within themselves. Azriel always seems to be moving constantly so as not to have to think about the *hérem* that would otherwise obsess him. But his innumerable trips across Europe offer him the opportunity to share with others his treasures of understanding and empathy. Before encountering the rudderless young man, the octogenarian had been a welcome guest across the whole political spectrum from the right to the extreme left. And proof of his immense gift for empathy, he is loved by young people from the most diverse milieus, because he tells them the truth in a disinterested manner.

The trigger mechanism that finally impels him to free himself from his oath of silence is his awareness that by enclosing himself in the past of his destroyed city, his existence has become a stagnant water. A prisoner of a tragedy that has left a permanent mark on him, Azriel realizes that he has sunk into indifference towards his own present. Even Moshe, who nevertheless had forced him to pronounce the terrible oath, often warned him against the vice of indifference, especially as concerned the suffering of others. To feel that he is still alive as well as to give a meaning to his imminent death, the octogenarian is now determined to talk to the young man about Kolvillàg. Azriel will thus see to it that his interlocutor will be a witness for his dead city and will in this way impose on the young man the moral obligation to remain alive. In turn, the latter will save the octogenarian's life in the figurative sense by giving him the opportunity to embody the Messiah one more time before his death. Azriel explains his decision in the following terms: "This is why I will speak despite everything. Out of gratitude. I will violate my oath not only to save you, but to save me as well. I am old and tired, but I am not yet dead: I want to live my death, after having lived that of Kolvillàg. And although I am older than the old people whose throats I saw slit, I am still capable of using their voices to evoke their childhood and mine" (*K*, 86).

While the novel traces Azriel's trajectory that takes him from an unconditional admiration of Moshe to revolt, it also orchestrates two related themes: antisemitic hatred and the transmission of memory. Indeed, the two combine to shed light on the decision taken by the old survivor of the pogrom and place it into stunning relief. As strange as this may seem, however, they prevent the novel from sinking into unremitting pessimism.

In *The Oath*, antisemitism appears as one of the most ignoble manifestations of human conduct. It consists in hating the other because he/she adheres to different forms of cultural and religious life, and in using that person as a scapegoat in order to have a convenient albeit false explanation for events that a given society can no longer control. It would never have occurred to the Christians of the little city to accuse their Jewish neighbors of the ritual murder of the adolescent, Yancsi, if the Jews had practiced the same religion as they did. What exposes the Jewish community to public condemnation is their desire to safeguard their cultural and religious specificity. And it is the leaders of the Christian majority, out of hostility towards this minority impervious to their dominant ideology, who create the conditions that are conducive to an eventual explosion of hatred.

The vile predator of antisemitism begins to emerge from its unstable sleep in the hearts of the villagers after the first search organized to recover the boy who disappeared. On returning to town, they hear what seems to them a strange noise. It is Jews chanting in a house of prayer. Immediately, their completely innocent chanting is interpreted by the peasants as an affront to the community's sorrow. Ancestral paranoia, sustained by centuries of poisonous indoctrination, is aroused once again. The Pope of the community pours oil on the nascent fire by the kind of remark that, on the surface, seems only subjective but turns out to be malevolent and skillfully calculated. Here it can only give free rein to a collective hatred held in check for too long: "This is nevertheless curious... Very curious... I have the impression they are singing louder than last year. I'm wondering...if they are doing it on purpose" (*K*, 95). After making this perfidious statement, the Pope can try as much as possible to calm the passions of his flock by maintaining that one must never accuse innocent people even though they are hostile to Christ. The damage is done. From then on, the novel describes the progressive deterioration of relationships between Christians and Jews who were beforehand good neighbors. Hatred in the end resembles an impending storm that is almost palpable in the atmosphere of the city, a storm that might break out at any time.

Yet however reprehensible hatred founded on ideological exclusion may be, the worst of antisemitism resides elsewhere. According to the novel, the Christians of Kolvillàg invoke their religious faith and the suffering of their Savior at the hands of the Jews to have a legitimate excuse for giving vent to their destructive urges without feeling monstrous. The proof of this lies in the fact that once the predator is fully aroused within their hearts, no human reasoning, no logical evidence will prevent them from assuaging their thirst for blood. Blinded by their own cruelty, intoxicated by the terror they wield, the Christians start massacring their own brothers whom they mistake for Jews. Their coreligionists can protest all they want that they belong to the same faith, they can implore their so-called brothers for mercy from today till tomorrow, the mob acts like an unstoppable infernal machine. Antisemitism, then, is an abomination not only because it claims innocent Jewish victims, but because it represents an outrage against human dignity. As the novel emphasizes, antisemitism is essentially the sadistic pleasure of hating and killing. As a result, it degrades the killers even more than their prey. Wiesel depicts the murderous insanity that continues being unleashed as the pogrom reaches its climax, and the brutal indifference the attacking Christians show towards their besieged coreligionists whom they mistake for Jews even when the latter call out in vain for their pity: "The mob, stupefied by violence, refused to believe. Its need to kill, to debase the human within man, to offer it as food to the night predators was not yet assuaged. Drunk with power and cruelty, the mob clamored for more blood, triumphs, victims" (*K*, 251). The fire that ends up devouring the whole city, victims and persecutors alike, serves as a metaphor to describe the destructive hatred of antisemitism that leaves nothing human alive in its wake.

Because hatred based on religious faith represents one of humanity's worst scourges, it is indispensable to bear witness for future generations. Azriel is convinced of this during his whole existence as a "Na-Venad-nik," even though, as we have pointed out, he has allowed himself to be mesmerized by Moshe's fiery fanaticism. Ever since his childhood, the elderly man felt an immense admiration for his father who was the official scribe of the community. For the latter, to preserve the memory of his dead coreligionists for future generations constitutes an article of faith, indeed, his reason for being. Thanks to the witness the victims do not die a second time, generations converse across time and space instead of standing opposite one another like strangers. Expressing his credo in front of Moshe, Azriel's father declares: "An act transmitted is a victory achieved over death. A witness who refuses to testify is a false witness. I, on the contrary, do not refuse, I do nothing but that, I yearn to do only that" (*K*, 172).

There is another reason that justifies the transmission of memory from one generation to another. The martyrs of the past can be inspiring examples for the living. They breathe their courage and pride into their coreligionists who exist in the present. They bring them comfort. They prove to the living that there exist transcendent values within a universe that seems abandoned to madness and cruelty. Several hours before the massacre of the Jewish community breaks out, Azriel glances through the *Pinkas*, and reads stories of various Jews who lived from the twelfth to the nineteenth centuries. They all embody the same unostentatious courage, the same moral integrity, the same generosity of mind and heart, the same dignity. All preferred to die rather than renounce their faith. But because they accepted to die for values that conferred a magnificent significance on their destinies, they seemed infinitely greater in death than did their executioners in life. In fact, their deaths represented their apotheosis. By rereading the chronicles, Azriel brings back to life the Jews of Virgirsk from the twelfth century who proclaimed their faith through their singing with such fervor that they remained oblivious to their executioners' sabers that beheaded most of them. He then focuses on the tragedy of the sovereignly beautiful young woman, Brakha, both morally and physically.

In 1553, she slashed her face and bosom rather than give in to the blackmail of the lord of the kingdom who wanted to possess her body. He is moved by the heroism of the young man Zemakh, so humble and self-effacing in appearance, who in 1803 held his ground in the face of the sadistic nobleman Lupu, and categorically refused to heap praise upon him, because, he maintained, "to glorify a torturer is the basest of servitudes..., to turn him into a god, the worst of perversions" (*K*, 238). Indeed, if the Jews as a people have been able to survive so many catastrophes, it is precisely because they considered themselves inseparable from a venerable history that they kept alive by drawing from it the spiritual strength necessary to confront the present and future. Having forgotten this truth, the renegade Jew, Stéphane Braun, a celebrated lawyer and perfectly integrated into Christian society, on the surface at least, is overwhelmed with shame. He uprooted himself culturally and spiritually without embracing the faith of the majority. And so he existed within parentheses, and realized to his sorrow that his son had deserted him and returned to his grandfather to rediscover his Jewish roots.

In his way, Azriel also kept alive within his heart the trials that his people had endured. Transmitting his testimony appeared so important to him that he finally went beyond the threat of eternal damnation. For him to save another human being was a saintly act. Because of this transgression committed by the octogenarian on the threshold of death, *The Oath* does not drag the reader down into despair. Elie Wiesel seems thus to exhort us never to let ourselves be downtrodden. But the old man is not the only one to show grandeur in this novel. Perhaps the most striking example of generosity, because it is the least expected, can be seen in the conduct of the non-Jewish Prefect of the city. After showing so much cowardice and venality, he resolves to save Moshe even at the risk of his own life. One will say that this manifestation of virtue is very little when one takes into account the destructive hatred that prevails in the city among the overwhelming majority of its citizens. No doubt, but in a world as imperfect as ours, Wiesel invites us to honor every act of goodness that allows us not to lose confidence completely in our fellow man.

The Testament

Some of Elie Wiesel's heroes like Michael, Grégor and David return to the Judaism of their childhood at the end of a spiritual journey marked by multiple tragedies. It is not so much a question of removing themselves from the faith of their ancestors, consciously or unconsciously, as of relegating it to the periphery of their existences until a crisis draws them back to it. The trajectory of Paltiel Kossover, the hero of the novel *The Testament*, is appreciably different from that of the others. This protagonist believed he had distanced himself definitively from his family's religion. At certain moments, he was even convinced he had jettisoned it in favor of the Marxist ideology which, according to its fanatical followers, was going to create paradise on earth. But, supreme irony, at the end of his life, a prisoner of the redoubtable Stalinist secret police in 1952 and knowing that he will soon be executed, Paltiel Kossover abjures the secular religion of communism to which he had adhered with a neophyte-like fervor and proudly reclaims the Judaism of his childhood.

As he tells us in the second volume of his memoirs, the author was captivated by the destinies of Jewish intellectuals like the hero of he novel after visiting the USSR in 1965 and remained caught up in them until 1979. During that period Wiesel never ceased wondering how a young Talmudic scholar could become a convert to Marxist-Leninist orthodoxy.[13] The novelist does not hesitate to inform us that he is particularly fond of *The Testament*. He believes he has explored the soul and the conscience of a Jew repressed or exiled at the frontier of Judaism (*ELM*, 118). It is not difficult to agree with him on that score. Indeed, such was the power of his imagination that without ever having met him, Wiesel drew an indepth and nuanced portrait of a real Russian-Jewish writer, Perez Markish, whose personality and tragic destiny bear an astonishing resemblance to those of his personage. When the son of Perez Markish read the novel, his was convinced that Wiesel had made his father's acquaintance.

The hero, Paltiel Kossover, moves us deeply because of certain characteristic traits which, although contradictory in appearance, harmonize to create a singularly rich individual: idealism and sorrowful lucidity, vulnerability and unostentatious heroism, naïveté and childlike enthusiasm tempered by the wisdom of a venerable old sage. He devotes himself to others unstintingly as though he were immortal. Nevertheless, he is agonizingly conscious of the fragility of man's/woman's destiny as an individual. In several places during the novel recurs, like a poignant leitmotif, a simple little phrase that the hero expresses as a question or a sad observation, either when he has the premonition that he is going to lose friends for whom he

---

[13] See Elie Wiesel, *Et la mer n'est pas remplie*, Paris : Les Éditions du Seuil, 1996, 117-118; referred to henceforth as *ELM*.

feels an immense sympathy, or when he discovers that they have left this earth. Before leaving his beloved mentor, Paul Hamburger whose death warrant Stalin has already signed without his being aware of it, Paltiel asks him: "Will we see each other again?" [14] When he learns, horrified, the news of the death of Lebedev, a Jewish military doctor both intrepid and compassionate, he says to himself: "I will never see him again, either" (*T*, 271).

To emphasize the spiritual and moral radiance of his hero, Elie Wiesel organizes his narrative like a musical score for five voices. The dominant voice is that of the poet whose assassination Stalin has ordered. It expresses itself eloquently through the testament that Paltiel Kossover composes in prison to reply to the accusations of his judges. Three other narrators will conserve this document piously so that the martyr's memory will be transmitted to posterity. The reader meets the first one at the beginning of the novel. It is the Israeli writer, Yoav, a transparent disguise under which Wiesel himself appears. Just like the novelist, Yoav overflows with joy on seeing the Russian Jews deplane at the Tel Aviv airport. They have come to settle in Israel to be able to affirm their Judaism without fear of reprisals. Moreover, he takes on as a sacred duty the responsibility of championing the works of writers persecuted by repressive regimes. Yoav welcomes into his home the son of the assassinated poet, Grisha, a very intelligent and sensitive young man but rendered mute, as the reader will find out later, following a traumatic experience.

Grisha assumes the function of narrator only once to tell us about the act of self-mutilation he felt he was forced to perform to put an end to the relentless cross-examinations that his mother's lover, Dr. Volodia Mozliak, was inflicting on him. A diabolically skilled psychiatrist, Mozliak figured out that having lost his father when he was still a baby, the adolescent had created for himself in his imagination a mythical father to fill the emotional void. To consolidate his position more easily vis-à-vis the boy's mother, the doctor endeavored to undermine the myth the child entertained with filial piety. Driven into a corner by Mozliak's ruthless interrogations, Grisha bit his tongue so violently that he cut part of it off, thereby making himself incapable of speaking and, as a result, liberating himself from his tyrant's hold.

Another narrator difficult to identify takes over from Paltiel Kossover's son to describe the emotions and events making up the web of his

---

[14] Elie Wiesel, *Le Testament d'un poète juif assassiné*, Paris : Les Éditions du Seuil/Points, 1980, 189; henceforth referred to as *T*.

existence before his act of self-mutilation: the desperate love he felt for his mother before she fell for the psychiatrist, the lacerating need for a father figure that he tried to satisfy by setting up a cult around the photos and poems his deceased dad had left, the erotic fever that a non-Jewish schoolmate, Olga, had aroused in him. This relationship could have helped Grisha accept himself, because the young girl, despite a playful and mocking temperament, was very moved by Kossover's poems that he would read to her before he became a mute. The same narrator picks up the thread of Grisha's life once he settles in Israel: his sentimental and sexual relationship with a young widow, Katia; his ambiguous sentiments of tenderness and hostility that he continues feeling for his mother since her liaison with Mozliak while awaiting her arrival in the Holy Land. But who is this voice? On the surface, it is inseparable from the unfolding of the narrative itself since it seems to relate the events like some invisible and neutral presence. When one scrutinizes the text, however, it is not far-fetched to perceive in it the novelist's discreet intervention. He views the fate of the young man with so much sympathy and compassion that the reader does not have the impression of dealing with an impersonal narrator. By identifying with his character's drama, Wiesel invites us to do the same.

The last word of the novel, however, belongs literally to the fifth narrator, Viktor Zupanov, the obscure witness thanks to whom the testament of the assassinated Jewish poet has been snatched from oblivion. What a singular guy this Zupanov is! A Jew living under Stalin's reign of terror, he manages to get by unnoticed. His discretion and taciturnity as a stenographer make him almost invisible. He succeeds in removing from the archives of the secret police, one after the other, all the pages of the final text that the poet composes in his cell before his execution. Totally devoid of heroism, his mind nevertheless has sufficient integrity to be shaken up when he discovers it in someone else, and his heart is sufficiently compassionate to want to ensure the posthumous triumph of innocence. As Zupanov explains to Grisha, one day he heard Kossover express his sadness to the magistrate at the idea that his son would never read his confessions. The stenographer decides then and there to take action: "And I, who do not have a son, I felt an iron fist squeezing my heart. I had tears in my eyes, and I have never cried or laughed in my life. Was it then that I decided to snatch a page here, a page there, and stuff them all in my drawer, where the devil himself would have trouble finding anything, and thinking to myself: you never know?" (*T*, 202).

It wasn't always that way. Zupanov had seen quite a lot before meeting Kossover. All the prisoners who passed through the sinister corridors of the prison had, in the end, broken down, and the stenographer considered it to be normal. But the Jewish poet was different. Despite his relative physical fragility, he resisted his tormentors with such determination, as much on the psychological as on the physical levels, that he finally aroused in this silent witness a profound sympathy and admiration. At the beginning of the interrogations and torture sessions, Zupanov felt irritation and impatience against Kossover. He expected the latter to collapse just like the strongest of the prisoners who had been brought in before. He wondered why this particular one was persevering in his crazy campaign of resistance. As the stenographer increasingly noticed the incredible strength of character that the poet was deploying during the sessions of silent torture even more than during the brutal beatings, Zupanov silently vowed his fraternal love to the prisoner. The latter's almost biological integrity, his dignity in the face of his torturers, his intrepidness in the face of death, all these traits of character had conquered the silent witness.

Once the Stalin reign of terror ends, Zupanov finds a way to show his solicitude towards Paltier Kossover beyond death. He guarantees the poet's posthumous triumph by entrusting a copy of the testament to Grisha and by talking to him constantly about his astonishing father. Having recycled himself after the terrible years in the city of Krasnograd, as the custodian of the building where Grishna lives with his mother, Zupanov strikes up a friendship with the adolescent and becomes a kind of spiritual father to him. By the most notable of paradoxes, it is because the late poet's son is now mute that the former stenographer does not hesitate to hand over to him this precious spiritual heritage. He even advises the boy to emigrate to Israel to assume his sacred filial duty of ensuring that that his late father's works attain the recognition they deserve. Once he arrives in the Holy Land, Grisha, as fascinated as ever by this father whom he has never known except through his writings and the custodian's stories, starts to peruse the poet's testament. In this way the reader discovers it, too. Interrupted from time to time by the voices of Zupanov, Grisha and the author, Paltiel Kossover describes the circular itinerary that led him to renounce the Judaism of his childhood in favor of the secular messianism of the communist ideology, then to reject the Marxist-Leninist doctrine on which that ideology is founded in the name of his Jewish faith. Thus, the novel answers two, rather than one, essential questions that the author was asking: why does a Jewish intellectual abandon his religion for

Marxism, and why, in some cases, does he finally repudiate this doctrine and embrace again the faith of his ancestors with a renewed fervor? To allow the reader to better assess the distance traveled during his spiritual journey, Paltiel Kossover begins at the end. Responding to the accusation directed at him by the magistrate of being a Jewish nationalist, the poet proudly proclaims his solidarity with his people. In fact, in a marvelously combative spirit, he goes even beyond the fallacious arguments put forward by the Communist Party to justify his death sentence and discovers in them new claims to fame. Indeed, his break with this Party so adulated in the past now represents for him a kind of spiritual deliverance: "I declare myself guilty for having sustained, a bit late, too late, an exaggerated, incommensurable love for a stubborn people, my own, which you and yours have never ceased scorning and oppressing. Yes, today, I cut my ties to the world which this prison protects and represents; I espouse the Jewish cause, I espouse it entirely, totally; yes, I show complete solidarity with Jews, wherever they may be: yes, I am a Jewish nationalist in the historic, cultural and ethical sense; I am a Jew above all, and regret not having been able to affirm it earlier and in other places" (*T*, 33).

This solidarity with his people has a breadth that goes infinitely beyond any notion of loyalty towards an ideology, party or country. Just like David in *A Beggar in Jerusalem*, Paltiel Kossover connects with a spatial and temporal continuum encompassing four thousand years of history and legends that each one of his coreligionists carries within their hearts the way he does. He is linked to a supra-national identity, the same one that has always represented for Jews their spiritual centre of gravity wherever they may have lived on the planet, and whatever might have been the particular cultures in which they have grown up. As he explains to the magistrate, a Jewish businessman in Morocco will get along better with a chemist from Chicago or a ragpicker in Lodz than with his own citizens. Because of the extra-territorial and even extra-temporal solidarity that binds them all, the term "solitude" has only a physical meaning for them. As soon as a Jew thinks of his own people, he immediately reenters his spiritual territory: "A Jew is never alone: he remains integrated into an intemporal community, even if it is not visible, even if it is geographically or politically unrealizable. The Jew does not define himself in geopolitical terms, citizen magistrate; he expresses himself and defines himself according to historic categories" (*T*, 57-58). Since the love Paltiel Kossover confesses for his people remains infinitely more significant than the notion of loyalty towards any political party, he dares make the following sensational statement that summarizes the whole drama of his life: "I have lived as a Communist and I die as a Jew" (*T*, 89).

When one examines closely the unfolding of his destiny, it is not at all astonishing that, as a young man, the hero embraced communism with the zeal of the neophyte. What brought him to that doctrine was not only his religion founded on messianic hope and the insistence on charity towards his fellow man, but also his awareness, from the age of five, of the Jew's precarious position in a Christian world resolutely hostile towards his presence.

At a time in his childhood when his mind was already sufficiently developed to understand the impact of a pogrom, Paltier Kossover witnessed an outburst of antisemitic hatred of a rare violence against his community in Barassy. Inebriated by the barbaric cry "death to the Jews!," the mob went berserk in the streets with two purposes in mind: to kill and pillage. The boy's family escaped by the skin of their teeth thanks to his father's foresight. Many others were not as fortunate. After the insane tornado spent itself, the survivors counted the victims. Gripped by anguish, the boy discovered to what extremes antisemitic barbarity could lead: men, woman and children with their throats slit, disemboweled, crucified, beaten to death, homes and businesses sacked or set on fire. Aghast, he attended the funerals of his unfortunate coreligionists, and it was then that he experienced an immense love for his people. If he converts to the Marxist faith in the secular sense, it will be with the hope of creating a new man and, consequently, of abolishing murderous prejudices that make such massacres possible.

On the surface there would seem to exist an organic link between Judaism and Communism. Both aspire to create a reign of justice and fraternity with universal dimensions. According to the religion of Abraham, man must seek knowledge for the purpose of understanding creation and acting on it and on its Creator. When the human spirit will have apprehended simultaneously the beginning and the end of the universe, it will free the Messiah and will bring about the reign of peace among men and women. This, at least, is what Mendel the silent one, the hero's teacher, thought. The communist ideology is in much more of a hurry. It is not a question of hoping to realize one day the advent of happiness on earth, it is rather the determination to create, through sheer force of will and perseverance, the new fraternal order within which men/women will respect one another as equals. Judaism, like all the other great religions, is wise enough to postpone indefinitely the creation of paradise on earth. It knows only too well the dark underside of our human condition. Communism eschews this reality and grants the human being a vote of confidence he/she no doubt does not deserve.

This irrational belief in brighter days for all time, this deification of history shine forth in the words of the hero's friend, Ephraim. Paltiel encounters him at the Talmudic school in Lianov, in Romania where he and his family have sought refuge before the end of the First World War. That Jewish apostle of the new Marxist doctrine burns with the faith of the unconditional believers. Convinced that he is moving in the direction of history, he proselytizes with a fanatical zeal. Through his fervor and his exciting rhetoric, he conjures up the mirage of a human paradise that does not fail to mesmerize a very naif Kossover. The key argument Ephraim uses to clinch his friend's support for the cause is that of the partnership that must exist between man and God. The Lord of the universe has entrusted to man the responsibility of taking care of it. He, then, must assume the heroic duty of freeing his brothers and sisters who are still enslaved and, by doing this, of restoring their pride and dignity. By acting in this way, man effects a synthesis between his own freedom and the all-powerfulness of God. Since the Creator of the universe has conferred upon us the freedom to act, let us show ourselves to be worthy of the honor by striving to fashion a better humanity. "We must make this Revolution," cries out Ephraim at the height of exaltation, "We must make it, because God orders us to do so! God wants us to be communists" (*T*, 68-69).

Ephraim is not the only one to share this insane recklessness in believing that man can direct the course of History, can accelerate its rhythms, indeed supplant the Messiah himself. When the hero settles in Berlin during the years preceding the rise of the Nazis, the communist milieus with which he associates embrace this credo as well. Above all, the two heads of the Berlin Communist Movement, Robert Hauptman and his mistress, Inge, both former Jews converted to Marxism, affirm their unshakeable faith in the triumph of their cause. Like Ephraim, they show the same enthusiastic yet naïve confidence in the ability of the masses to make the right choice, the same tendency to deify History, the same certitude about the imminent arrival of a glorious future since they are moving in the right direction. Paltiel Kossover falls under their influence all the more easily because he admires Hauptman's intellectual rigor, and he manages to arouse the latter's mistress. Since Inge has initiated him into realm of love, the Marxist ideology that she represents becomes his evangel as well. But the German elections that bring Hitler to power in 1932 hits them with the force of a whiplash, negating their ideal. Like over-excited dope addicts who must sooner or later come down to earth after many exciting "trips," they learn with a mixture of stupor and despair that the masses in whom they believed have repudiated them in favor of a racist and brutal megalomaniac. Detoxified at last, Hauptman resolves his dilemma by committing suicide.

Despite this solemn warning, Paltiel pursues the same path. Armed with his Romanian passport, he can leave Berlin and seek refuge in Paris. In the City of Light, the irrational enthusiasm he deploys, as a journalist for the Jewish revue *La Feuille* (The News Sheet), in favor of the international communist movement guided via remote control by Moscow, reaches a new paroxysm. Since he and his colleagues were persuaded that they held the monopoly on Truth, they waged a ruthless ideological war against their conservative competitor that was also Jewish, the *Pariser Haint* (Paris Today). As the hero remembers, "Everything they were preaching was bad; everything we did was sublime. We were defending truth and justice; they were lying and practicing idolatry" (*T*, 164). Pushing sectarianism towards total insanity, Kossover accuses the Zionist Jews of his time of having minds perverted by a ghetto mentality. Instead of enclosing themselves within nationalistic walls, they would be well advised, according to him, to show an openness of spirit to the ideal of a humanity without borders. It is only when he hears about the pain his virulent article has caused his father that he regains control over himself and feels genuine sorrow.

From that moment on, periods of ideological sobering up and blind if not fanatical exaltation will alternate in the hero's life. As the evidence multiplies underscoring the falseness of the new faith to which he had abandoned himself body and soul, more and more anguished doubts will develop about the true nature of Communism. Kossover will wonder more than once if the noble ideal that had inflamed so many hearts and engendered so many hopes is not in the process of becoming irreversibly adulterated. Because he is very intelligent, he realizes that behind the notion of universal brotherhood looms at present something shameful, indeed, monstrous: a party governing the USSR composed of fallible individuals that functions as though it were magically invested with the gift of infallibility. In the name of this fallacious omniscience, this party claims for itself the right to enslave and annihilate any human life whose disappearance will serve its ideology and its interests. Behind this party lurks a power even more evil: that of the megalomaniac killer, Joseph Stalin, crowned as the "father of the people" by his warped admirers, who in his paranoia and murderous thirst for power ruthlessly persecutes all who refuse to subjugate themselves unconditionally to the line of conduct he dictates. However, and this represents the ultimate horror, as Kossover will find out much later, behaving towards the party with exemplary loyalty will not be enough to put any fervent communist in the clear. All the master of the Kremlin has to do is suspect a man or a group of wanting to cause him harm for the lightning bolt to strike dead the unfortunate wretches at that very instant. Without being aware of it, then, right from his sojourn in Paris, the hero will be the victim of a tragedy unfolding inexorably and rigorously controlled by this psychotic master who is totally unworthy of the love his worshippers lavish on him. Because this false god possesses a whole collection of diabolical tricks, Kossover, like so many other victims, will lull himself into believing that the train of history has been put back on its tracks and is advancing towards a messianic future. But sooner or later will come the time when it will no longer be possible to let oneself be mesmerized by a mirage. The ugliness of reality will vanquish the need to believe. And the hero, like so many believers forced to accept a more balanced analysis of the world, will sorrowfully admit that he has been caught in a trap. Like some giant octopus, Stalin will extend his tentacles to seize his supposed enemies one after the other. Once he liquidates the most dangerous, he will go after the others. In this second batch of victims will be Paltiel Kossover.

The first harbinger of the catastrophe that will eventually swoop down on him is the arrest, torture, confessions of guilt and execution of Lenin's former companions. Still carried aloft by his neophyte faith, the Jewish poet sincerely believes that these innocents are guilty of subversive acts against the USSR. He is convinced, moreover, that the communist state never went about torturing the accused to wrest confessions out of them. But his boss, Paul Hamburger, a communist militant from the very beginning and director of an immense network of international contacts, thinks the opposite. He has just been summoned urgently to Moscow, which confirms his pessimism. This brilliant, generous and compassionate man had lived the revolutionary movement from its very beginnings. He remembers that when Communism was born it was really a generous yearning for the equality of all people. He tells his young friend about the pride he felt at the idea of being able to approach the most important men in the political organization of the USSR without the slightest embarrassment. He suspects that a poison has infected what had been a wholesome and robust organism. This thought anguishes him. He would like to push it away. His lucid mind prevents him from so doing: "Lenin's companions, traitors to the country of the Revolution? Double or triple agents? Is this conceivable? If it is true, we are done for; and if it isn't true, we are done for even more" (*T*,186).

If Paul Hamburger's anguish shakes up Paltiel Kossover, the conduct of the communist militants during the Spanish Civil War devastates him. We should make clear that the hero pays homage to the numerous volunteers practicing different professions who came from many countries for the sole idealistic purpose of helping their brothers fight against tyranny. Nevertheless, his admiration for the disinterested generosity that those people showed throws, by contrast, into a very unfavorable light the Marxist fighters who joined up with the Republican forces. The latter commit acts of unimaginable savagery just like the Fascists that they execrate. But there is worse still. It is the cynical flippancy with which the leaders of the international communist network set out to liquidate purely and simply all those who, according to Moscow (which means, according to Stalin), do not adhere with unconditional docility to the ideology laid down by the Pary in the Soviet Union, or go beyond the orders, thereby arousing the implacable jealousy of the dictator who manipulates for personal gain all ideological arguments. The hero is appalled to learn of the disappearance of his comrade, Bercu, a young man of utmost integrity and completely devoted to the revolutionary cause. Yasha, the representative of the Security organs, speaks of Bercu's death as a simple detail, and exhorts Kossover to acquire an overall view of history. So the Revolution can be made against the innocents rather than for them, and all crimes can be justified by referring to a hypothetical future.

The traumatic experience of the Spanish Civil War plunges him into a torpor from which he is brutally awakened by an even more devastating shock: the signing of the non-aggression pact between Germany and Stalin's Russia at the very beginning of the Second World War. Declared a *persona non grata* in France because of his ties to the International Communist Movement directed by Moscow, Paltiel Kossover return to his country of birth, rebaptized the Soviet Union since the October Revolution. Shortly after his return, he is dealt another blow: following the agreement concluded between Hitler and Stalin, the Jewish community strives to go unnoticed. The writers and artists that he encounters in Jewish circles seem hunted down by fear to the point of appearing shriveled up as much on the physical as on the psychological levels. The hero discovers that behind its egalitarian façade the country of human fraternity, just as at the time of the Tsars, continues oozing the same antisemitic poison. As he remarks sorrowfully: "If Hitler had demanded the deportation to Siberia of a million Jews, they would have studied his request with the greatest seriousness; and I do not think that they would have rejected it in Moscow, my older colleagues knew this better than I did" (*T*, 240). It is necessary for a phenomenon to be unleashed that is even more monstrous through its capacity to sow terror and destruction, namely, war, for the communist Jews to feel liberated from their ancestral fear. Supreme irony, it is the aggression by the German army against the Soviet Union that allows the Jews to demonstrate their loyalty towards the regime and be accepted as full-fledged citizens. Among so many other coreligionists, Kossover, as a stretcher-bearer, distinguishes himself through his bravery in the face of enemy fire and his generosity in snatching Russian soldiers from the very jaws of death. As a diabolically skillful demagogue, Stalin succeeds in galvanizing the Russian people by an eloquent speech. Since the struggle against Nazi tyranny devours the energy of the country, antisemitism is put on the back burner. At the end of the war, Kossover's career as a writer really takes off. Since memory is selective and tolerance towards the Jews seems to have returned, he forgets the solemn warnings he had received. In fact, his convert-like fanaticism regains the upper hand.

Wiesel analyzes with admirable mastery the process through which an orthodox Jew installs himself comfortably in the communist doctrine. The mental structures do not change. It is simply a matter of substituting one content for another. In this way the majestic God of Israel is replaced by the false god of the Party, a group of fallible and vindictive mortals endowed by the poet's misguided imagination with the powers of omniscience, omnipotence and omnipresence. The immutable Jewish moral law advocating respect for the Other is replaced by the law dictated by the Party. Unfortunately, that law can change overnight and can also incite its followers to hate as well as to worship. Finally, love of God is transformed into an unconditional adherence to the Party's will. But, alas, in the Jewish faith, the love one offers to God remains inseparable from the love one feels for man/woman. In the new communist religion, however, devotion to the Party often manifests itself by the exclusion of certain individuals who, according to the decrees put out at a given moment in time, have committed ideological crimes. Once Kossover recovers his lucidity after his terrible ordeals, he describes thus that period of his existence: "All I had to do was remember my youth and substitute the Party for the Law of the Lord. In that way I could accept everything without reservations or hesitations. Occult, omniscient and transcendent, the Party had the truth and the keys to the future in its possession; it knew where the most tortuous roads would lead and was familiar with all the components that made up happiness" (*T*, 307).

Kossover needs the resumption of persecutions against the Jews to shatter his illusions and underscore the falsity of his new religion. Like so many other Jewish intellectuals, Kossover is subjected to imprisonment and torture to force him to make false confessions. If he never breaks down, it is because he is sustained in the hour of his greatest distress not only by his courage but by his Jewish faith that watches over him like a living, protective presence. He remembers his friends with deep affection, and especially certain women whose images he conjures up in his cell: Inge, so strong and maternal; Sheina, whose voluptuous lips caused vertigo; his wife, Raïssa, whose emotional robustness he admires while dreading the sentiment of guilt that pushed her into his arms. But it is above all his faith that breathes into him the heroic moral energy in the face of which his torturers remain powerless.

In a sense, the religion of his childhood never left him. Throughout his spiritual trajectory are revealed numerous manifestations of a nostalgia for his Jewish identity that persist despite all his efforts to transform himself into a Marxist revolutionary. First there is the issue of the phylacteries. These are little square boxes containing strips of parchment or vellum on which are inscribed verses from the Bible. Orthodox Jews are supposed to put them on their arm and forehead during the morning prayer. Before he leaves Lianov definitively, Paltiel Kossover promises his father to put them on assiduously every day as a sign of his fidelity to his faith. Even though he does not keep his promise, he persists in taking them with him wherever he goes. During the period of his life that precedes his arrest, at a time when he no longer conserves the slightest illusion about the regime that he had praised to the skies, the hero puts them on again one day while he is watching over his new-born. This gesture that immediately follows the circumcision of his son signifies his return to Judaism.

His reaction as a Jew first breaks out during the Spanish Civil War in which he participates. Noting the dreadful carnage unleashed by the Republican forces, Kossover does not fail to emphasize that the soldiers of Jewish origin fighting alongside them have always abstained from such barbaric practices. Later on, reflecting on this atrocious conflict between citizens of the same country, he puts forward a gripping interpretation of it. According to the poet, five centuries earlier, the Spanish people, fanaticized by a ruthless Inquisition and totally contrary to the spirit of Christian charity, began persecuting Jews with unimaginable brutality. Having debased themselves by such conduct, it was inevitable that sooner or later the Spaniards would strive to exorcize the hatred and disgust they felt towards themselves for centuries by combating one another. In fact, for the hero, this civil war can be described as an act of collective suicide that a whole nation commits through self-loathing.

His nostalgia for the Jewish faith is revived each time he meets the enigmatic David Aboulessia. A personage who seems to emerge straight from the domain of legends, a man whose gait has dignity and majesty, a person radiating intelligence and charisma, he meets Kossover on three occasions and always at a turning point in the poet's existence. Paltiel sees him once more in his cell through his imagination and memory. Like a consoling presence, Aboulessia watches over his friend and encourages him to stand his ground vis-à-vis his tormentors. An eccentric man who also possesses a very sharp, lucid mind, that Jew spends his time globe-trotting in an unflagging endeavor to track down the Messiah. Does David Aboulessia really exist or is he the hero's alter ego? In certain episodes, such as the train trip from Berlin to Paris and the conversation in a Parisian hotel, the reader is convinced that this singular personage really does enjoy an autonomous existence. At other times, he is less sure. In the long run, this question matters little. This man who fascinates Paltiel Kossover constitutes a kind of piercing gaze on the latter's conduct, compelling the poet to become much more conscious of his aspirations and identity. In Paris, as though to test him, Aboulessia asks the hero to entrust his phylacteries to his care. Paltiel's refusal to comply with this request represents the confirmation that the Judaism of his childhood remains rooted within him. When the hero finds him again in the Holy Land where he had to go on a secret mission for the Party, the Messiah tracker gets him to reflect on the nature of the legendary figure who is supposed to bring comfort and justice to the whole of humanity. Kossover notices that the views of Paul Hamburger and David Aboulessia converge on that subject. The first maintains that one must have the courage to amputate the world in order to save it. The second believes that a cataclysm must unleash its fury against this earth before the Messiah can come and ensure the redemption of mankind. The poet deems both these positions as inadmissible: "If, to appear in his immaculate splendor, the Messiah must be preceded by the howls of massacring and massacred people, let him stay where He is. And yet my two friends call for him, each one in his own way, each one using methods that would repel the other. Poor Messiah: all these things that are done for You, in Your name; all these things that others make You do" (*T*, 177).

The hero encounters the mystic adventurer for the last time in Barcelona during the civil war. Paltiel was striving to persuade himself that he had enlisted in the Revolution as much as a Jew as he had as a communist. Aboulessia makes the poet see his error. In addition, his friend forces the hero to separate the role of the revolutionary he is performing, even if he is performing it with passion, from the Jewish identity that he continues claiming for himself: "It is the communist who has come here to strip himself of his name and his past to become an international soldier" (T, 222). The poet will have all the time he needs to verify the correctness of this observation once he has gotten over all his illusion about the international communist movement.

Three other experiences that he lives through immediately after the war confirm the indissoluble links uniting him with his people, and consequently, the permanence of his Jewish identity. The poet visits the site of Drobitzky Yar, near Kharkov, where fifteen thousand of his coreligionists were massacred by the Nazis. He returns there again and again. He feels he is on familiar ground, as though tragedy were an integral part and for all time of his vision of Jewish existence. He returns to Lianov, hastens to see once again the family home, expects to meet his next-of-kin while knowing full well that they have already perished in the Holocaust. He feels "crushed under the mass of an infinite, unspeakable, tumultuous and dark sadness" (*T*, 275). Yet another proof that his people have been singled out for tragedy. Finally, he spends a whole day within the Majdanek concentration camp in Poland. As though to express his solidarity towards the thousands of victims who were herded into the crematory ovens, he tries, through his imagination, to put himself in their place at the supreme hour when they were going to die. In a paroxysm of despair, he is tempted to remain there forever. It is necessary for a voice surging from the depths of his consciousness and representing his irrepressible will to live to pull him away from this nightmarish scene.

It is not farfetched to conclude that these three experiences prepare, well in advance, the illumination that Patiel Kossover will have in his cell, several hours before his execution. He will understand then that through his personal suffering he is connected in a visceral manner to his people, one of the most martyred in history. He will also have the certainty that through this very suffering he is proclaiming his indefectible commitment to the faith of his ancestors. Thus, when he thinks he sees his father in his cell, this harbinger of death does not frighten him. All he feels is a profound sadness: "A fundamental but calming sadness, that of creation which accepts its creator" (*T*, 319). Beyond its tragic character, this awareness reveals something infinitely exalting. It signifies that the poet's life does not simply unfold over a finite duration but is placed under the aegis of an eternal present. He will soon die even though he so longs to live for this son he does not know. And yet, he will always belong, beyond death, to this immense history of his people that goes from the mythical epochs of the Bible to infinity. If death removes him in the physical sense, it will not triumph over him on the spiritual level. From the very beginning of his testament, when speaking to the judge, he expresses this morally comforting sentiment, even though he knows that the magistrate will not fail to burn the document he is writing once he is assassinated. But it doesn't matter. No force on earth or heaven will ever be able to destroy the fact that he has borne witness to his pride as a man of integrity and freedom in this text. This evidence will remain indestructible for all time: "The words that you strangle, that you assassinate, produce a kind of original, impenetrable silence; you will never succeed in killing such a silence…"

But, without his being aware of it, Paltiel Kossover will have another powerful ally: the silent and almost invisible stenographer who felt a fraternal love for him. As Viktor Shupanov points out to Grisha, executioners are stupid, that is why they are executioners. They had erased every vestige of the assassinated poet's presence so that he would be swallowed up in eternal oblivion. But they never figured out that Paltiel Kossover had an unknown friend who witnessed all the cross-examinations and torture sessions. He is the one who will confound the executioners, indeed, will annihilate them, by handing over to the poet's son the testament that he had stolen, page by page. Thus, having helped his friend achieve a magnificent victory over his torturers, Victor Shupanov will laugh uproariously for the first time in his life. And with his assistance a significant chapter in the history of the Jewish people will enrich the generations to come.

CHAPTER 4
ANGUISHED QUESTIONING AND
FRAGILE VICTORY

U p till now the reader has been able to follow in Elie Wiesel's novels the trajectory that goes from despair to an affirmation of confidence in life. The irreducible pessimism of the narrator in *Night* and the heartbreak of the heroes in *Dawn* and *Day* yield to the renewal of faith in the human condition to which Michael in *The Town Beyond the Wall* and Grégor in *The Gates of the Forest* bear witness. Even the three following novels, *A Beggar in Jerusalem*, *The Oath* and *The Testament* do not negate this spiritual victory. Despite their anguished awareness of the tragic element inherent in human destiny, David, Azriel and Paltiel Kossover realize that their mystic solidarity with their people and the transmission of their coreligionists' collective memory confer a transcendent significance on their existences. In the author's next three novels, however, *The Fifth Son* (1983), *Twilight* (1987) and *The Forgotten* (1989), one comes across a certain ambiguity. Although the heroes do not avoid fighting for what they believe is right, they are not at all certain of achieving victory. Doubts infiltrate their minds like a poison against which their spiritual vaccines do not always fight effectively. The atmosphere darkens appreciably yet without the black despair of *Night* or the unresolvable anguish of the first two novels reappearing. It is not that the author denies the possibility of a victory over the forces of evil; but now he insists much more on all the factors capable of undermining it even if his protagonists resolutely refuse to give up their belief in the Messiah.

The Fifth Son

When Jews gather to celebrate Passover with its accompanying meal, they organize this service of gratitude towards God, called a *Seder*, with the help of a little book of prayers and legends titled the *Haggadah*. One of the stories told there deals with four sons from the same family and their attitudes towards the question to be asked about the relationship between God and his people. The first son knows the question and accepts its consequences. The second knows it but refuses the responsibilities it entails. The third remains completely indifferent to it. As for the fourth, he is not aware of it at all. For Elie Wiesel, in the aftermath of the Shoah, there must be a fifth son, the one who is absent and does not appear at the *Seder* because he perished in the concentration camp hell. In the novel he is called Ariel. He is not found in the *Haggadah* narrative but for his father, Reuven Tamiroff, he is far more alive than Tamiroff's son born after the Holocaust and seated next to him at the table. This is the tragedy that tears apart the heart and mind of the former prisoner of the death camp. It is also the tragedy of his living son who is the narrator of the novel, a narrator whose first name is never mentioned, thereby suggesting that he lacks a clear sense of identity. As for the fifth son, the reader must peruse two thirds of the novel before discovering who this absent and enigmatic young person is. Once he makes this discovery, he realizes to what extent the fifth son dominates the text. Indeed, Ariel, the six-year-old child brutally murdered by a sadistic SS officer, remains omnipresent in the novel. We meet him at the very beginning of the book in a series of poignant letters that his father, Reuven Tamiroff addresses to him. The man's constant obsession with the dead boy finally elucidates the secret sorrow that has been torturing him for more than twenty years. The bereavement of his mother, Rachel, explains the mental illness that is progressively undermining her health. The anxious, even desperate,search for an identity that their son, born after the Second World War, is still carrying out, acquires its full significance only in relationship to this little brother whom he has never known, but for whom he feels, just like his parents, a heartrending tenderness.

Elie Wiesel's extreme skill as a novelist consists in acquainting us with Ariel from the beginning of the narrative while maintaining our uncertainty for so long about the child's identity. But by proceeding in this manner, by refusing to reveal everything right away, the author is not seeking to create suspense. We realize retrospectively that this delay is indispensable to focus the novel on the parents' moral torture and on their living son's distress. An invisible barrier has been erected between the narrator and his parents. He is instinctively conscious of its existence without being able to put his finger on the cause of his ill-being. The discovery he will make much later of the phantom still floating within the minds and hearts of Reuven and Rachel Tamiroff will represent the last piece of a puzzle reconstituted with so much difficulty. It will prompt his bizarre decision to designate himself as the dispenser of justice as a means of exorcizing the curse that has been hovering for so long over his family.

Thus, the novel traces the narrator's spiritual itinerary starting with his desire to satisfy his curiosity concerning his parents' past and ending with his determination to punish the former SS officer responsible for their tragedy and, indirectly, for his own. At the same time the narrative evokes in a jerky fashion, without always respecting the chronological order, the existence of his parents whose secret pain weighs so heavily on his own. Just as the narrator's discovery of Ariel's identity comes to us in fragments, similarly, his own journey that leads him from New York to Reshastadt in Germany to seek out his brother's killer, is not structured in a linear manner. We learn as of page 7 that the hero wanted to commit an assassination by traveling to that little German town. Here again it is not essentially a question of keeping up the suspense by arousing the reader's curiosity about the deep motive behind an action that appears insane. Elie Wiesel seeks rather to keep the reader's attention fixed on the dilemma of a child of Holocaust survivors who must thrash his way through the thickest of silences and shadows to gain control of his own history. While describing the narrator's struggle to acquire a personal destiny, the author orchestrates a grave and moving meditation on crime, punishment and forgiveness.

Very complex emotional ties are woven between the narrator and his father. The son adores him, ardently longs to draw closer to him, but comes up against an invisible wall. This is because Reuven Tamiroff is not eager to open his heart. In fact, he cannot confide in his son since he himself is haunted by a terrible secret that will deprive him of joy forever. His son finds his father all the more fascinating because the latter envelops himself in an aura of tragic taciturnity and opaqueness. As soon as his son broached the subject of the war, Reuven Tamiroff would disappear mentally. As the narrator observes with resignation: "He did not budge. He became distant. Subjugated by a great sadness from the past which blended into an unnamable anguish. All right, I would give up right away. I changed the subject, thinking: I'll try again another time."[15]

In the father's anguish lies something dreadful left unsaid: his loss of faith in God. This does not mean that Reuven Tamiroff renounces practicing Judaism. He attends synagogue services assiduously. He observes all the holidays on the Jewish calendar. He is proud of his people who were able to safeguard their spiritual and cultural specificity despite the innumerable traps set up for their perdition during their epic history. He admires his coreligionists for having bounced back after so many ordeals that should logically have annihilated them all. In one of the rare moments when he allowed himself to share secrets, Reuben Tamiroff related a discussion he had with his friend and Talmudic guide, the Rabbi Aharon-Asher, well before the outbreak of the Second World War. Tempted by assimilation and agnosticism, he seemed on the verge of moving away from Judaism without quite repudiating it. It was then that the religious man persuaded him, through his eloquence and the fire of his convictions, not to desert a history that had defied death and had triumphed over it on so many occasions: "Our history, our prodigious history is a permanent challenge to reason and fanaticism, to persecutors and their power! And you would like to desert this history?" (*CF*, 38).

His indefectible attachment to the people of Israel, to their spiritual and moral patrimony, his admiration for the Jewish will to survive that is something of a miracle do not, however, extend necessarily to the God of Israel Himself. In the postscript to a letter addressed to his dead son, Ariel, he expresses sentiments of revolt against this God who abandoned a whole generation of innocents to the Nazis' destructive fury. Reuven Tamiroff even wonders whether he is as dead in the spiritual sense as are the deceased victims of the Holocaust, since he remains incapable of feeling any gratitude towards the Lord of the Universe: "Is it true that God always intervenes? The dead do not sing the praises of God, said King David. Have the dead shut out gratitude? Conversely, are the living who are incapable of gratitude dead themselves? Facing you, son, what am I?" (*CF*, 40). As long as Ariel was alive, his father could still believe in God's loyalty towards the people who had chosen Him. During the last Passover celebrated in the ghetto before the Jews were shipped off to the death camps, Reuven did not hesitate to intone with his friend Simha a song of praise to the Eternal. In it he blessed the Lord for always having rescued

---

[15] Elie Wiesel, *Le Cinquième fils*, Paris : Grasset, 1983, 41; referred to henceforth as *CF*.

His faithful when the enemy sought to exterminate them. His little son's presence filled him with pride. All he had to do was look at his six-year-old child in order not to sink into despair. As he reminds himself in the same letter, on the eve of the terrible ordeal that the Jewish community would face, he, Reuven, had not yet renounced hope even though his wife had trouble fighting back her tears. Besides, it was said in the ghetto that Ariel's smile shone brightly on everyone like a blessing. But the brutal death of his child inflicted on Tamiroff an incurable wound.

From that moment on an abyss opened up in his life. Keeping up the cult of this dead child thus represents for the father the only way to hang on to the period of his existence when life, despite its multiple tragedies, still held a meaning for him, when he still considered himself a fully alive human being rather than a semi-phantomatic survivor. The loss of Ariel, however devastating it was, would not perhaps have been enough in itself to enclose Reuven Tamiroff in an almost impenetrable mutism about his experiences during the war. Two other events contributed powerfully to his despair. One preceded the death of his child, the other followed it; combined with his fatherly sorrow, they finally took away his appetite for life.

Designated by the SS Commander, Richard Lander, as President of the Jewish Council of the Davarowsk ghetto, Tamiroff had to walk a tightrope between the demands of a sadistic enemy and the imperatives of the Jewish moral law. His coreligionists suffered from dreadful living conditions. It would have been so tempting for him to abandon the weakest elements of the community. But he strove constantly to apply the fundamental principal of Judaism according to which every human being, as a reflection of the divine presence, remains infinitely precious. He would continuously repeat: "The day when a human tragedy, no matter which one, will be treated by us like an ordinary event without any importance, that day will mark the enemy's victory" (*CF*, 110). Now this moral stand of his ended up causing him terrible remorse. Having learned that a detachment of fifty men from the ghetto were shot without any reason by the German soldiers, Reuven Tamiroff sought out the Commander to tender his resignation. The explanation the officer provided for the massacre seemed so cynical and so implausible that the President of the Jewish Council refused to go back on his decision. Outraged by being unmasked, Richard Lander cooked up an unusual act of vengeance that was also profoundly satisfying for his megalomania. He chose at random the names of half the members of the Council and ordered them shot on the spot. From the intellectual point of view, Tamiroff knew that if he continued dispatching his duties as President he would be overwhelmed with shame. The destruction of six colleagues, however, shattered him to such an extent that long after the war their unjustified deaths continued to haunt his conscience. In one of the letters addressed to Ariel, he still reproached himself for not having groveled at the feet of the Commander to entreat him to spare his coreligionists. He persisted in questioning his bravado that cost so many innocent people their lives: "Indeed, my son, I feel responsible for the deaths of my colleagues on the Jewish Council. If I had put aside my ego, they would have lived a year, a month, a day longer. And for those who are going to die, one day is a long time, you know that well: to live one day, one more day, means a long time" (*CF*, 53). When Richard Lander predicted to him that his life would henceforth have the "odor of a tomb," he described in advance the mental torture Tamiroff would suffer. Indeed, more than twenty years after the Holocaust, the former President of the Jewish Council was still unable to tear himself away from the ghetto.

The other event that engendered atrocious torments for him was his participation in an assassination attempt on Lander in 1946. His decision to try to kill the SS Commander was taken after a particularly odious manifestation of the latter's character. In the autumn of 1942, during the Day of Atonement, the most solemn day in the Jewish calendar, that diabolically sadistic ham actor—the Jewish community referred to him as the Angel of Death—ordered the prisoners to direct their prayers to him instead of to the God of Israel. In the face of their categorical refusal, the German officer vented his anger by having two hundred of them shot on the spot. But it was only after the murder of Ariel that Tamiroff decided to act on his decision. A fat lot of good it did him. This act of vengeance did not bring him any satisfaction at all. More than twenty years after the assassination attempt, he would meet every month with his closest friend, Simha, another member who was part of that punituve mission, to try to justify their action retrospectively in the light of the Jewish moral law. Another letter written to Ariel gives an account of the remorse that was still plaguing the distraught father: "Even if one could execute the Angel a thousand times, six million times, justice would not be done; the dead are dead, my son, and the death of the killer will not bring them back to life. I think of my friend the Rabbi Aharon-Asher who, from the very beginning, had expressed his opposition to our behavior. And if it was he who was right?" (*CF*, 164).

Consequently, Reuven Tamiroff never stops trotting out his tragic past and, as a result, never stops upsetting, fascinating, exasperating and shaking up his living son. The novel's protagonist strives to lead a normal adult life, first as a university student, then as an intellectual. But it always seems that the principal, if not obsessive goal of his existence consists in penetrating the silence in which his father envelops himself, in ferreting out the secret that the latter persists in wanting to repress. On that condition alone will he be able to put an end to his distress and become an individual with his own distinctive existence. Since the narrator suffers from an event that he did not live himself, it behooves him to understand it in depth so that he can exorcise it once and for all. Before reaching the threshold of adolescence, the hero must be content with secrets that come to him in snatches. During a Passover dinner, Simha urges Tamiroff not to treat his living son like the fifth one and to talk to him about the past. Appreciating this argument, the father begins to relate to his son the beginning of his brilliant career as a scholar and academic, his progressive disinvolvement with Judaism in the name of social conformism and the renewal of his faith under the spiritual tutelage of the Rabbi Aharon-Asher. Just before the narrator's Bar-Mitzvah, he pours out his soul to his son by describing the ambiguous sentiments he felt, and which he continues feeling, after having made the decision with his wife to recreate a genuine family life in the United States at the end of the war. Having survived the Holocaust, the Tamiroffs judged it necessary to create life to make sure that Hitler did not triumph over the Jews beyond death. But once they engendered their son in New York, the father started asking himself anguished questions. He wondered whether he and his wife had the right to burden their child, by bringing him into the world, with a past that seemed cursed.

The protagonist will learn only later exactly what this curse is. The unexpected presence in his life of a comrade of his father from the time of the ghetto, Bonchek, allows him finally to light up a whole series of dark zones. On the surface, nothing could explain why these two men would be drawn to one another. Bonchek was a big, strapping fellow with sensual appetites whose intelligence was not in the least refined. Reuben Tamiroff's whole person was characterized by a patrician and almost ascetic elegance. But a deep mutual esteem, founded on integrity and courage, enabled them to bond. Since Bonchek admires the narrator's father and loves to talk, he opens wide doors leading back to Tamiroff's past, and his son, more and more fascinated, drinks in all the stories. The more Bonchek divulges, the more the narrator yearns to hear. His thirst for knowledge about his father's past becomes insatiable. In this way the protagonist discovers unsuspected aspects of his father's character: his exceptional goodness that bordered on saintliness, his intrepidness in situations that could have made nerves of steel crack, his talent as a consummate diplomat in the face of the sinister Commander. This information, however precious it may be, still does not help the son establish a bridge between himself and his father. It merely makes it easier for him to access some repressed zones of his father's past. Reuben Tamiroff and his child born after the nightmare of the war have yet to draw closer to one another. In fact, the gnawing anger that the young man feels when he crashes constantly against his father's taciturnity finally explodes towards the end of the 1960s. Caught in the storm of systematic protests like so many people of his age at the time, the narrator revolts against this father whom he really adores and accuses him of being responsible for his mother's nervous depression. He seeks undoubtedly in this way to heap guilt upon himself, to suffer atrociously so that he may share, if only indirectly, the sorrow of his nearly elusive dad. But it is only an illusion. His attempt at drawing closer to his father fails, just like his endeavor to penetrate Reuven Tamiroff's soul by experimenting with hallucinogenic drugs like LSD.

The great revelation does not occur until the unloved son discovers by accident the series of letters written by his father to Ariel. The question he asks of this man normally so withdrawn, "Who is Ariel," touches off an emotional cataclysm in the latter. The living son sees his father cry for the first time in his life. Naturally, Reuben Tamiroff's tears betray the incurable wound of which we have already spoken. This time, however, the father's sorrow will be fruitful, because his son's question has the effect of tearing him away from an ossifying past. No longer walled up alive in his terrible secret, he can pour out his heart in the narrator's presence. His emotional growth, immobilized for so many decades, can at last resume. Having become vulnerable again, he can henceforth receive the filial love that the narrator brings him in a surge of compassion. Now that he knows his distraught father needs him, the hero agrees to assume the identity of the child that had perished in the extermination camp. The very moving dialogue that follows marks a new stage in their relationship: "Ariel, my little Ariel," he whispered like a guilty, unhappy child. "Yes, father," I said. His eyes grew misty, his breath became heavier as he repeated: "Ariel." "Yes, father" (*CF*, 168-169).

Through his father's sorrow, the narrator not only draws closer to him but becomes obsessed by Ariel's killer, Richard Lander. As we noted, the narrator had already heard about the sinister Commander thanks to Bonchek's stories. There was, nevertheless, a difference. Beforehand, the SS officer was only for him the tormentor of the Jews in the Davarowsk ghetto. Now, he is the sadistic murderer of his brother who would have been the elder one had he still been alive. The hatred the narrator harbors towards that German whom he has never met, galvanizes him. When he finds out that Lander, far from having been being killed in the assassination attempt like Reuven Tamiroff thought, is now living under an assumed name, his plan for revenge becomes a fixation. Indeed, the narrator views it as a means of liberating himself from his father's tragic past and fulfilling his own destiny. In one of the letters that he himself writes to Ariel, the protagonist describes this new exaltation that has taken hold of him: "In truth, hatred draws me to it. The Angel draws me to himself. I need to hate. Hatred seems a solution for the time being; it blinds, it intoxicates, in short: it keeps me busy" (*CF*, 180).

But who exactly is this former Nazi Commander reconverted into the president of a large German company and a philanthropist under his new identity as Wolfgang Berger? An egocentric ham actor? The embodiment of Evil, devoid of any feelings of guilt towards his victims? Rather a vain and cynical opportunist and endowed with a remarkable ability to adapt to widely different circumstances. During the Second World War, his sinister narcissism manifested itself in the role of an SS Commander. He was able at that time to use terrorized Jewish prisoners as magnifying mirrors that would send him back an ultra-flattering image of an unlimited diabolic power. In front of his powerless victims, he could delude himself into thinking he was a god. Did he not proclaim himself the God of Death vis-à-vis his Jewish captives? After the war, circumstances having radically changed, Richard Lander recycles himself into a respectable and honored citizen of a country once held in contempt that was now doing its utmost to turn over a new leaf on the moral level. The narrator's feat will be to unmask the imposter, to strip him of his flashy rags of civic and moral respectability, and to denounce him as a piece of filth.

Why does the living son of Reuven Tamiroff not assassinate the war criminal after having vowed to avenge Ariel and the Jews of the Davarowsk ghetto? His decision to spare that former Angel of Death can be explained in part by his impulsive and vacillating temperament inherited from his father. In fact, there is a moment during their conversation when the narrator is on the verge of slaying him. If Wolfgang Berger had tried to justify his sadism in the presence of Ariel's living brother, the assassination would have been committed. But the narrator's impulsiveness provides only a partial explanation. The profound reason that prevents him from murdering the former Nazi is his Judaism. Despite half-hearted attempts at revolt during the 1968 student uprisings in New York, he remained attached to his ancestral faith. Now, according to the Jewish religion, every human life is infinitely precious because it is created in the image of God. Only the Master of creation has the right to decide on the fate of His creatures. Thus, man is forbidden from transgressing the divine law by putting himself in God's place. Even if one were to interpret this law in a purely metaphorical fashion, it would signify an interdiction to be scrupulously respected in order not to debase the human being.

The theme of justice, indissolubly linked in the novel to those of crime and punishment, appears for the first time in the novel after the massacre of two hundred Jews from the ghetto ordered by the Angel of Death. The Rabbi Aahron-Asher was firmly opposed to the vengeance project conceived by Reuven Tamiroff and his friends. Citing Jewish law, he reminded them that the guilty person had to be judged by a tribunal of twenty-three members. In addition, the accused had the right to be defended. About thirty years later, when the protagonist is getting ready to fly to Germany to commit the assassination, the Rabbi Tzvi-Hersh of New York refuses to bless him when he guesses the latter's intentions. From then on, the theme will be magnificently orchestrated. Going beyond the words pronounced by Aharon-Asher in 1942, Tzvi-Hersh solemnly declares that the Torah forbids murder in all circumstances. Certainly, the Old Testament teaches us that we have the right to kill a person who wishes to make an attempt on our life. But that does not allow us to put an end to the life of anyone we consider threatening. We should first of all acquire the proof that our aggressor really intends to kill us, and how do we plumb the labyrinthine depths of the human heart to zero in on the motive that impels him to act? Even if a man utters threats, they may only be verbal ones and not reflect his true intentions.

It is in Germany that this question acquires a very sharp focus. This is because despite his wish to be equitable, the hero has trouble overcoming his antipathy and distrust towards the nation that had been responsible for his family tragedy as well as for the extermination of six million of his coreligionists. His ambiguous attitude is first perceived in his reaction to a German woman about thirty years old, called Thérèse, whom he encounters in the train taking him to Reshastadt. He acknowledges the validity of her assertion when she protests against the world's tendency to include all Germans in the same reprobation, whether or not they participated in Hitler's diabolic project, and whatever their age had been at the time of the Holocaust. Nevertheless, he politely rejects her attempt to show him sympathy. And while he is waiting for his connection in Graustadt, he daydreams. He imagines attending the funeral of a German who is totally unknown to him. For a reason that escapes him, the widow of the deceased person invites him to pronounce the eulogy. She lavishes praise on the narrator, declares that he is the only real friend her late husband every had, and she insults one after the other all those who had known the dead man for a long time. But as soon as the hero announces to the crowd that he is a Jew, they forget the widow's insults, and form a tightly knit group hostile to his presence.

He finally confronts Ariel's killer in a climate of profound uneasiness. Having successfully passed himself off as an American journalist who has come to do a story on Reshastadt, the protagonist has absolutely no difficulty in obtaining an interview with the former SS Commander recycled into a model citizen. When one reads the beginning of the novel where the living brother relates his failed attempt to assassinate Richard Lander alias Wolfgang Berger, one is inclined to think that this crazy plan has turned out to be an abysmal failure. The narrator seems to despise his vacillating nature, his congenital inability to carry out a project that was so close to his heart. When he gets on the plane to return to the United States, the Angel of Death is still alive. But as one observes towards the end of the novel, the latter has been shaken to his very core. On the moral level, Ariel's brother has achieved a triumph. The vengeance has been exemplary.

Representing his coreligionists massacred in the ghetto as well as his murdered brother, the hero arouses within Wolfgang Berger an emotion he was not in the habit of feeling: fear. The fear of being denounced in the media, of being reported to the police as a notorious criminal. A fear all the more terrible because his new, respectable identity will be in danger of collapsing under the weight of his infamous past. But the repercussions of this denunciation are even worse. By underscoring the abyss between the sadistic criminal that the German industrialist had been and the citizen above suspicion he is now, the narrator unmasks Berger's hypocrisy as well as his cowardice. The SS who appear in *Night*, *Day* and *The Fifth Son* are all killers who take pleasure in killing. One should point out, however, that one of the most notorious of the SS, Eichman, is supposed to have been only a kind of human robot, a conscientious worker, who simply performed the task assigned to him. This kind does not exist in the fictional world of Elie Wiesel. Lander alias Burger enjoyed torturing thousands of defenseless victims and never even had the courage to acknowledge this.

Under his soul from which emanates a stench of death, the only thing that has changed is the shroud of social respectability that covers it. It is enough to read the narrator's description of the progress fear is making as it moves across the former killer's face to realize that he is in the process of undergoing a virtual execution: "As I speak, the features on his face grow more tense and gaunt, his pallor increases from one minute to the next, from one episode to another. He is afraid, oh yes, the Angel of Death is dominated by fear, transfixed by fear; Death has finally caught up with the Angel of Death. For one brief instant, I feel a mute jubilation rising within me: bravo, Ariel! So you are capable of inspiring, of inflicting terror! Are you satisfied, Ariel? Are you proud of my deed?" (*CF*, 219).

Having ripped the mask of civic and moral virtue from the former executioner's face, all that is left for the protagonist to do is to send him back into his spiritual vacuum. And into this void will rush headlong the whole ghetto of Davrowsk with its thousands of innocents whom their sadistic master though he had crushed once and for all under his boot. For this reason, in the end, Ariel's brother leaves Berger's office without killing him, without feeling the slightest hatred toward him or interest in him. This is no longer necessary. The hero has killed the executioner and replaced him with a man who has finally acquired a conscience. To live for the rest of his life in the resurrected ghetto will be for Hitler's former lackey the worst of punishments: "The Angel no longer aroused either hatred or a desire for vengeance: I had disrupted his existence, refreshed his memory, spoiled his future joys, that was enough for me. He would no longer be able to carry on, or live, or laugh as though the Davarowsk ghetto had not served as a stage and magnifying mirrors for him." (*CF*, 223).

Ten years after his confrontation with the former Nazi Commander, the narrator assesses his existence. He considers it " not as a failure but as a defeat" (*CF*, 223). Certainly, his relationship with his father has been strengthened. He offers Reuben Tamiroff an unconditional filial love and agrees to be for him the child lost during the nightmare of the Shoah. Hence the feeling he has of being incomplete as an individual. Almost forty years after Ariel's death, the hero of *The Fifth Son* remains convinced that he does not have a life of his own. To this sadness is added the painful awareness that less than twenty years before the beginning of the new millennium, the world has already entered the catastrophic realm that Orwell predicted. Because the narrator is Jewish, he refuses, despite everything, like so many other heroes of Elie Wiesel, to succumb to despair. Continuing to believe in the Messiah's coming, despite all the evidence pointing to the opposite, already constitutes a form of redemption: "...the Messiah may very well arrive too late; he will come when there will no longer be anyone to save. So much the worse: I'll wait nevertheless." (*CF*, 229).

Twilight

When we move from the novel *The Fifth Son* to the following one, *Twilight* (1987), we are gripped by the darkening moral and philosophical climate we find there. Reuven Tamiroff's living son was far from being a happy person. But even though he was thrashing his way through an identity crisis, the nameless narrator did not feel his life had been a failure. This is not the case for the hero of *Twilight*, Raphael Lipkin, whose tormented conscience Elie Wiesel evokes vividly. Even if this former detainee of the Nazi hell does not abandon himself completely to despair at the end of his spiritual trajectory, the tone which prevails at the conclusion of the novel remains rather ambiguous. This is because the author depicts here the obsession with insanity. The hero does not drown in it; nevertheless, he is fascinated by it to the point of brushing against it on several occasions. The enigmas he strives to resolve simply grow thicker and become more and more disconcerting.

In this respect, the novel's title has been judiciously chosen. Twilight is the metaphor for the protagonist's state of mind where disquiet, anguish and even terror dominate. The invasion of the earth by shadows corresponds with the obscuring of the consciousness as a result of moral and metaphysical questions that must remain unanswered. At a turning point in his existence, the inner peace and fragile balance that Raphael Lipkin had succeeded in restoring are suddenly disrupted. Night begins falling on his interior landscape just as it takes possession of the heavens. This, then, is how the author conjures up the anguished powerlessness of all those, including the protagonist, for whom twilight is the equivalent of threat: "The twilight far off is no longer so far away. In an instant it will invade the earth, the way it has just subjugated a radiant and peaceful sky. As it approaches, all beings hold their breath, bow their heads and commend themselves to the fierce, mute, golden elements of an inexorable power. Escape? One would still have to know where to escape. The twilight breaks open all shelters and overturns all walls. Twilight is an implacable invader. Man cannot hide from it."[16] Since night prevails ineluctably

---

[16] Elie Wiesel, *Le Crépuscule, au loin*, Paris : Éditions Grasset et Fasquelle/Livres de Poche, 1987, 261; referred to henceforth as *C*.

over day, this period of transition symbolizes the relentless struggle during which hope slips away in the face of helplessness and even despair. By the end of his spiritual trajectory, Raphael Lipkin realizes that the truth he had been pursuing tirelessly has receded into the shadows.

This forty-year-old university professor lets himself be submerged by the twilight of the soul following a phone call. It hits him like a bolt from the blue and provokes the worst crisis of his life. An anonymous interlocutor informs him that his best friend, Pedro, the man for whom he feels boundless admiration, was really a cynical betrayer, responsible for the torture and death of innocent prisoners in the Soviet Union in the years following the Second World War. The hero is all the more devastated by this denunciation because the anonymous voice provides concrete details that testify to a genuine knowledge of the prison in which Pedro had been locked up. The interlocutor was anxious to contact Raphael Lipkin because the latter, according to him, had drawn in one his books a far too flattering portrait of his friend. If the author really wishes to discover the truth, the voice adds, he has only to go up to the famous Clinic on the Mountain, a psychiatric hospital located in the State of New York. The hero vehemently rejects these accusations of the man without a face and calls him an odious slanderer. But the keystone on which his whole existence was resting—his faith in Pedro—begins to sag. He cooks up a university research project that necessitates a stay at the clinic, settles in there as a librarian during the summer and endeavors to track down either the slanderer or his friend whom he lost thirty or so years before behind the Iron Curtain.

During the two months that he stays there, Raphael feels real empathy for the sick people in the clinic, each one appearing more disconnected from reality than his neighbor and manages to wend his way through the tortuous networks of their minds. Running parallel to the description of this singular experience are the memorable episodes of the hero's past and the history of his family before, during and after the Holocaust. Elie Wiesel thus uses in *Twilight* the same technique of shifting between the past and the present that proved itself so effective in his preceding novels. But here, the subject seems to require such a structure more than ever. When Raphael enters the clinic, he believes he is on the verge of breaking down. The perhaps too idealistic image he has kept of his friend has just been sullied. This sorrow is just the last of a series of tragedies and personal disappointments that have punctuated his existence since the Second World War. By itself, the denunciation of Pedro by that anonymous voice would not have been sufficient to make the hero plummet into despair.

By itself, the succession of personal hardships that he endured since his youth would not have borne down on him heavily enough to arouse in his soul the fascination with the void. Combined, they drag him to the edge of collapse. But the worst is yet to come. His shattering encounters with various patients in the clinic that unfold in the present, simply increase the stress caused by the other misfortunes inflicted on him in the past. Hence the perfect appropriateness of the structure for the vision that the novel projects. The evocations of his relationships with the mentally ill is frequently interrupted by flashbacks relating events that have fashioned his very bruised consciousness. These references to the past end with the recollection of the most recent episode, that of the phone call. At that very moment, his past reconnects with his present. Unfortunately, it is just about the last straw that may break the camel's back. Especially because that traumatic experience occurs shortly before Raphael has a conversation with the most disturbing and heartbreaking patient in the whole clinic: the one who believes he is God. Naturally, we know from the beginning of the novel why the hero has gone to the clinic. But the impact of the anonymous interlocutor cannot be fully measured until the end of the professor's journey. Given the seemingly unending distress he has suffered and the doubts that torment him concerning God's mercy towards His creatures, Raphael had to believe unconditionally in Pedro's virtue. From the moment the voice on the telephone calls into question the nobility of that friend, Raphael, propelled by motives that he has trouble understanding completely, feels the need to speak with the madman who thinks he is God so that the latter can explain why the cosmos is in such a horrible mess.

When Raphael Lipkin heckles God in the person of the sick man, his list of grievances is long. In the first place, the hero has it in for the Creator of the universe for having broken his alliance with the people of Israel. For the hero, the cruel fate inflicted on his own family constitutes a gripping illustration of this. Like hundreds of thousands of families living in Poland before the outbreak of the Shoah, the Lipkins lived in the love and fear of God. Like so many other Jews, Raphael's next of kin were deserted by the Almighty to whom they addressed fervent prayers while being subjected to the murdering fury of the Nazis barbarians or ground under by Stalin's totalitarian regime. One of his older brothers, Hayim, was captured by the Hungarian fascists as he was trying to make his way to the Holy Land by using a fake passport to cross through eastern Europe. He was tortured by the secret police, then almost lost his life during a massacre of Jews perpetrated by the Germans at Kolomei, and finally perished like his father, mother and sisters when supposedly "good Christian souls" divulged their hiding place to the Nazis. Ezra, the oldest brother whose heart was tender and compassionate, was caught on the day he showed insane foolhardiness by leaving his hideout to visit their parents during the New Year. Yoël, the youngest, was locked up in a sinister Soviet prison for having believed literally in the Communist dream of paradise on earth. Having told the truth with unabashed naïveté to the police as soon as he arrived in Moscow, namely, that he had fled the Nazis and was awaiting the imminent arrival of his communist girlfriend, he was taken for a dangerous spy. He escaped death by pretending to be mad. Unfortunately, by dint of playing a mentally unhinged person, he ended up becoming one. That timid and contemplative young man wanted nothing more than to live a great love with the woman of his life, the ardent and idealistic Mirele. Seized by the irrational forces of History, he would rot forever in a cell for the mentally ill and would be dead on the spiritual level.

To these family tragedies are added other subjects of sadness. Like the first ones, the second ones seem to reveal a woefully dysfunctional universe. One would think that malevolent forces were determined to poison the joys and certitudes on which Raphael was striving to build his life in the United States after going through the Nazi hell. His marriage is a disaster. And yet, he loved passionately his wife Tiara and their daughter, Rachel. His wife fascinated him as much by her witticisms and her tyrannical whims as by her surges of unexpected tenderness. But being older than him, she was anxious to be the first to put an end to their marital union for fear of being abandoned one day and of suffering in her pride. The fact that she became pregnant a second time following mad nocturnal embraces was enough to touch off in her an irrational fury against her unfortunate spouse. She took revenge by getting an abortion. Despite their divorce and the memory of the dreadful tantrums Tiara would throw, Raphael still feels nostalgia for her presence.

After the disintegration of his marriage, Raphael suffers another affliction: death through sorrow of his two dearest American friends, Marcus and Alma Natanson. University professors like the hero, they, too, emigrated to the United States after the war, both having nearly perished during the political convulsions that ravaged the European continent. Without being particularly religious, they were anxious to safeguard the Jewish traditions. One day they discover with horror that their only and adored child, Lidia, a very gifted university student, has joined a cult practicing systematic brain washing using a pseudo-spiritual kind of gibberish.

As though he has a premonition of his imminent death, Marcus, overwhelmed with grief and shame, remembers the mourning that Meilekh Harziger, the father of a young girl in his native city, went into when she informed him of her decision to marry a Polish Christian doctor. The father did not live long after that marriage, which he deemed nefarious for himself as a Jew. In a similar manner, Marcus dies of anguish over having lost his child to a false religion with fascist tendencies that has deprived her of her free will and anesthetized her mind. His wife follows him into death shortly after. Lidia was finally able to regain her lucidity and return to her parents, but it was too late to save them. Raphael lived through the Natansons' family tragedy as though it had been his own, so close did he feel to them, especially after his divorce.

An even more terrible endurance test will crash down on him: the anonymous phone call. At that precise moment the hero relives that heaviest sorrow he has experienced since the Shoah: the loss of his friend Pedro. The author does not relate this episode in detail before the intervention of the interlocutor with his neutral voice in order to emphasize to what extent Raphael still feels traumatized as much by his bereavement in the spiritual sense as by the defamation of his beloved friend. Indeed, this slanderous accusation opens up a wound that has barely healed despite the many years elapsed since the event. The hero believes he is all the more guilty for Pedro's imprisonment because the latter had sacrificed himself in an attempt to free Raphael's brother Yoel. Pedro, an intrepid and compassionate man, longed to lessen his friend's grief after the Shoah by bringing him the only joy likely to lift his spirits: reuniting him with the only surviving member of his family held in a penitentiary hospital in Krasnograd. To that end, Pedro penetrated behind the Iron Curtain in East Berlin, then, dressed in uniform and carrying the appropriate forged documents, assumed the identity of a soviet officer entrusted with the job of taking the prisoner to Moscow. This crazy adventure could have succeeded if Yoel had controlled his emotions instead of arousing the guards' suspicions by yelling out that he wanted to be freed from prison to be reunited with his brother. The result: the prisoner remained in the hands of the N.K.V.D., the redoubtable soviet secret police, and the man who was supposed to save him became a prisoner himself. As though he is determined to intensify his guilt complex, Raphael remembers having slept in West Berlin with Pedro's collaborator, Doshka, after the mission's failure, to attenuate his own despair.

The tragic irony of the situation hits its peak when the hero rushes to the Clinic on the Mountain to try to save the honor of his best friend thirty or so years after the latter had risked his life to bring back to him a brother who was supposedly mentally insane. But there is another reason why Raphael Lipkin agrees to visit the psychiatric institute. Madness has fascinated him since his childhood in Rovidok. In that respect, he resembles the author of the novel who never fails to include in his works of fiction at least one character whose mental balance remains in doubt. To underline the primordial importance of this theme in *Twilight*, Elie Wiesel quotes as an epigraph the words of the great Jewish medieval scholar, Maimonides: "The world would not have subsisted without madmen." Madness exerts an irresistible attraction on the author as well as on his principal character because it gives access to the infinite realm of the imagination. No longer hindered by questions of logic and realism, this faculty can expand in total freedom and create all sorts of possibilities of thought and being. Thus, in its way, madness that allows the breaking down of all barriers imposed by reason can represent an instrument of knowledge. It is precisely to the extent that madmen take their fabulous and terrifying dreams for reality that they hold up to us a magic mirror in which are reflected, disproportionately magnified, some of our deepest and most repressed tendencies. From this angle, madmen can compel us to envisage our spiritual and metaphysical problems in a stunning new light. Evidently, the price to be paid can be very high. Too high, in fact. By letting the imagination unfurl without constraints or limits, the mind is in danger of sinking into chaos. Reason by itself does not contain all of knowledge, but its function is to impose a structure on existence without which we would be powerless to apprehend it. Reason also provides indispensable safeguards to the extent that it establishes a clear line of demarcation between the fantasies of a delirious imagination and the external world which, often, contradicts them. Hence the hero's very ambivalent attitude towards this mental phenomenon.

On the one hand, Raphael Lipkin remains fully aware of the fact that madness erases the frontier between imagination and reality. He knows that it engenders deformed perceptions of existence. He realizes that it can enclose its victims in a universe of illusions that make them dysfunctional, because they think they are what they can never be. This is why the protagonist mocks himself during his conversation with the mentally ill person who believes he is God. Realizing suddenly that he was on the verge of taking the patient seriously, Raphael pronounces the following judgement: "This takes the cake, I say to myself. Here is a madman who thinks he is God, and here I am, myself, whom he takes as his interlocutor.

Yes, this takes the cake: God in a clinic for the mentally sick..." (*C*, 263).
On the other hand, however, despite all the dangers inherent in madness,
Lipkin marvels at the limitless possibilities of invention towards which it
propels the initiated. They seem to escape the laws of gravity and, with
their minds liberated from the hard exigencies of the material world, they
get drunk on the sovereign freedom they enjoy in their imaginary uni-
verses, as unfathomable as any ocean. The professor explains his attitude
in an interior monologue put into italics to underscore its seriousness:
*"When one is mad, one loves or hates whomever one wants: one is free.
Freed from social or logical constraints. When one is mad, one considers the other like a prison for which one holds the key. When facing this
prison, when facing those imprisoned eyes, those imprisoned words, one
laughs, one cries, one jumps in the air, one breaks down doors, even
those that don't exist, one scales mountains, even those that rise in the
bowels of the earth, one plays and one watches oneself playing; when
one is mad, one is everywhere"* (*C*, 182). Hence the touch of contempt
combined with annoyance that Raphael shows the director of the clinic,
Dr. Benedictus—a name with rather ironic resonances—for whom everything can be boiled down to psychiatry and according to whom the task of
that discipline consists in bringing the mentally ill back towards the middle ground by restoring their balance. In other words, one must impose
on the mentally sick person a superficial rational structure at the cost
of repressing the vibrant forces that are gushing from his imagination.
It means impoverishing the person spiritually. This is how the doctor will
proceed vis-à-vis the patient who thinks he is God. When Raphael asks
Dr. Benedictus whom God needs most, the mystic or the psychiatrist, the
director replies with a trace of nastiness: "We could ask him that. God has
honored us by asking us to come to his rescue. Now, he lives under our
roof, you know" (*L*, 44).

The immense empathy the hero feels for the madmen can be traced back
to his contact with a sweetly smiling old man who lived in the psychiatric
ward of his native city, Rovidok. Young Raphael would go there every
Saturday to bring him, as well as the other patients, fruit and cakes. But
it was with the old man that he struck up a friendship. In fact, it was infinitely more moving than merely affectionate ties. The old man would mesmerize him by the richness of his imagination and his belief that he was
literally living all the experiences and adventures he was inventing in his
inner world. Casting off all the cables of reason that fasten the mind to the
shores of reality, the old man would navigate, like an unsinkable ship, on

the unleashed seas of the fantasies he would whip up. And the child would drink the words of the old patient without really understanding them. This is because the visions the latter cooked up were fabulous and he believed them: "The old man spoke of God and His attributes. He evoked an invisible palace surrounded by flaming walls where the Creator of the world awaits the *Shekina* [the creative force of existence] to give the world back its original purity. He described the eagle's nest where the Messiah, alone and melancholy, prays for time to accelerate its rhythm, for words to open unto the Word..." (*C*, 139-140). The lackluster eyes of the sick man from which nevertheless emerged a mysterious light symbolized his ambivalent state. Indifferent towards daily life that devours the energy of most of his fellow men, living in an elsewhere to which ordinary mortals did not have access, he was passionately engaged in a spiritual adventure with cosmic repercussions.

The old man at the Rovidok hospital was convinced he was invested with a sacred mission: to console his fellow men, to suffer by their sides, and to die with them whenever they had to confront the supreme trial. As a child, Raphael had proof on two occasions that this sublime madman believed he was a kind of Messiah who had come down to earth to lessen the pain of his brothers. Afflicted with typhus during the epidemic that struck the city and in the throes of terrible suffering, the boy was transported to the hospital. He received the visit of his old friend whose compassionate presence signaled the subsiding of his illness. At the beginning of the Second World War a truly hallucinating scene unfolded. The Nazis had just taken Rovidok and rounded up its citizens on the public square to force them to witness the execution of a Jew accused of having attacked a German soldier. Raphael, horrified, figured out that the condemned man would be the old madman. And yet, one instant later, he discovered the same friend, who was supposed to have already been hanged, standing next to him in the crowd, exhorting him not to despair.

As he matured, did the hero continue believing literally in the powers of that man suspended between heaven and earth? The reader never receives a clear answer during the novel. Moreover, it does not matter. As Raphael Lipkin's destiny unfolds or, rather, unravels, the question becomes irrelevant. No doubt the old man at the asylum deludes himself just like the other sick people there about his supposed ability to vanquish death by submitting to it. The essential lies elsewhere. He possesses the gift of compassion, a genuinely messianic quality, and his madness reflects his yearning to incarnate the Savior for his fellow man. He remains gravely ill because he is constantly leaping over the abyss in his imagination between this yearning and its impossible realization.

But since the hero knows how to differentiate between reality and illusion and he is anxious to safeguard his judgement despite his empathy for madmen, how does one explain the hallucinations he himself experiences on several occasion as an adolescent and a mature adult? They all involve the same old man from Rovidok. He pops up unexpectedly when young Raphael returns to the ghetto to look for his parents. His crazy friend informs him that they were part of the first round-up of Jews made by the Germans and at the same time orders the young man to live so that their memory will be preserved. The orphan finds him again after the war reincarnated as an elderly Rabbi who had come to preside over the New Year celebration at a centre in France for young Jewish refugees. The survivors of the Nazi hell refuse to pray to God. They are convinced that the Master of the universe has broken His alliance with His people. At that very moment, the Rabbi begins to weep softly. His tears become sobs that "shake him up and suffocate him" (C, 150). His expression of grief so moves the future academic and his comrades that it serves as a prayer for them. As a mature man, Professor Lipkin sees the old man of his native town one last time when the latter's image appears in the depths of the starry sky that is eagerly scrutinized by the sick man at the Clinic on the Mountain who believes he is God.

Obviously, it is tempting to see nothing more in the successive appearances of the madman from Rovidok than the effect of the hero's overexcited imagination which, by his own admission, hovers over insanity without ever plummeting into it. Does he not define himself as belonging to the category of people who "remain at the threshold, undecided, not knowing whether they should advance or back away" (C, 182). But I think it would be much more appropriate to interpret Raphael Lipkin's visions on the metaphorical, and consequently, spiritual level. They represent the projection on the screen of his imagination of his most ardent and unrealizable yearning: the presence on earth of a Messiah identifying entirely with all the suffering men and women who inhabit it, capable of lessening their pain, of dispelling their despair and breathing into them an unshakeable will to live. Even in the form of poignant nostalgia, this ideal can provide comfort and attests, as an aspiration, to the nobility of the human person. In this respect, it is very significant that at the end of the novel, when Raphael perceives the face of his old friend at twilight, he notices a startling change: "His eyes, his eyes infinitely human and wise

and overwhelming in the truth they express, no longer look lackluster..."
(*C*, 279). Thus, the hero's conscience continues speaking to him through
the madman of Rovidok.

The old man from his native city enjoys an immense advantage over
the madmen that the hero encounters in the Clinic on the Mountain. Not
only is Raphael's old friend conscious of the fact that he is escaping from
reality, but once he lands in the realm of imagination, he draws from it a
genuine plenitude of being. The patients in the clinic in New York State,
however, are all profoundly unhappy. The unreal worlds they have con-
cocted for themselves and in which they have sought refuge have not
brought them the peace they long for. Besides, in their madness one can
perceive a bizarre mixture of lucidity and unreason. They are all conscious of having been marked indelibly by a traumatic experience. They
know their problems have overwhelmed them. But the solutions they have
devised to alleviate their pain have only submerged them more. Most of
them have recourse to biblical archetypes to try to better understand their
affliction. When all is said and done, this approach remains completely
legitimate provided they do not identify to such an extent with the legendary personages that they end up believing they literally embody the latter.
Now this is exactly what their insanity consists of; the archetypes they
assume become false identities in which they imprison themselves. They
then get trapped in a dead-end street. When they don't attempt to merge
with the great figures of the Old Testament, they immobilize themselves
in sorrowful attitudes that bring on sclerosis as much on the emotional as
on the spiritual levels.

The order in which the hero meets these mentally ill people is based on
a progression. As Professor Lipkin visits each one of them, we advance
from the legendary eras of the Bible to contemporary times and end up
in the intemporal domain when he finally makes the acquaintance of the
patient who considers himself to be God. First, there is Adam. He is very
unhappy that God has not deigned to heed his advice and acknowledge the
failure of His creation and proceed in the opposite direction, namely, to
go backwards in time and make it possible for man to have never existed.
Then, there is Cain who cannot stop killing an imaginary brother to punish
his billionaire father who is indifferent to human misery. Cain is followed
by Abraham, a survivor of the Nazi terror. He does not forgive himself for
having instilled in his son a love of the sacred texts. If Abraham had taught
his son how to make his way in life, his child could have escaped from
German barbarity. Then Nadav, son of the high priest Aharon, appears.

He still mourns the disappearance of his father who died of sorrow in the face of his coreligionists' ingratitude. After him, it is Joseph, convinced that his father sent him to his death to rid himself of a child he did not love. Then comes Moshe, tormented by the fear of being swallowed up in the "kef-hakéla" or unfathomable black hole infinitely removed from divine mercy where all aspirations, all glimmers of hope, all life are enveloped in an impenetrable oblivion. After these Zelig arrives, a sweet and distinguished gentleman, but so distraught by the extermination of six million of his fellow Jews that he spends all his time searching the sky, since he is convinced that the cinders of the victims of the crematory ovens have found their burial ground there.

The encounter with God represents the point of convergence of all the lines in Raphael Lipkin's destiny. As a quadragenarian who survived the Nazi cataclysm, was affected by so many trials and tragedies, it is normal that he should desire to ask the Creator for explanations. It is equally normal that the hero should want to heckle Him. This final episode of the novel where the hero engages in a dialogue with the sick man who thinks he is God is all the more heartrending because he knows that he is dealing with a patient of the clinic. Nevertheless, the university professor is so racked by anguish that he feels the imperious need to unburden his heart by asking the sick man questions about the meaning of human existence and the relationships that supposedly exist between the Creator and His creatures. In this respect Raphael Lipkin is Elie Wiesel himself. In fact, the relationship the author entertained with God after Auschwitz was characterized by incessant questioning, revolt verging on blasphemy and, however strange this may seem, love mixed with pity.

The conversation between Raphael and God also constitutes the outcome of all the soul-searching he has carried on since his childhood concerning the Latter's nature and His attitude towards the people with whom He had formed an alliance. As a child on the eve of the Nazi occupation, the hero refused to believe that God could abandon the Jews. The old madman of Rovidok did not share his illusions in the least.: "To the question the boy asked him, 'you think God will let it happen?' his friend replied, 'God? You were saying: God?' and burst out laughing" (*C*, 266). Later, when the German tidal wave was washing over the terrified Jewish communities, he wondered whether the Master of the universe was indifferent towards the fate of His creatures. The consequences of that question were to frightening too envisage: "If the enemy can build a ghetto of hunger, a ghetto of shame, a ghetto of death, without God being interested in it, then the human adventure is condemned in advance" (*C*, 268). After the war, he overheard by chance a conversation between two former prisoners of the death camps: "The were talking about selections, hangings, beatings, blows to the head as though they were comparing their school memories" (*C*, 269). At that moment, for the first time in his life, the adolescent dared formulate a sacrilegious thought: and what if God was cruel? What if He was determined to make fun of His servants by rewarding their love with whip lashes? When he became an adult, Raphael returned to the interpretation of his Talmudic teacher in Rovidok. According to the latter, God is the one who needs pity as much as men do, "because he suffers from the decline of His creation that is ridiculed" (*C*, 272). Thus, it is the King of the universe and not man who howls the phrase of Ecclesiastics, "because all my days are nothing but sorrow" (*C*, 265).

And yet this conception of divine nature, however reasonable it may appear, does not quite satisfy the Professor. God is defined by omniscience, omnipresence and omnipotence. Why then does He not rearrange the circumstances of human history in such a way that the Holocaust would have never been unleashed? Why does he not take the trouble to erase suffering inflicted on the innocent? In addition, since He is love in the infinite sense, why did He remain immobile, why did He maintain an impenetrable silence during which His creatures were drowned in blood? When the hero asks these aggressive questions of the sick man who thinks he is God, all the poor mental patient can do is reply with a mixture of sweetness and pain: "You are hurting me... You can't imagine how much you are hurting me" (*C*, 265). Whether He manifests himself in the guise of a madman or in the holy books, God never delivers the message likely to put an end to the doubts that have tortured human beings from time immemorial. Indeed, the hero feels so tormented by this dilemma that within the space of one second the appalling thought occurs to him that God Himself, like the sick man, is perhaps also crazy and that all His creation is affected by His sickness.

In the absence of a clear and irrefutable sign of God's solidarity with His creatures, what can one do to justify life and commit oneself to it? Evidently, flight into madness is not a viable solution, since it represents an escape from the concrete problems of existence. Once again, it is anthropocentric messianism that presents itself as the ideal to follow. This is what confers eminent nobility on our human condition. And this ideal can take on a multiplicity of forms. It triumphs in the friendship that Pedro felt for the young Raphael. Thanks to this closest of friends, a representative of the Briha,[17] the adolescent who had lost everything during the Shoah was able to give life a vote of confidence again and accept new challenges that could turn his existence into the most exalting adventure imaginable. The ideal also appears in loyalty to the deceased. As the old man from Rovidok reminds Raphael, the survivors had the moral obligation to survive so that they could welcome into their memory the victims of Hitler's murderous fury. The Messiah manifests himself in the compassion that the hero feels for the sick patients in the clinic and in his determination to lessen their pain. Finally, this anthropomorphic Messiah comes alive at any moment when a human being draws closer to another in a spontaneous surge of tenderness. No reply in this novel is more moving than the one pronounced by Mirele in front of her father. Captured by the Germans and on the verge of being executed, they walk hand in hand towards their death. Here is how their last conversation unfolds: "Father… Yes?… How does one tell someone that one loves that one loves him? -That is easy, daughter. One tells him so and one smiles. So, she smiled: I love you, father" (*C*, 85).

In a universe too often given over to insanity, it is these glimmers of firefly light, however fragile they may seem, that illuminate the darkness and prevent men and women of good will from succumbing to despair.

The Forgotten

In *Twilight*, Moshe, one of the mentally sick patients, is convinced he is going to disappear in the Kef-hakéla—literally—when the Angel of Death will knock at his tomb, ask him his name and he will be unable to remember it. Elhanan Rosenbaum, the hero of *The Forgotten* (1989), knows he is going to sink to the bottom in the same abyss in the figurative sense. According to his doctor's diagnosis, he suffers from a kind of cancer that takes the form of extreme amnesia: the progressive and irreversible destruction of his memory. This illness is tragic to the extent that it attacks his intellectual and affective reservoir containing his impressions, experiences, values and spiritual as well as moral landmarks. In other words, it undermines his identity. For a religious Jew like this university professor and therapist, the tragedy entails an added dimension. By forgetting the history of his people that extends from legendary biblical times till 1988, he becomes separated from the eternal memory of Israel, and through it,

---

[17] An international Jewish organization constituted after the Second World War having as its goal to help refugees from the death camps emigrate to Palestine.

from the memory of God as well. Even worse: since he is forgetting God, he will, in turn, be forgotten. Not that the Lord of the universe abandons any of His creatures. But from the moment Elhanan Rosenbaum will have lost any remembrance of Him, the relationship between the two will simply disappear.

Consequently, in this novel Elie Wiesel again underlines the extreme vulnerability of our human condition. Here again, however, the author, through his characters, refuses to be vanquished by despair. Joy exists alongside anguish and triumphs make defeats more bearable. *The Forgotten* orchestrates this whole thematic network. Woven into the theme of memory are revealed so many others that the novelist has explored since the beginning of his career: filial love, conjugal tenderness, the necessity to bear witness, the Jew's commitment to the people of Israel through time and space, the responsibility towards the Other based on justice and compassion, and the sorrowful questioning of God's designs. A structure of redoubtable complexity encompasses these pressing issues.

The novel is framed by Elhanan Rosenbaum's two interior monologues. The first marks his anguished awareness of the irreversible ravages that have taken place in his memory. It is a heartbreaking prayer addressed to God in which he entreats Him not to allow to be dissolved into the void his identity as a Jew connected to the history of his coreligionists from the time of the prophets till the epoch of the Nazi concentration camps. He also affirms his will to preserve everything of his personal history, the sorrows as well as the joys. The second monologue betrays the distress of a man whose mind has now been almost entirely overwhelmed by darkness. The old father is heartbroken that he can no longer bequeath his spiritual testament to his son, and that he is undergoing the death of the soul even before his bodily functions stop for good. Between Elhanan's prayer and his words of farewell three major narrative lines stand out in striking relief.

The first relates the journey undertaken by Malkiel Rosenbaum, the son of Elhanan, to the town where the latter was born: Fehérfalu in Romania. The events that make up the narrative are spread out over about a month in 1988. Out of filial piety, Malkiel, a journalist for the *New York Times*, carries out a mission there the true meaning of which does not, however, reveal itself to him until the very last moments of his sojourn, when he meditates at the grave of his grandfather and bids the latter farewell. The second traces the tragic life of Elhanan from his happy childhood in a loving family, through the nightmare of Hitler's "Final Solution" and his sorrow as a young husband in Israel till his discovery of a new equilibrium in the United States and his unequal combat against his terrible illness. The third deals with Malkiel's life before his journey to Romania. It evokes his intense love for his father as well as his experience of love with several women among whom Tamar will remain the true beloved. These lines crisscross continuously as the novel unfolds, which allows the author to shed light on and explain one through the other the destinies of the father and son.

This shuttling back and forth between the past and the present for which the author has a real predilection does not, however, rigorously respect the chronological order. This is because Wiesel prefers to present an episode and characters at the precise point in his story when they are likely to throw into sharp focus the nature of a relationship or the modification that occurs within it through time. Thus, the novelist interrupts his retrospective on Elhanan Rosenbaum's youth to depict his wife, Talia, the woman he adored and whose death he still mourns. A death that was all the more tragic since it took place after the birth of their son. By so doing, the author accentuates by contrast Makiel, the son's wariness towards romantic passion and helps us understand the anguish he feels when reflecting on the fragility of relationships founded on love. Similarly, the novel describes the young Rosenbaum's erotic adventures with his very enterprising cousin, Rita, the girl who initiated him into the mysteries of sex, and with an anti-Zionist Palestinian woman at two moments in his life when he experienced feelings of guilt towards his sick father. Finally, Malkiel remembers his quarrel with Tamar as he is meditating at his grandfather's grave. This breakup occurred before his journey to Romania. Nevertheless, the author does not make it known to us until that precise point in the story to underline the fact that at the end of his filial pilgrimage Malkiel has evolved appreciably. He has overcome his fear of marriage and has realized that he ardently yearns to devote his life to the woman with whom he has had a rather stormy adventure.

Malkiel's illumination in the Jewish cemetery of Fehérfalu would not perhaps have happened so quickly without his father's fatal illness. It is precisely the tragic disintegration of Elhanan Rosenbaum's memory and its influence on his son that represent the organic centre of the novel. This is why Wiesel's text has such a heartbreaking intensity. The cruel fate that will not fail to swoop down on the professor manifests itself at first by relatively insignificant signs. Elhanan forgets the words of the Kiddush, a prayer pronounced over the wine and which he had already recited thousands of times. He has difficulty remembering the name of a colleague whom he has known for many years. Then, the assaults become more and more aggressive. One would think that a sacrilegious and malevolent demon is in the process of ripping out pages of his memory where had been printed the most significant experiences of his existence. Although he is free to move about physically, from the spiritual point of view Elhanan remains the prisoner of a dissolving force which, by depriving him of his past, disconnects him from himself. To delay this encroachment of spiritual death on his consciousness, Elhanan fights against time to record his memories. This is a deeply moving combat, because even though the events he has lived through will be preserved through this recording, he, Elhanan Rosenbaum, as the subject uttering these words, will soon no longer remember them. What defined him as a human being will disappear like ashes blown away by the wind. Nothing is more poignant in this respect that Elhanan's reaction while he evokes the Sabbaths of his childhood over which his mother presided: "My mother, I think of her especially on the Sabbath. I will never forget her, because I will never forget the Sabbath. (Sorry, while dictating these pages, I realize that I am saying things in which I no longer believe: how can I say that I will never forget, since I am falling deeper into oblivion? The day will come when I forget everything. My mother also? She also. The Sabbath also? It also. What can I do to hold on to what enables me to live? I don't want to forget, do you hear me, mama? I don't want to..."[18]

As the shadows encroach on his memory, the conversations he has with his son acquire resonances that are more and more heartbreaking. They appear in italics to underscore their importance. At one time, Elhanan is convinced that his deceased wife is in front of him. He would like his son to believe in the real existence of what is only a hallucination at worst or an illusion at best. Out of respect for the superior intelligence his father used to enjoy, Malkiel refuses to play the game. At that moment Elhanan entreats him: "If you are right, son, then help me: help me to not see your mother in front of me as I see you, help me, I need your help so badly" (O, 149). The father is desperate to safeguard his memory and to transmit its contents to his son for two reasons. First, he witnessed the most diabolical enterprise of racial extermination in human history. Of course, the world knows of the murder factories at Auschwitz, Sobibor or Treblinka. On the other hand, few people have heard of the acts of butchery perpetrated by

---

[18] Elie Wiesel, *L'Oublié*, Paris: Les Éditions du Seuil/Points, 1989, 220; referred to henceforth as *O*.

the Nazis in Kolomey and Stanislav. The anguish that grips Elhanan in this period when his past is disintegrating more and more, is the possibility that the victims of these genocidal deeds may be relegated by posterity to the "second category" (*O*, 105). If future generations stop thinking about these innocent people, the young man who was Elhanan Rosenbaum at that time will have borne witness for nothing, and the victims will have perished for good.

The other reason is of a personal nature. It can be found in the love bordering on veneration that he still feels for Talia and in his cult-like devotion to her beyond death. That ardent and mischievous young woman possessed the power to pull Elhanan away from his tragic past thanks to her ability to create happiness around her. Moreover, she firmly believed that redemption took place on this very earth, in this finite existence, through human joy rather than through divine intervention. Tenderness being the generator of happiness, Talia performed the miracle of bringing happiness to the refugee from Fehérfalu by making him fall madly in love with her. A Jew of Yemenite origin and representative of a Zionist agency, she enchanted the heart of the timid and shy young man with the promise of a new start in life after the trauma of the Second World War. In this promised land that had become the state of Israel in 1948, they lived a most exalting conjugal relationship founded on the need to always be more worthy of one another. The letter Talia sends Elhanan when he is a prisoner of war in Jordan illustrates the nature of their love. To comfort him, she tells him why she continues loving him with the same intensity. She conceives their union not so much as a symbiosis but rather as an exhortation to the two of them to transcend themselves. Talia is in love with Elhanan not because she sees in him a model of perfection to emulate. She sees in him her own image but embellished and idealized.

This awareness of what she represents for her husband thrills her and inspires her to strive even more towards perfection. Since Elhanan reveres her, she will do her utmost to deserve the sentiments she has aroused in him. Obviously, Talia cherishes her husband for his vulnerability and compassion. But it is the idealism engendered by their love that confers on their union a transcendent dimension. Let us listen to the young woman: "What do I love in you? Your pathological timidity? The way you are attentive to the fears and desires of other people? The way you avert your gaze when certain memories invade your mind? You know what, I am going to surprise you: what I love in you is me. Don't laugh. I love the image

128

you receive from me. In you, thanks to you, I feel purer, more deserving. Because of you I feel closer to God" (*O*, 235).

Despite the dogged determination with which the hero fights oblivion, he never deludes himself into believing that his victories will be anything but temporary. "I refuse to get bogged down," he tells his son proudly (*O*, 72). As though to taunt the malevolent destiny that is demolishing, one after another, entire sections of his memory, he does his utmost to convert each instant into an eternity. These magnificent outbursts of revolt are unfortunately of short duration. His degeneration hurts him so much because he has been conscious since his childhood of the human creature's extreme fragility. One of the terrifying myths of Jewish spirituality is wired into his consciousness since his childhood days in Fehérfalu and still constitutes, fifty years later, an essential component of his interior landscape. It is the myth of the Tempter. As God's implacable enemy, the Tempter takes delight in sullying His creature as a means of mocking His work. He appears for the first time in the boy's life in the form of a diabolical snickering emanating from a well. Gripped by fear, young Elhanan rushes to Rabbi Sender. Through his spiritual energy, the latter reduces the Tempter to silence. At the end of his trajectory, Professor Rosenbaum is again assaulted by the snickering of the same dreadful presence; but this time he no longer has the Rabbi to protect him. Alone, helpless, his mind already in its death throes, Elhanan knows that night will soon take him away. The Tempter's work frightens the old man so much because its aim is sacrilegious. Its purpose is to break the organic bonds linking him to the eternal memory of Israel.

As I have already pointed out, for every practicing Jew the eternal memory of Israel signifies the reservoir of ethical and spiritual values that the legendary heroes and sages of biblical times as well as the individuals of the more recent history of the Jewish people embody. Their trials, defeats and triumphs seem as real and meaningful as any great contemporary event. Connecting to this venerable history composed of legends and real occurrences magnified to legendary proportions means conferring an intemporal dimension on an individual's life. It also implies for millions of Jews like Elhanan the possibility of acquiring a kind of immortality during their time on earth. Now, when individual memory collapses, the consciousness of participating in an intemporal history disappears simultaneously. The individual finds himself spiritually shrunk and directionless.

The primordial importance for the hero of this collective intemporal consciousness can be observed in the moments of his life when he grieves over having committed immoral actions. In many respects Elhanan's conduct towards his fellow man/woman has been exemplary. But given the lofty exigencies that Judaism imposes on those who practice it, he judges himself with ruthless severity. Thus, he is disgusted with himself after the partisans attacked a restaurant frequented by SS officers. Instead of running away immediately like his comrades after throwing grenades against the building, the hero works himself up to a paroxysm of murderous fury against Hitler's henchmen who have tortured and killed his next of kin. It matters little that those murderers have done everything to deserve such reprisals. When the partisans celebrate their victory, Elhanan cannot swallow anything. A little later, his native city is liberated by the Russians. Propelled by a vengeful rage, his friend Itzik rapes the wife of the sadistic leader of the Niylas, an antisemitic Hungarian organization. Since the rapist is stronger physically than him, he witnesses with a broken heart this negation of human dignity. He entreats his friend not to commit that act, a sacrilege according to Jewish law. He returns later to offer his compassion to the traumatized victim. He condemns Itzik, breaks with him. Several years later, he encounters his former war comrade in Israel, in the old, besieged city of Jerusalem. Again, Elhanan accuses him of having glorified evil by his act, of having sullied the Torah by acting without justice and compassion towards his powerless victim. But his conscience is not relieved of its pain. A feeling of guilt torments him till the end of his days. He is persuaded that God has punished him and continues punishing him for not having succeeded in preventing this moral blight. More than forty years after the event, in the throws of feverish agitation, he confides in his son on his hospital bed: "You know why your mother died? Because I witnessed the rape of a human being, the rape of her sovereignty, the profanation of her divinity, and I witnessed it without reacting. Here is the devastating lesson I bequeath to you, son: Itzik blasphemed, and I watched, but it is your mother whom death took away" (*O*, 196).

Is old Elhanan, then, trying to rid himself of his guilt by exhorting his son to make the trip to his native city? One is inclined to think so, despite the rather enigmatic terms in which he expresses himself. Since his memory is failing more and more, he cannot manage to state precisely what he yearns for his son to find there, but he is convinced that Malkiel must go there at once: "There is an essential point... -Which one? -It is at the centre of my recollections that are fading: it is thanks to it that they are still part of my memory. -What do you want to talk about? – You will know in good time. -When? Over there? -Yes, over there. Or when you return. To know it, you must first go there" (*O*, 94). We will understand later that this is one of Elhanan's reasons for exhorting Malkiel to go there, but it is not the only one, and perhaps not the most important one either.

The father certainly places a crushing burden on his son's shoulders, but he had been loading heavy moral responsibilities on him for a long time by putting Malkiel at the centre of his universe. In fact, Professor Rosenbaum was anxious for his son to be not only his present but also his whole future. He wished that his son would insert himself into God's memory so that he, Elhanan, as the father, would have the certitude that his finite existence would be prolonged beyond death. Given these demands, it was inevitable that Malkiel would revolt from adolescence onward. The Professor's son refused the patrimony of sorrow that his father was thrusting upon him. He did not want to embody Elhanan's hope: "Let me live my adolescent life, don't make me age too much, he cried out" (*O*, 134). To this refusal was added an unconscious jealousy. Elhanan was practicing a cult-like devotion to the mother that he, the son, had never known. When he reached adult age, a feeling of guilt replaced his hostile opposition to his father. It crystalized around short-lived amorous adventures that his father, a man of lofty moral principles, would never have approved. Elhanan would perhaps have felt empathy for Inge, a young German journalist whom his son met in New York. She loved Malkiel because of the atrocious suffering Nazi Germany had inflicted on the Jewish people. But she realized that the very memory of the Holocaust would have prevented them from sharing an enduring happiness.

Now, as his father is sinking into the night, Malkiel, who had nevertheless always adored him, overflows with filial solicitude. Heeding the advice of a Hassidic Rabbi in Brooklyn, he is resolved to sanctify his father's life by experiencing joy in his place. In addition, he agrees to travel to Fehér-falu. To retrieve a father's past is a sorrowful and disappointing enterprise, because no man can live in another one's place. A person's living, direct experience cannot be transmitted, as is, to someone else. The son can walk through all the areas where, as a child and a young man, his father had known great joys and immense sorrows, but it won't make any difference because Elhanan's memory can only be communicated to Malkiel as a pale reflection of the reality lived by another human consciousness. The son cannot substitute himself for his father and relive the important events of the latter's life as though they were his own. As he walks in Elhanan Rosenbaum's footsteps, Malkiel senses he is heading towards failure. In an interior monologue where he speaks to his absent father, his son shares with the latter his certainty that he has made the trip for nothing. Again, the use of italics accentuates the gravity of his dilemma: *"I see and hear everything that you have done, everything that you have seen, and yet, father, I know, yes, I know that it will be impossible for me to keep my promise. Certainly, I will bear witness for you, but my testimony will be lightweight compared to yours; it will be lightweight and meager. What can I do, father? You life and memory are one and indivisible. They cannot survive you, not really"* (*O*, 194).

Despite this acute discouragement, Malkiel's visit is far from being a failure. I will come back to this later. It suffices to state for the moment that the son endeavors to exorcize his father's guilt concerning the rape of the wife of the fascist leader, Zoltan, and he succeeds. The gravedigger of the Jewish cemetery, Herschel, the only survivor of the Nazi roundups and killings, puts him on the right track. He relates to Malkiel the circumstances in which he strangled the sadistic Nazi collaborator. This story touches off an association of ideas in the journalist's mind. He asks his official interpreter, Lydia, to get information on the widow of the man who had terrorized the Jews of Fehérfalu. She discovers the lady's identity. The latter is now called Mme. Calinescu. She remarried after the end of the war and is determined to bury the shame of forty years ago in an impenetrable silence. Even more, she wants to erase all traces of that dreadful event from her memory. But Malkiel's questions break into the sanctuary of her consciousness where Mme. Calinescu had repressed it. The journalist's interrogation seems inhuman. Why torment an old woman who has already undergone dreadful suffering? An interior voice urges Malkiel to stop, because the reminder of that episode of her past is sheer torture for her. Yet another voice incites him to pursue implacably this search for the truth. And then a kind of miracle takes place. Mme. Calinescu admits she was a rape victim. She also acknowledges that thanks to Elhanan Rosenbaum's compassion she did not become cynical towards men. At that precise moment Malkiel reveals his identity to her: he is the son of the man who had so wanted to save her from shame. The kiss Mme. Calinescu bestows on him has a double significance. It affirms that she had never considered Elhanan responsible for her degradation, and that finally, through his son, the old wound would be able to heal. Malkiel has thus succeeded in accomplishing an essential part of his mission. Will he be able to work as effectively to guarantee his own happiness? Nothing seems less sure before the end of the novel.

On the surface, Malkiel has everything to be happy. He loves and is loved by a woman of exceptional beauty and intelligence. Tamar, star journalist of the *New York Times*, bears an astonishing resemblance through her character and physiognomy to the mother that Malkiel never knew. Dynamic, bold, overflowing with self-confidence and determined to devour life, she would seem to be able to breathe into the man she loves this same passion for fighting in favor of joy. But Elhanan Rosenbaum's tragedy has left an imprint on his son. Even though he is captivated by Tamar's charm, anguish has too much of a hold on him and creates in him a fear of the long-term relationship that marriage implies. He is haunted by the curse that a cruel history constantly leaves hanging over the earth. He quotes for Tamar the thought of a man who refused to have children: not because he did not love them, but because he did love them. He felt pity for them. He kept thinking of the future that was awaiting them and would say: "It would be better for time to unfold without them" (*O*, 47).

This attitude of anxiety and pessimism when facing the future aroused Tamar's fury. Since destiny has been generous to her by lavishing on her the gifts of a goddess, she intends to exploit them fully to exalt life. Not that naïve optimism is obscuring her mind. She is just as aware as Malkiel of the fragility of our condition. But this awareness engenders in her a diametrically opposite reaction. In her magnificent pride, she defies fatality and death: "To accept this would be to resign oneself to defeat and shame, and that is what she would never admit" (O, 47). I would venture to say that a woman of Tamar's caliber almost needs the forces of Evil to triumphantly proclaim the intrepidness of her heart and her mind. This exuberant confidence can be seen in her relationship with Elhanan. She has a filial love for him. She knows as well as Malkiel that the sickness with which his father is stricken causes irreparable damage. But she maintains that it is possible to prolong Elhanan's life well beyond his spiritual and physical death. By incorporating into both of their minds the best that he has stored up in his own, they will protect him from the ravages of time. When Malkiel remembers their conversation on the subject, even he, the anguished one, lets himself be carried away by his beloved's ardent conviction: " – I have confidence. You know why? – Tell me.- Because I love your father's stories. We will not forget them. Is that not the beginning of a victory? Blessed Tamar" (*O*, 265).

Tamar and Malkiel are ready to move heaven and earth to bring Elhanan courage and comfort. But is the God whom the latter entreats at the beginning of the novel not to let the shadows of night invade his consciousness really attuned to the affliction of His servant? The Creator seems so far away, so unwilling to bring succor. At various times the same question keeps coming back like an obsessive leitmotif: "and God in all of this?" Where does He hide when men need Him? Why did He remain so obstinately silent during the terrible ordeals the hero and his next of kin endured? Does He want to test the weakness of His creatures rather than their strength? As usual, Elie Wiesel raises these anguished questions without providing clear answers. Even the religious characters in the novel seem to think that events set off by the insane agitation of men unfold according to a rhythm by turns capricious and ineluctable that has nothing to do with divine intervention. God no doubt remains sensitive to the suffering of those who pray to Him but does nothing to end the reign of injustice.

This very pessimistic interpretation of the human creature abandoned to his/her own resources without being able to count on the God he/she worships, an interpretation that the writer himself would perhaps judge unacceptable, seems to be justified on many occasions in the text. The journey undertaken by Elhanan Rosenbaum from his childhood till his old age illustrates the presence of a destiny where chance and/or injustice predominate. Throughout the Second World War he avoids death, as though others, just as innocent, had been designated to die in his place. Sent by his father to Stanislav to verify the rumors of genocide perpetrated by the Nazis, he thus avoids an anti-Jewish roundup in his city the consequences of which are disastrous not only for his whole family but for almost all his coreligionists in Fehérfalu. A prisoner of the Stanislav ghetto when the Germans decide to encircle it, he manages to escape thanks to his friendship with Itzik who is already enlisted in the work brigade. While other comrades perish from cold or get shot by sadistic German officers, he continues leading a charmed life. The same thing happens when he is a fighter in the insurrection movement of the Jewish partisans. The woman he knew briefly and loved, Vitka, is killed during a raid whereas Elhanan again escapes by the skin of his teeth. Then, in Israel, during the capture of the old city of Jerusalem by the Arab Legion, the young lad with a generous heart and immense courage, Avsholem, is mowed down by bullets. Itzik, whom the hero encounters again in the besieged city, is also felled. Elhanan is taken prisoner but in the end is liberated. Talia, his beloved wife, dies when bringing Malkiel into the world. Why her rather than her husband? But the height of absurdity is reached in the United States. After having skimmed past tragedy so many times, it is finally Elhanan, an almost saintly man through his goodness, who serves as a victim for a cruel fate. His luminous mind tumbles into night without God intervening to stop this undeserved punishment. No wonder Malkiel would prefer that his father blasphemed against God rather than endure his misfortunes as though he deserved them.

As though the life of Elhanan Rosenbaum was not sufficient to demonstrate the Creator's non-intervention in the tragedy of His creation, the gravedigger of Fehérfalu, Herschel, provides yet another example. He tells Malkiel the phantasmagorical story of the Great Meeting in the Jewish cemetery of the town. Appalled by the threat of genocide that hovers over the community of their coreligionists, the deceased Rabbis wake up from their deep sleep, leave their tombs, take counsel among one another, and are resolved to come to the rescue of the unfortunate Jews. But even these saintly souls close to God are powerless to stop the catastrophe. Since they are unable to leave the place where they have been buried, all they can do is lament in vain over the fate of these innocent deportees.

Inasmuch as God appears powerless, it behooves man and woman to do better than Him. They must assume the sacred responsibility of not only consoling their unhappy brethren but above all of coming to their rescue even at the peril of their lives. They must, once again, reincarnate the Messiah during this terrestrial existence. The father of Elhanan and grandfather of Malkiel, who bears his name, was a sublime manifestation of this messianic presence. After the Germans captured Fehérfalu, the grandfather was ordered, as the leader of the Jewish community, to give the names of ten coreligionists who would be held as hostages. These would be shot if other members of the ghetto attempted to escape. Grandfather Malkiel refused to commit such a base act. Instead of presenting the Nazi Commander with a list of ten names, all he did was write his own ten times. Furious over having his authority ridiculed, the SS officer tortured his victim until the latter was reduced to an inert, bloody and shapeless mass. Malkiel's grandfather died on the spot from the torture he had endured, but the glory of his death crushed all the victories the Nazis had won through brute force.

Malkiel, son of Elhanan and grandson of old Malkiel, knew of the martyrdom of that admirable man before undertaking the voyage to Romania. Young Malkiel already resembled his revered grandfather in the sense that he, too, was moved by the suffering of innocents. He had already travelled to the refugee camps in Cambodia to bring succor to the victims traumatized by the brutal Pol Pot. But only when he meditates at his grandfather's grave does an illumination take place in his soul. As though that saint was inspiring his grandson beyond death, young Malkiel, before leaving

Fehérfalu, fully assumes his Jewish identity and agrees to completely identify with the history of the people of Israel. Without perhaps having been aware of it, Malkiel has just accomplished the whole of the mission his father had entrusted to him in enigmatic terms. Evidently, his meeting with Mme. Calinescu was a part of it. But there was something even more important. By exhorting his son to return to the city of his birth, Elhanan no doubt hoped young Malkiel would make a pilgrimage to the cemetery where the saintly Malkiel, the latter's grandfather, was buried. Despite the irreversible disintegration of his mind, Professor Rosenbaum sensed instinctively that a soul-to-soul dialogue would occur between the grandson and his grandfather, and that, through the latter's agency, he would succeed in bequeathing to his son, Malkiel, his spiritual legacy before his death.

In this respect nothing is more revealing than a comparison between the last words pronounced by Elhanan and the thoughts unfolding in Malkiel's mind when he bids farewell to his grandfather. Elhanan yearns for his son to always remain a Jew and maintains that by safeguarding his Judaism he will connect with the universal. Malkiel fulfills this yearning by entreating his grandfather to watch over Mme. Calinescu and over his guide, Lydia, a young woman dragged into a nightmare because of her love for the son of the Chief of the Romanian secret police. Elhanan ardently wishes that Malkiel will marry Tamar. His son has decided that he will become reconciled with her as soon as he returns to the United States. They had quarreled over an article written by Tamar that denounced the use of torture by Israel against the Palestinians. Out of visceral loyalty towards the Hebrew state, Malkiel accused her of endangering its security. Tamar maintained come hell or high water that Israel owed it to itself to remain faithful to the lofty ideals that founded it. Now ready to forget their quarrel, Malkiel will marry the woman he has never stopped loving. Finally, his father wanted his son to have children to ensure the survival of the strange and marvelous community of Israel that extends from Moses to himself.

Malkiel will fulfill this wish as well. By agreeing to become a father, not only does he affirm his love of life, an affirmation that is typically Jewish, but he will guarantee Elhanan's survival in the memory of the grandchildren that the latter will never know. Speaking mentally to Tamar and his grandfather, he paints a vision in lyrical terms of the kind of immortality Elhanan will enjoy thanks to his decision to generate a large family. He does so in an invocation carried forward on an anaphoric rhythm which recalls certain biblical texts:

"And the memory of my father will sing and cry in mine.

And ours, Tamar, will blossom forth in that of our children.

You are the one who wins: children, we will have many of them, Tamar.

And one day, they, in turn, will tell the story of your sons, grandfather.

Elhanan son of Malkiel.

Malkiel son of Elhanan (*O*,311)

At the end of the novel, Elhanan's memory disintegrates completely. As though to accentuate this brutal end of the death of his mind, the speech he was in the process of recording stops at the conjunction "because." Naturally, he will never know that his son has made the resolution in the cemetery of Fehérfalu to transmit his spiritual legacy to the grandchildren who will one day be born and thus to preserve, beyond death, that which was most precious in his spirit. But at least this gift will be bequeathed to the next generation. In this way, Elhanan will continue living in the consciousness of his future grandchildren exactly as Abraham had lived in his. A fragile victory, no doubt. Elie Wiesel would reply that in a world victimized so often by the forces of Evil, one must rejoice whenever a victory testifies to the dignity of our human condition.

CHAPTER 5

THE COMPLETELY
SECULARIZED MESSIAH

I n Elie Wiesel's five last novels that are spread out between 1991 and 2010, one notices that the ideal of the Messiah becomes more and more secularized. With few exceptions, the protagonists embody their lofty moral convictions without alluding to a coming they consider impossible. Moreover, not only adherents to the Jewish faith are capable of surges of sublime generosity and abnegation. Through the agency of several of his heroes, the novelist pays homage to certain non-Jews who, in their way and without being aware of it, embody the sacred duty of all Jews to commit themselves to repairing a damaged world and, as a result, to form a partnership with the Creator to make humanity continuously more human.

As concerns the quality of these texts, admirers of Elie Wiesel's oeuvre are confronted by a dilemma. They are obliged to compare the author to himself. In other words, they notice, almost reluctantly, that the last novels of the master are not all worthy of the ones written between 1959 and 1989 when his talent was in full bloom. *A Mad Desire to Dance* and *The Sonderberg Case* are masterpieces that equal the best the novelist has ever produced. On the other hand *The Judges*, *The Time of the Uprooted* and *Hostage* betray a flagging or falling off of his inspiration. But even in these three novels that do not appear to us to be on the same level as the two others one can discern passages of great literary beauty, and so they, too, deserve to be approached with sympathy and respect.

The Judges

Various critics have sometimes reproached Elie Wiesel for his inability to escape the obsession of the Holocaust. His novel, *The Judges* that appeared in 1999 after a decade of silence, refutes this reproach. Here, references to the Shoah are brief and indirect. The essential lies elsewhere. It resides in the individual's confrontation with his/her soul. The novelist structures his narrative in such a way that he compels his characters to practice painful introspection during which arise irresistibly questions about the meaning of their existences. In *The Judges* the author again orchestrates the main themes that constitute the moral and metaphysical richness of his works: the importance of memory, the need to assume responsibility towards our fellow humans and to embody the Messiah in our relationships with them, the beauty of friendship and love, the mystery of death which, paradoxically, confers an essential meaning on life. Certain passages of the novel that celebrate human relations are extremely moving and recall Elie Wiesel's magnificent texts that preceded it. And yet, one ends up experiencing a sentiment of malaise, as though we were witnessing an ebbing of his talent as a writer of fiction. He has constructed a powerful motor to propel his vehicle. He does not, however, fully exploit the potential his text contains. The motor is not working to its full potential. As Jean-Pierre Denis remarked in the Montreal newspaper *Le Devoir*, by its plot *The Judges* reminds us a bit too much of the play *No Exit* by Jean-Paul Sartre and especially the novel *The Breakdown* by Friedrich Dürrenmatt.[19]

During a violent snowstorm, a flight from New York to Tel Aviv makes a forced landing at a little airport in the state of Connecticut. Five of the passengers are picked up by a man from the neighboring village, who offers them hospitality. At the beginning, overflowing with gratitude towards their host, they do not take too seriously his strange, indeed disquieting words and behavior. But they soon realize that this weird personage is a real mental case. He presents himself as a judge and invites his guests to participate in a game that will become more and more terrifying during which he will pass judgement on them. To satisfy the gods of which he calls himself the emissary, he informs them that one of them will have to die and the five passengers themselves will have to designate the expiatory victim. The Judge locks them up in a room to prevent them from escaping. In addition, thanks to a sophisticated electronic system, he has them under

---

[19] Jean-Pierre Denis, "Le pouvoir du Mal," *Le Devoir* (Montréal : samedi, 22 mai, 1999).

constant surveillance by a deformed servant called "The Hunchback" who seems unconditionally devoted to his master. During this sleepless night, the five prisoners who did not know one another beforehand entertain relationships that are, by turns, cordial and hostile and try to figure out the Judge's motives while their anguish mounts. At the same time, they enter the labyrinth of their past to uncover its deep meaning. They become the judges of their own existences. They intend in this way to justify their right to be spared not only in their own eyes but in the eyes of their co-detainees. By the end of this period of introspection they succeed in better understanding their attitudes towards life and death.

Wiesel devotes the largest part of the novel to following the five travelers as they advance in their adventure of introspection which is as unexpected as it forced on them. Of the five, Razziel is the one who seems most affecting because he has had a close call with hell and madness. As an innocent man persecuted by a ruthless communist regime in Romania, he had undergone multiple kinds of degradation to destroy his memory. For the Jew that Razziel calls himself, depriving a human being of his memory is an act of sacrilege. When this faculty disappears, the consciousness sinks into chaos. Everything that defines the individual and constitutes his identity—name, family ties, spiritual and moral values, experiences lived—vanishes and the human being degenerates into a living wreck: "I didn't remember anything. As soon as I looked backwards, I felt my brain floating over a dark and opaque ocean. And a familiar anguish rose within me, preventing me from breathing: I was afraid of sliding, of falling. I was drowning in myself." [20]

Like movie censors determined to cut out long sections of a film to render it inoffensive, his tormentors had injected drugs into him to annihilate his past and turn him into a docile rag. Unfortunately for them, they were unaware that Razziel had a companion in his cell, a Jewish wise man, mysterious and compassionate, by the name of Paritus. Did Paritus really exist, or did Razziel create the Sage in his imagination as a means of combatting this dispossession of the self? It doesn't matter. A soul of inexhaustible generosity and endowed with an unbeatable faith in his fellow man, he quickly realized that to save his co-detainee he would have to give him a new identity by refurnishing his memory. Paritus thus offered him the gift of his own first name, Razziel, then began filling the void dug out by his torturers by telling him the story of his life with all the joys and

---

[20] Elie Wiesel, *Les Juges*, Paris: Éditions du Seuil, 1999, 88-89; henceforth referred to as *LJ*.

sorrows that accompanied it. Just like Michael in *The Town Beyond the Wall*, Paritus was finally able to resurrect the consciousness of the living corpse that the young prisoner had become and used almost the same words to express his tenacious will to tear him from the shadows: "Wake up, in the name of God! This is our only chance! One of us will finally win! And if I don't, we are both lost! Futile efforts, vain tears. You were occupying a fortress the entrance of which was forbidden to me. And then, one day, or one night, how could one differentiate between the darkness and the penumbra, you looked at me, and I understood that you and I, or both of us, were worthy of miracles. You looked at me like before but more intensely: you were drinking in my gaze, you were receiving my voice, you were absorbing my words. I wanted to laugh or cry. I was witnessing your birth into the world" (*LJ*, 91).

Having emerged into the light, Razziel was able to acquire from his benefactor values and convictions that would give him the courage to live and the pride in belonging to the human condition. The keystone of his regenerated consciousness was friendship. Unlike Pedro in *The Town Behind the Wall*, Paritus did not envisage this human relationship as a symbiosis. Pedro affirmed that one and one equaled one to underscore the fusion of hearts and minds that took place between two human beings. The Sage substituted another equation for the previous one: one and one equal two. He was anxious in this way to show that contrary to what happened in love, the relationship between two friends resembles parallel lines that lateral ones connect. While preserving their autonomy, "each of the two is enriched by the other and for the other" (*LJ*, 85). To this ideal of friendship is indissolubly linked the concept of the Messiah. After so many other personages in Wiesel's novels, Paritus expresses himself without any ambiguity on this matter. The savior is man himself and no one else can embody him as he relates to his fellow man. Miracles unfold exclusively in human contexts. People do not free themselves from their pain and brotherhood does not surge forward until men and women perform acts of justice and charity for one another. To await the coming of the Redeemer is tantamount to madness. This is how Paritus speaks to Razziel in a dream the latter has: "Do you really think the Savior so longed for will appear tomorrow, or next year, as though he came from nowhere, to give you his light and grace? Don't be foolish. Don't wait for the end any longer. We have gone beyond it. The end is behind us. The Redeemer will no longer come. And supposing that he does, he will need our pity more than we will need his. That is because he has lost his powers, this Redeemer... He has tarried too much along the way, your good man. He has allowed the opportunity to pass; it has slipped between his fingers" (*LJ*,128). Having become Razziel's alter ego during their stay in prison, the mysterious Sage always remains by his side even when they are separated by time and space.

Another blessing that illuminates the life of this traumatized man: after his liberation from the communist hell, he comes to the United States, becomes the director of a Talmudic school and discovers love. Wiesel conjures up the relationship that Razziel sustains with his beloved Kali in a very delicate manner. Instead of analyzing intellectually the nature of this sentiment, he suggests the profound harmony that reigns within the couple by describing its various manifestations. Their understanding raises them to the rank of the elect of this earth. The following passage reflects the sense of wonder felt by two human beings who seem predestined to bring joy, comfort and plenitude to one another:"-I love listening to you, Kali said to him while taking his hand. -But I haven't said anything. -I love listening to you even when you say nothing. They were happy. They needed so little to forget everything that threatened their happiness. Taking a short walk together on the banks of the Hudson. Sharing a raspberry ice cream. Listening to a recording. Watching children as they played in the garden. Guessing the contents of a book before opening it. What would his life have been without this incomparable woman?" (*LJ*, 74). Kali's death at the very moment when they were expecting a baby devastated Razziel and opened within him an abyss that the spiritual presence of Paritus was this time incapable of filling. In this snowed-in enclosure where he is forced to confront his past and assess his portion of responsibility for his acts, the Talmudic master wonders in anguish whether he had not wounded his wife on various occasions without meaning to. He would sometimes neglect her in favor of his students. His connection to Paritus would arouse his companion's jealousy. His obsession with his past smothered by his communist torturers would sometimes erect a barrier between him and the woman he loved. Having drawn up the balance sheet of his existence, Razziel begins to think that his death would perhaps be a form of deliverance.

The only woman passenger in the group, Claudia does not share the anguished sentiments of her fellow-passenger. Proud, witty, vivacious, she is experiencing at last, after reaching the thirty-year stage, the joy of loving and being loved. It is not surprising that she arouses Razziel's immediate empathy and reminds him of his beloved Kali. She, too, is compelled to examine her past to justify her right to life. Before her exciting encounter with David, this press agent for a drama company had lived her relationships with men rather as a spectator. Married in the past to Lucien, she had deluded herself into believing that she was living a veritable passion with him. But she did not in the least have the certitude of blossoming forth in this conjugal situation. An essential part of her being remained unfulfilled. She never gave herself to him body and soul: " A part of her didn't participate, remained at a distance, like an observer whose senses were blunted: when love dies out, one forgets the fire that made it sing" (*LJ*,110). Then David came upon the scene unexpectedly and it was the exaltation of the mind, the heart and the senses, a fullness of being so intense that the two lovers believed they had temporarily gone beyond their mortal condition: "Thank you, David my love. Thank you for showing me, thank you for letting me show you that the night, that of the couple, transcends its limits and becomes eternal" (*LJ*, 166). Obviously, Claudia intends to remain alive to meet up with her lover in Israel.

Bruce Schwarz, the repentant playboy, is just as resolved as Claudia to save his life. He also has finally found the great love of his life implying the gift of oneself, but he has reached it by a radically different path. Before falling madly in love with Stacy, he had cynically exploited, as a Don Juan drunk with his conquering masculinity, the good faith or gullibility of his numerous feminine victims. He would conjure up for them the glittering mirage of a great passion, and once they allowed themselves to be subjugated, he would make fun of their stupidity and coldly informed them that he had been playing a game all the time. This insatiable need to vanquish women's resistance resulted from a traumatic experience he underwent during his youth. Returning home unexpectedly, he saw his father making love to his mother's best friend on the bedroom floor. As though he intended to sully as much as possible a humanity in which he no longer believed, he decided, from that moment on, to show his contempt for it by behaving without any scruples. He made it his life's work to betray men and dominate women sexually.

Bruce, however, was not entirely successful in killing his moral conscience. One day he felt shame invading him. The old father of one of his victims who, in despair, had committed suicide, came up to him and asked him to explain why he acted so wickedly. In the snow-bound prison where he finds himself now, the former playboy relives through his memory this heartbreaking scene where the old man's reproaches put an end to his career as an apparently impenitent seducer: "Bruce was going to recite his habitual refrain, that it was only a game, a game the cruel consequences of which escaped him, but in front of this bereaved father, crushed under grief and solitude, he could not open his mouth: the words, in his throat, were turning to ashes. If only he could say something, do something to dispel the sorrow in front of him. If only the ground that was giving way under his feet could swallow him up...Was it at that moment that he understood that he had to change course in order not to sink into the void?" (*LJ*, 164-165). From then on, Bruce had only one idea in his mind: to do penance. He would fly to the religious kibbutz in Israel where Stacy had taken refuge. She would forgive him and would agree to marry him.

Claudia and Bruce are committed to life with all the energy of their being just as George Kirsten is tempted by death. And yet, when he embarked on this unfortunate flight to Tel-Aviv, he seemed at last to have found a reason to live. Better still: a mission of the utmost gravity to accomplish. This archivist bogged down in a mediocre existence had just discovered a document carrying within it the potential for a scandal of international proportions, and he was going to bring it to the Israeli secret services. There was in it enough to ruin the career and reputation of an Austrian statesman known for his extremely favorable attitude towards the Hebrew state, because the document contained proof that this warm friend of the Jews had belonged to the Nazi party during the Second World War. But his unexpected detention obliges him as well to dig into his past, and he once again sinks into despair. In the balance sheet he draws up of his life a profound incompleteness is evident.

As an adolescent, George was torn between a scientific grandfather with a sceptic mind whom he adored and a rationalistic father who repulsed any demonstration of tenderness. The future archivist found that man so redoubtable and withdrawn that he did not dare show him the slightest visible sign of filial affection even on his deathbed. Moreover Mr. Kirsten realized before dying how tragic their relationship had been when he declared to his son how much he regretted never having had with him the so necessary and longed for conversation. As concerns love, another failure is noted. At the height of their sexual ecstasy, his beloved first wife, Betty, cried out the name of a former lover. Then, his second marriage to Marie-Anne had already been failing for a long time. That bitter woman never missed an opportunity to remind her husband that their conjugal union had spoiled her life. The atmosphere of bitterness and recrimination that dominated their home made their children want to leave. Only his adulterous liaison with a woman of Jewish origin, Pamela, brought him any comfort.

There was failure, too, in the professional domain. Perusing old documents did not bring him any enduring satisfaction. Certainly, George felt admiration for some exalted spirits driven by ideals that conferred a transcendent dimension on their lives, and he would often detect traces of this exaltation in his work as an archivist. But devoid of energy and self-confidence, and having lost his ability to dream and, consequently, to hope, he admitted to himself his inability to be inspired by their examples. Thus, summoned by the Judge like the others to designate an expiatory victim, he thinks seriously about sacrificing himself:

> I expect nothing, George Kirsten says to himself. He had never revolted against anyone or anything. He had let Marie-Anne dominate him. He was born resigned. Even his liaison with Pamela was an abdication more than a revolt. The discovery of the document and this trip to Israel? He had thought up till now that it would be the big event of his life. But now it had scarcely any importance…

> Disabused, the archivist had lost even the taste for discoveries. Life was unfolding without him, outside of him. He had not killed himself, the other day. What if he did it now, quite simply, by volunteering" (*LJ*, 189-190).

By temperament and character, Yoav, the fifth passenger sequestered at the Judge's home, is diametrically opposed to the archivist weighted down by the circumstances of life. A Captain in the Israeli army and leader of many commando operations, he always revealed himself as energetic, decisive and enterprising. He always knew why he was acting. He is fulfilled in a loving relationship. Furthermore, as a supreme blessing for a man not inclined to externalize his sentiments through words, his wife, Carméla, possessed the gift of deciphering them without his having to pour them out. Nevertheless, the thought of death has encroached upon him just as it has on George Kirsten.

The Israeli officer was devastated on the night his best friend and comrade in arms, Shmoulik, lost his life in an ambush. Since then, the image of the latter's shredded body never stopped haunting him. For Yoav, the lightning swiftness with which his friend was killed bordered on the unreal. For a long time he persisted in wanting to deny the evidence of Shmoulik's death because the loss of his friendship seemed irreparable: "Something inside of him refused to admit that a man like Shmoulik, who had stood his ground in the face of Death more than once, in more than one circumstance, could be extinguished like the flame of a candle in the wind" (*LJ*, 66). The officer's anguish was intensified by his knowledge that Shmoulik's wife, Lidia, was lusting after him, Yoav, and that his unfortunate friend was aware of it before dying. Out of nobility of soul, he refused to accuse Lidia of having thrown herself at him. As for Carméla, she had recourse to all the treasures of her intelligence and heart to persuade Shmoulik that all there was between his wife and Yoav was an affectionate friendship. But as the letter given to Yoav after his friend's death proved, the latter had never been duped by their attempt to preserve his illusion of marital happiness.

To this bereavement was added another, far more devastating: the death of his father. The latter's disappearance could not have come about at a worse time for the officer. By participating in these bloody events and seeing the destruction of his comrades, Yoav had lost his enthusiasm for life. It is not that he had succumbed totally to despair, but his soul was at a standstill: "It was over, my quest for nocturnal exaltation against the enemy" (*LJ*, 118). As though this existential sickness were not enough, the commando leader learned that he was dying of a brain tumor. In this crisis he had to face, only his father, an idealist of unbreakable fervor, could have come to his rescue. Speaking to him beyond the grave, his son asked him sorrowfully: "You who, in your way, believed in miracles, can you not perform one for me as well? Because I need one, now, to breathe in the freedom that you bequeathed to me on dying" (*LJ*, 119). Abandoned to his reflections while a vicious storm is seething, Yoav remembers the spiritual trajectory that brought his father back to the faith of his ancestors at the end of his life. Like Paltiel Kossover, this man venerated by his son had embraced Communism with the ardor of the neophyte before recoiling in horror and disgust on witnessing the application of the inhuman principle that the ends justified the means. Hating Evil and Death, its inseparable companion, he nonetheless accepted that war had to be waged against Isrrael's enemies so that his coreligionists' fragile chances for happiness would be safeguarded. When he gave up his military career, it was to immerse himself in the sacred texts of Judaism. They reinforced his belief that whenever men reincarnated the Messiah for one another, they were performing miracles.

Unfortunately, Yoav did not believe in miracles. The German doctor who was caring for him at the New York clinic had, however, strongly advised him to believe in them. Eager to repair the evil caused by the generation of his parents mesmerized by Hitler's diabolical magic spells, Dr. Heinrich Blaufeld would have done anything to save the life of the Jewish officer. Much more fatalistic, Yoav was waiting for the inevitable to occur. But although knowing he was condemned in the short term, he was not at all disposed to offer himself as a sacrificial victim to save the other sequestered people because on the one hand, they were nothing to him, and on the other, if he would agree to die in their place, he would be obliged to tell them why. Being a very proud man, he did not want their pity.

In front of these passengers racked with incertitude and anguish, stands their torturer in the psychological sense, the Judge. A pitiful megalomaniac and impenitent exhibitionist who bases his metaphysics of evil on shaky reasoning, the Judge deludes himself into thinking that he is implementing the will of the God of Death. His past is enveloped in rumors and mystery. From time to time, he provides the sequestered passengers as well as his acolyte, the Hunchback, with information on his life. Thus we "learn" that his mother had been a prostitute and his father a saint and that his wife and daughter had been raped and killed by a sadistic criminal. But being a congenital mythomaniac, all his declarations must be taken with a grain of salt. If we are to believe what he tells Razziel, his obsession with Evil was born after his encounter as a young man with a cynical guru who was all the more frightening because he knew how to decipher the most shameful secrets buried in the unfathomable depths of the being. Before that fateful event, he had been a loving son and destined for a brilliant future. As soon as he fell victim to the influence of that diabolical personage, he was overcome by vertigo and plummeted into the abyss. Quoting his former mentor, he says: "There is no perfection other than in evil…To do good is convenient; it is the first rule we teach children. To do evil is not. Only a courageous soul burning with energy is capable of revolting against thousands of years of laws, social contracts and religious dogmas" (*LJ*, 178).

The Judge, therefore, seeks transcendence through Evil. But it is a false transcendence, because crime leads to destruction and destruction ends in the void. Hence the incoherence of his arguments according to which God only shows his strength when he flies into a rage against His creation: "For me, life is a curse. By giving life, God reveals His weakness, except when he incarnates Evil. Then, and only then, does he come out victorious" (*LJ*, 177). To say that the Creator of the universe is powerful only when he embarks on destructive projects means acknowledging that He is a lamentable failure, since in that case He remains powerless to make cosmos triumph over chaos, love over hatred, and life over death.

But why is the Judge so anxious to venerate such an evil divinity? By analyzing his declarations and the Hunchback's observations on him, the answer becomes evident. This crazy man takes delight in sadism. He confesses to Razziel the intense pleasure he felt the first time he let a handicapped young man slide on the sidewalk. He also remembers with satisfaction the day he shoved an old man to make him fall. Towards the end of the novel, the Hunchback reveals to the detainees the psychological tortures his master enjoyed inflicting on him. Among the most monstrous was the diabolical script of the crucifixion. The Judge forced his slave to play the role of one of the robbers crucified by the side of Christ while he took on the part of a "corrupt and hateful Redeemer" (*LJ*, 194). And how can one explain his sequestration of the five passengers as well as his death threats against them other than as a manifestation of a sadistic craving for power?

Even when the Judge is, fiercely and unrelentingly, bent on punishing criminals, he is simply trying to assuage his appetite for domination and violence. Only then does he manage to rival God: "Man has only one desire, one ambition: to become a god of Death by assuming his power. Truth is no longer in life, but in death" (*LJ*, 179). This is why the Judge remakes God over in his own corrupted image. Absolute power resides for him in destruction and the latter remains synonymous with death. In this nihilistic context, killing innocent victims represents the supreme pleasure. By its nature, innocence escapes judgement. To annihilate it, is to prove to oneself that just like the diabolical God he venerates, he has the right to exert his absolute and arbitrary power wherever and whenever he chooses. But obviously committing evil does not provide him with any lasting satisfaction, since he feels the need to multiply his acts of cruelty. He has thus locked himself up in a vicious circle. Eager to escape the emptiness of his existence, he commits reprehensible acts to demonstrate his all-powerfulness, but this so-called all-powerfulness merely betrays even more the emptiness of his existence. This is perhaps why at the end of the novel the Judge allows himself to be "suicided" by the Hunchback and accepts his death as a form of deliverance.

Do I dare state that despite all my admiration for the novelistic talent of Elie Wiesel, the character of the Judge seems lacking in psychological complexity, therefore, in credibility? This personage seems crushed under the allegorical weight the author wishes him to bear. His rapid capitulation in the face of evil and the pathetic arguments he invokes to justify it prevent the reader from accepting him as an emissary of the God or gods of hell. I would like to propose another scenario. One could imagine a young man overcome with vertigo while peering into the abyss, overwhelmed with shame at the idea of discovering in himself this potential for evil. He would invoke the help of the God of mercy in whom he desperately yearns to believe and, in the face of the impenetrable silence of the Master of the universe, he would throw himself headlong into a destructive project to defy Him and punish Him for having created in him such a weak and despicable creature; then, overcome with self-loathing, he would commit suicide in front ot the five passengers while proclaiming that he was a sinner to whom God had refused His grace.

I feel an uneasiness of another kind concerning the Hunchback. As Jean-Pierre Denis remarks, he sometimes reminds us of the chorus in ancient Greek tragedies. This is evident in the highly oratorical style of his tirades. But then there occurs a break in tone that disconcerts the reader. The author wants us to accept the five passengers and their sequestration as being plausible. Now, by introducing a personage whose discourse belongs to a ritual tragedy, he creates an incongruous situation. As a result, the reader can no longer suspend his disbelief. This is all the more unfortunate since the Hunchback's personality carries within it extremely moving possibilities. A deformed soul just like his body, he nevertheless aspires to righteousness, he hides within his heart a secret, impossible love for Claudia, the sparkling redhead. Even though the author never alludes to it, the temptation is irresistible to see in the Hunchback an avatar of the character Quasimodo in the novel *Notre Dame de Paris* by Victor Hugo. Just like Quasimodo felt a heartrending tenderness for the beautiful Esmeralda, the Hunchback in Elie Wiesel's novel knows that his love for Claudia will remain unrequited. The novelist could have developed this tendency more and show how this unreciprocated passion served as a catalyst for the character's moral redemption.

One can also formulate criticisms as concerns the structure of the narrative. The sequestration of the five passengers and the attraction-repulsion relationships that their characters and interests represent contain an extremely dramatic potential that Elie Wiesel did not consider exploiting. He could have written an extraordinary novelistic *Huis-Clos* (No Exit) with gripping moral resonances that would have rivaled Jean-Paul Sartre's play. Given their increasing anguish and the necessity of reaching a decision, Claudia and Bruce who, nevertheless, experienced a profound antipathy for one another, could have contracted a singular alliance to save their right to love, drive the three others into a corner, and demand that one of them serve as the sacrificial victim. Their proposal would have finally touched off an explosion of anger in the taciturn officer, Yoav. He, too, would have clamored for the right to love, the right to return to Israel to die in the arms of his wife. Razziel and George would have then confronted one another to determine which of the two had the least to lose by sacrificing his life for the others. At times the author suggests the very fertile tensions that exist between the five characters, but these never fully materialize. The reader waits impatiently for an explosion that never takes place.

It is no doubt foolhardy and vain on the part of a literary critic to propose other ways in which an author could have organized the material of his novel. But this act testifies indirectly to one's immense admiration for the novelist's imaginary universe. Because if the hallmark of a literary work consists in its ability to make of the reader a creator to the second degree by firing up his mind, this novel, despite certain flaws, obviously deserves to be read and discussed. It also shows that in an author of Elie Wiesel's stature, nothing is negligeable.

The Time of the Uprooted

It was inevitable that, sooner or later, Elie Wiesel would devote a whole novel to the theme of uprootedness. Many of the memorable characters from works of fiction he produced before the beginning of the 21st century find themselves uprooted as much in the physical as in the spiritual sense. Let us recall that, among others, Elisha in *Dawn*, Michael in *The Town Beyond the Wall*, Grégor in *The Gates of the Forest* and David in *A Beggar in Jerusalem* all feel they have been exiled. In the case of Paltiel Kossover in *The Testament*, it is a question of rediscovering the roots he had torn out himself in his insane endeavor to participate in the transformation of humanity according to the Marxist doctrine. The subject, therefore, contains a very grave significance. On reading the text, however, I experienced the same kind of malaise I felt when perusing *The Judges*. Certain passages are among the most beautiful the author has ever written. Other parts left me with the same impression of a weakening of his inspiration that I had noticed in his previous novel.

The Time of the Uprooted (2003) is organized around an event taking place unexpectedly that causes an upheaval in the life of the hero, Gamliel Friedman. An old woman of Hungarian origin, Zsuzsi Szabo, has been very seriously injured and disfigured as a result of a car accident. She is dying in a New York City hospital. The lady doctor who is caring for her asks Gamliel, a former citizen of Hungary, to serve as an interpreter since the elderly woman does not appear to speak any other language. When he hears the news, a searing pain mixed with strange hope flashes through his heart. Could she be the marvelous cabaret singer, Ilonka, her mother's best friend and a sublimely devoted saint? She was the one who had risked her own life many times to save his during the Nazi reign of terror in Budapest. She was the one who had been a mother to him after his parents were denounced by antisemites, shoved into cattle cars and shipped to the crematory ovens. Ilonka was supposed to have joined him in Paris after the failed insurrection in Hungary against the tyrannical communist regime in 1956. She had promised to meet him there and had always kept her promises. This time, however, she missed the rendezvous. Gamliel never again saw the woman whom he still reveres.

During a period of forty-eight hours that elapses between the first visit Gamliel pays to the old Hungarian lady enclosed in her mutism and the final one when he witnesses her death, he reflects sorrowfully on an existence that seems a failure from almost all points of view. All kinds of memories flood his consciousness, and not necessarily in chronological order. At sixty years old Gamliel is tired of living, disenchanted, helpless, convinced he has not fulfilled his artistic potential or his possibilities as a human being. He wends his way through the fragments of his memory as though he were walking through the corridors of a labyrinth without an exit, desperately searching for a comforting reality or at least a unifying principle likely to give a meaning to his interior chaos. In reality, the seemingly fragmented and disconnected structure of the novel, oscillating between the present and the past, serves as a metaphor to depict the protagonist's tormented personality. The events of his life resemble the scattered pieces of a gigantic puzzle that he has not been able to put together even on the threshold of old age.

The novelist organizes this apparent disorder with extreme skillfulness. He reveals elements that are indispensable for understanding Gamliel's character at the moments when they will produce their maximal effects. Two examples will illustrate the author's masterful technique. We know as of the first quarter of the novel that Gamaliel's experience as a father has been a disaster: "Gamliel thinks about his daughters, Katya so far away, Sophie so estranged, both hostile and, just like before, a pain sharp enough to take his breath away traverses his body." [21] But we will have to wait until

---

[21] Elie Wiesel, *Le Temps des déracinés*, Paris : Éditions du Seuil, 2003, 68; referred to henceforth as *TD*.

almost the end of the book to understand the reasons for the girls' hostility. Gamliel rereads the last letters his daughters sent him before breaking off with him for good at the very moment in his life when he has the impression of being swallowed up irreversibly into a spiritual black hole. In the second-to-last page of the novel, the hero remembers the reverence with which his mother would celebrate the Sabbath when lighting the candles despite the Nazi peril that threatened them. This memory forms a stunning contrast with his reading of his daughters' letters. The recollection of these fragments of his past as a boy touched off by the discovery of two candles among the personal effects of the deceased old Hungarian woman enables Gamliel to resolve the enigma of his own destiny and, consequently, not only to move beyond his depression but to triumph over it.

Before being reconciled with himself, however, Gamliel is tormented by the sentiment of his uprootedness. He is not the only one either. His closest friends, all Jewish like himself, all traumatized by the murderous events of the 20th century, feel the same helplessness. For them as well as for the hero, the uprootedness they suffer is not essentially of a geographic order, even though that element is not excluded. It is rather an incurable wound caused by experiences that seem to deny man the possibility of dominating the primitive brute he carries within him. After traversing their own forms of hell, after witnessing the unleashing of the worst passions during the final years of the 20th century, not one of the friends in this group can believe any longer in the ideals of their youth. They no longer have a spiritual magnetic pole towards which to direct their lives. Not one of them can accept himself fully. Each one feels he is living on the periphery of a human condition and civilization that he cannot willingly assume. Hence the extreme wariness that the idea of happiness brings out in them. Let us listen to Gamliel: "An old man struck dumb in front of his sons whose throats were slit, in Rwanda. Cadavers in a common grave in Bosnia. A universe of barbed wire and smoke under a bloody sky. When one of the members of our little group of crazies would dare evoke happiness as a goal, a duty or an eventuality, Diego would yell out, roaring with laughter: Hey, you guys! Look at him! At last, someone who believes in happiness! He deserves a prize! The century's Grand prize for imbeciles!" (*TD*, 250-251).

Diego has cast aside all ideologies that promise man a radiant future, whether they come from the right or the left. With inexhaustible verve and energy, he flays all those who allow themselves to be mesmerized by idealistic mirages. Neither does Iasha believe in social doctrines that will save us from ourselves; he does not have any confidence in History to lead humanity inevitably towards a better future. As a translator during Stalin's reign of terror, he was indirectly responsible for the death of a very talented Jewish poet who was totally devoted to the communist regime. By interpreting a few anodyne allusions of one of the poet's texts to imply a criticism of Russian socialism, Iasha, to his horror, provided proof of the guilt of his coreligionist. As a result, the latter was shot like so many other innocents in that dreadful period. Gad, another comrade within the group of friends, never forgave himself for having played an infamous role as a secret agent for the Mossad, Israel's information agency. A Jewish American journalist with a big heart towards whom he felt a deep attraction, took him for a Nazi sympathizer, a role he played to perfection in order to worm his way more easily into antisemitic Arab milieus. She showed utter contempt for Gad and he was powerless to reveal the truth to her.

But of Gamliel's four chums, Bolek was the one who hid behind a serene façade the most devastating anguish. One day, he shared a terrible secret with the hero. As the leader of a group of resistance fighters in Poland during the Second World War, Bolek discovered to his horror that the traitor responsible for having delivered information to the SS about the places where coreligionists of theirs were hiding during a raid in the ghetto, was the son of one of the members of the Jewish community, a man of utmost generosity and integrity. Bolek was torn between his conception of justice demanding that the guilty perish and Jewish law that forbids murder. His dilemma was complicated by the fact that on the one hand, the spy had handed over his own family to the Nazis, and on the other, that the father of the treacherous young man was overcome with a sorrow that aroused sincere pity in Bolek's heart. A half-century after that event, Bolek continues being tormented by remorse, as though he could not forgive himself for not possessing divine omniscience. Thanks to a lightning-swift intuition, Gamliel understands the moral agony that Bolek and his comrades endured during that time, and that they continue enduring at present. He formulates it in the form of a question: "Were they afraid to resemble their own executioners by punishing one of their own?" (*TD*, 195). Bolek strives to deaden this permanent pain through paternal love. He has a daughter, Léa, whom he adores, to whom he seems even more attached than to his charming wife, Noémie. But, as we will find out later, this precious relationship remains extremely fragile. It will take very little for it to break.

Although Rabbi Zousia is not part of Gamliel's band of chums, he nevertheless exerts a considerable influence over him, especially on the spiritual level. On the surface, this venerable wise man seems the opposite of an uprooted person since he is sustained by an ardent faith and possesses, as a result, a spiritual centre of gravity that prevents him from getting lost in the shadows of doubt. Indeed, he reproaches Gamliel more than once for drowning himself in dark despair and exhorts him to commit himself fully to life. But in his way, Zousia, too, feels he is in exile. There exists an unbridgeable distance between himself, a creature as imperfect as he is mortal, and the God of Israel, infinite Wisdom, and soul of the universe as inexhaustible as it is indestructible. Hence the anguished question he asks about the need the Creator supposedly has for his creatures: "For what reason would He need them, He who is the beginning, the end and the rebirth of all that is, of all that will be? I no longer understand" (*TD*, 78). In the face of the Creator's refusal to intervene in the unfolding of history to prevent the massacre of innocents, Zousia calls out to Him in vehement terms, and even threatens to put an end to their spiritual partnership which is the duty of every practicing Jew: "...if You have forgotten the nighttime procession of Jewish children walking towards the flames, God of charity, I will tell my prayer to scream, I will no longer have the strength to invoke your sacred name, I will order my mind to close in on itself forever" (*TD*, 78).

These reproaches blasted out against God reflect an individual with exemplary energy. Moreover, Zousia will fight to the death to accelerate the coming of the Messiah. What a contrast, then, with Gamliel Friedman who admires this Rabbi. Do I dare admit it? The hero, as Elie Wiesel has depicted him, seems to me the most obvious weakness in the novel. This is because I have inevitably compared him to other protagonists in the author's fictional world who have aroused my enthusiasm by their strength of character and their will to live, by their refusal to accept the world as it is without at least trying to modify it. He pales in comparison to Michaël, David and Paltiel Kossover, all three uprooted individuals in their different ways. Even the narrator of *The Fifth Son* shows more initiative.

What adds to my disappointment is the break in the development of Gamliel's personality. As a child under the Russian occupation after the defeat of the Nazis and the end of the Second World War, young Gamliel shows immense and spontaneous courage in defending his benefactress, Ilonka. When a drunken Russian soldier is on the verge of grabbing hold of her to rape her, the boy protests with such moving vehemence that he draws the attention of an officer of the Soviet army. The latter not only puts an end to the soldier's violence but insists that Ilonka and her protégé jump the queue in front of the bakery to be able to obtain bread. Later in the novel, two Hungarian officers plus a Russian one and a civilian burst into the apartment where Ilonka and Gamliel are shuddering in fear and cold. They are about to arrest the cabaret singer for being a Nazi collaborator. The boy saves her a second time by declaring that without her, he, as a Jew, would have already perished. His devotion towards his benefactress is unconditional. He tells them he is ready to follow her to prison. He insists on sharing her suffering. The Russian officer is so impressed by Gamliel's generous conduct that he orders the others to release Ilonka. In 1956, when the insurrection breaks out in Hungary against the Russian presence, Gamliel, now a young man, bravely participates in it.

Why then is it that the hero seems to lose this magnificent combativeness once he has left Hungary to remake his life in the West? Once he arrives in Paris, Gamliel becomes exasperatingly spineless. He tends to submit to events instead of endeavoring to modify them in his favor. Naturally, one can understand that his feeling of being an exile intensifies with time. It is normal to feel overburdened after having endured such heavy losses. But other heroes created by Elie Wiesel have suffered as much without allowing themselves to be dragged down into passive acceptance of what fate imposes on them. They can draw from within their inner reservoir enough energy to reconstruct themselves. Why can't Gamliel do the same? We will answer this question by analyzing the nature of his uprootedness.

Geography counts for practically nothing in Gamliel's distress. He does not express any nostalgia either for his native Czechoslovakia or for Hungary where he grew up. His sickness comes from elsewhere. The first major wound inflicted on Gamliel is the disappearance of his father during the Nazi occupation when he was a young child. As a result, he suffers from an emotional and spiritual void that he still cannot fill. His father could have been his closest friend. Tormented at sixty years old by the absence in his life of a paternal presence, Gamliel is convinced, a half-century after the Holocaust, that it would have been preferable to share his barely known father's fate than to live with hazy memories: "And if I had accompanied him to prison, then to the camp? Gamliel wondered. I would not feel the void which, sometimes, drags me down like a black whirlpool." (*TD*, 204). He misses the mother he adored, too, along with the tender and comforting solicitude that radiated from her person as well as her unostentatious courage. But at least he had Ilonka to alleviate his solitude during the terrible years following his mother's deportation.

To this family uprooting is added a kind of intellectual alienation. To survive in France, Gamliel becomes a ghost writer for authors devoid of talent but hyper-endowed with money. Whenever he is overcome by despair, he almost considers himself a purveyor of lies, a kind of literary prostitute who simulates emotions he does not feel in the least. In that respect, he compares himself to Samaël, an impenitent seducer, an imposter of consummate cynicism, whose goal is to project pernicious illusions as a means of snaring multiple victims: "As for his trade: all those pages filled with signs, all those ideas, those situations, those conflicts he imagined and which others appropriated, was that not yet another deformation of the truth? And, in that case, what was the difference between him and Samaël? Was it conceivable that a Samaël existed in each human being, thus in him as well? But then, how to eliminate it without dying the same death?" (*TD*, 260). To redeem himself, the hero undertakes a grandiose work titled *The Secret Book*. We read excerpts from it scattered through the novel. He would like his text to evoke magnificently the confrontation between two great religions, the Christian and the Jewish, two divergent visions of the idea of redemption. He yearns to suggest the tumult of different historical epochs that collide. He is eager to orchestrate in his text the essential themes of our human condition. In other words, Gamliel wants so much for this book he believes in to be a major contribution to universal knowledge. Based on the fragments that he affords us in *The Time of the Uprooted*, his *Secret Book* deals with a monumental confrontation between a Hungarian Catholic archbishop, Jànos Bàranyi, a religious fanatic and, therefore, a virulent antisemite, and a Jewish spiritual master, Hananël, a specialist in the Kabbalah. The latter possesses the power to penetrate the sanctuaries of people's souls like a laser beam and to extract from them the most shameful secrets that are hidden there. In an exciting scene, Hananël has recourse to his spiritual energy to floor the archbishop and force him to save the Jewish community from persecution. In a sense Gamliel is attempting to redress on the level of fiction the innumerable wrongs inherent in real life by creating a character who combines within him stature, idealism and purity.

When he has the time to devote to literary creation, Gamliel lives a most exciting drama with words. For him, they are not simply signs or intellectual concepts. They vibrate with a mysterious life, conduct themselves like independent beings that one must know how to dominate. Sometimes they put up fierce resistance against the writer's will, at other times they allow themselves to be cuddled. Here is what the hero notes: "They can be the writer's best friends, but also exhausting challenges. When they refuse to submit, or at least to let themselves be tamed, Gamaliel suffered like a sick man in need of a fix. But when they consented to allow themselves to be led and harassed by his inflamed imagination, he blessed his happiness and the whole of Creation" (*TD*, 29-30). Given his unusual talent, the reader often wonders why Gamliel doesn't have the courage to abandon his galley-slave trade, complete the volume, leave anonymity behind him, and assert himself as a writer recognized by the public at large. Is he not worth infinitely more than the laughable braggarts who have exploited his ideas to strut around in front of the media? Why this inability to act on his own behalf? Why this inertia? The publishing world is a cramped and almost incestuous place. People know one another. If the hero had shown determination, could he not have found an editor of quality or an influential intercessor capable of launching his career? Gamliel's creator, Elie Wiesel himself, began his career thanks to the support of François Mauriac. There was also another possible way for Gamliel Friedman to gain success. He could have practiced legitimate blackmail against the publishing houses for which he worked as a ghost writer. He could have threatened to circulate rumors according to which certain of their most popular writers had their novels composed by others. He could have made good on that threat unless the publishing houses agreed to produce his own books under his real name.

His spinelessness manifests itself equally in his disastrous marriage with Colette, a very singular woman he encountered by chance in Paris and reinforces the impression that in the domain of love, too, Gamliel is unable to find fulfillment. Despite his lucidity, Gamliel lets himself be dragged into a relationship with a woman who will never be able to offer him the emotional and comforting plenitude that is missing in his life since the death of his mother. Colette is authoritarian, domineering, explosive. Very cut and dried about everything, she constantly behaves like an actress in a melodrama. Either she loves someone to distraction, or she hates him with a vengeful fury. Gamliel must have known intuitively that this passionate attraction could never last, because even after moving in with her, he refused to give up his own apartment and had no desire to stop visiting as often as in the past his comrades Bolec, Diego and Gad.

Why then does he agree to marry her? Several motives explain his decision. There is first of all the excitement of the senses that she sets off in him. Colette is like a force of nature in bed. Her nocturnal inventions are cunningly calculated and conceived for the purpose of making her husband live tumultuous dramas. Secondly, she seems to truly wish to fill the emotional void that has opened up in his uprooted heart. She seeks to recreate her husband to make him forget his tragic past. She even wants to exorcize it. For this reason, she insists on calling him Péter, the Hungarian name used by Ilonka to hide his Jewish identity, even though Colette is Jewish herself. But like any tragic heroine of the 17th century French playwright, Jean Racine, who burns with passion, to bring happiness to the beloved means to constitute this happiness exclusively.

Aware of her hyper-possessive and tyrannical nature, Gamliel should have sensed that the worst would occur in this long-term relationship. Colette's tendency to multiply her hare-brained ideas should have put him on his guard. He thought that perhaps the acquisition of French citizenship through marriage would make up for the annoyances he would have to endure, and that all he had to do was suffer in silence. What a pitiful illusion! He did not reckon with his wife's perspicacity. She was no doubt crazy, but she was far from being stupid. Realizing that the man she though she adored could not be transformed, she finally spewed out all her contempt for him: "I loved you, I married you for one reason: I wanted to offer you the happiness of which life deprived you. Apparently, I have failed. You are happy only with your uprooted chums. You have more to share with them than with me. All right, go back to them. Leave this house. Let us separate. The sooner will be the better for everyone" (*TD*,210). Once their twin girls become conscious enough to observe that their parents are living an infernal relationship, Colette succeeds in poisoning their mind, encouraging them to hate their father as much as she does. Katya and Sophie will always hold their father responsible for their mother's suicide. Thus, through his lack of energy, the hero becomes the artisan of his own misfortune.

What a contrast one notes between Gamliel's spinelessness and Ilonka's exceptional energy. She was the sublime lady who protected him during the Nazi occupation of Budapest! Here was a fighter! A practicing Catholic without complications or states of mind, she did not need to know about the mystics of her religious faith or those of the Jewish one to understand that the relationship of man and woman with the Creator of the universe resembles a partnership. In her own simple and moving way, Ilonka knew that we must all embody the Messiah in our daily life to help God improve the world. Indeed, we are indispensable to Him for curbing or at least slowing down the progression of evil. According to her, miracles exist, but people must create them themselves by deploying all their psychic, spiritual and physical energies towards that goal. This is how she explains her philosophy to the little boy that Gamliel once was: "If you want the Lord to help you, son, you must help him, too. One must not let him cope alone with the crazies, the imbeciles, the bastards who run about in his miserable little world inhabited by scoundrels more than by saints: why would you want all this to fall on his shoulders? You must give him a helping hand, do you understand?" (*TD*, 76).

Ilonka is a woman of uncorruptible integrity. She knows instinctively how to distinguish between what is noble and what is ignoble. She knows that to persecute vulnerable Jewish children in the name of a false ideology of racial superiority is a crime. She does not reach this conclusion through deep intellectual reflection on the responsibilities that each individual must assume towards his fellow man/woman. There is no Kantian categorical imperative that influences her conduct. No religious illumination commands her to act virtuously in favor of the oppressed. It is her immense, natural and inexhaustible goodness that inspires her at every moment. This is what Gamliel thinks a half-century later when he evokes the memory of the cabaret singer with tenderness and admiration during a conversation with the doctor, Lili Rosencrantz: "She was a religious person, but her saintliness had nothing to do with her religion. Only with her heart, a good and generous one that can no longer be found. Do you understand? Ilonka was human, admirably human. For me, this places her higher than any saint" (*TD*, 117). Without being aware of it, Ilonka would illustrate at every hour of her existence one of the fundamental principles of Judaism: fighting tirelessly to make humanity always more human. The great Franco-Jewish philosopher, Emmanuel Lévinas would have applauded heartily.

Ilonka's idealism is what makes her soul rust-proof on the spiritual as well as on the moral levels during the worst degradations she is forced to endure to protect her "Jewish child." At various times the Hungarian fascist police subjects her to brutal cross-examinations that include rape and physical blows that make her cry out in pain, so that she will denounce Jews who are hiding in the city. She is obliged to sleep with repulsive Nazi collaborators to keep her job and guarantee Gamliel's safety. But these dreadful experiences have no effect whatsoever on her nature. Ilonka sets up an unsurmountable line of demarcation between the conduct she cannot avoid adopting to survive, and her noble conception of human relations that she is determined to put into practice once the dirty war is over. A woman of unshakeable courage, she bears the sordid present as best she can, but projects herself into a radiant future so that her morale will never flinch. Let us listen to the words that pass through her mind after little Gamliel falls asleep in her arms at the cabaret: "One day... I will sing for him, I will give him joy, I will make him laugh, I will rid him of his fear; I will show him the beauty of happiness. One day, I will talk to him about my childhood; one day, I will make love for love. One day, I will look at a man's body without being disgusted. Then, I will think about myself without repulsion, without remorse. One day, I will really live, I will live from morning till evening, I will smile when I want to, I will give pleasure to men who please me, one day I will wait for the evening without anguish" (*TD*, 90).

Another time, before sleeping with a repugnant man, the head of the Hungarian fascists, she kisses the forehead of Gamliel asleep on the sofa of her apartment. The words she utters express the same poignant nostalgia for the kind of purity that no human contact will ever sully: "Péter, are you asleep? That's good. Sleep, my little boy. Sleep. Have beautiful dreams. It is better that way" (*TD*, 119).

It is not far-fetched to think that in every woman he falls in love with Galiel persists in looking for another Ilonka as well as the mother he lost. He needs the protective generosity of the first as well as the soft radiance of the second. Thanks to a blessed chance encounter, at sixty years old the hero finally finds the ideal woman in the person of the doctor Lili Rosencrantz. But before attaining this happiness, he will have to live exalting as well as heartbreaking experiences with three other women: Colette, Esther and Éve. We have seen how the first adventure ended in tragedy. With Esther and Éve one might venture to say that he was stumbling towards an ideal that he had trouble defining clearly. This is because those two lovers realized his dream very imperfectly. Esther, of Moroccan origin, fascinated him as though she were a living oriental tale. From her voice, her eyes, her whole body floated a mystery impossible to pin down. If Gamliel had been more enterprising, he could have conquered the heart of this young woman. But paralyzed by his inexperience, he let her escape and never saw her again.

When he encounters Éve, he is much more mature and has been settled in New York city for many years. Éve is a very experienced lady. She does everything to discourage him from loving her: "I bring bad luck," she asserts solemnly (*TD*, 213). Indeed, she drags behind her a tragic history. She lost her husband and daughter in a car accident. Her conjugal life is a forbidden zone that one must never attempt to enter. She refuses to use the word "love" even when their relationship acquires a dimension of ardent sensuality. Gamliel should have been on his guard. But Ève possesses an intellectual vivacity, a physical beauty and a charm that finally captivates him. Moreover, when they are together, he is convinced that she is as indispensable to his blossoming forth as he is to hers. He is certain that the soul of that woman holds the key to the understanding of the universe. Through the agency of their love, he will learn how to decipher its secrets:

> Yes, it was her.
>
> He would use her to open nocturnal doors in her body and in his soul.
>
> And they would achieve a happiness grounded in their humanity and forever expanding (*TD*, 229).

Unfortunately, Gamliel's exalted dream evaporates like a mirage in the desert. One day Ève informs him that she is going to leave him. Despite the aversion she supposedly felt towards marriage, she is going to marry a satanically cynical, notorious seducer, Samaël, of whom we have already spoken. We never find out the real reasons that have impelled this woman who is rather whimsical on the edges to make such a bizarre decision, and this seems to me yet another weakness in the novel. Here the author could have developed a series of episodes that would have lent themselves to exciting psychological analyses. He could have kept the reader in suspense by answering the following questions during the unfolding of the narrative: Did Ève leave Gamliel because she remained pessimistic about how long passion could last? Did she believe that theirs had already reached its apex and was going to wither away? Did she see in Samaël an exciting challenge? Did she decide to marry him in a spirit of self-sacrifice or because she suffered from a martyr complex, so that Léa, Bolek's daughter, would be saved from a sinister predator? Was her belief in the tragic dimension of our human condition so ingrained in her that she resolved to self-destruct as a way of practicing existential overkill?

Whatever her motives, without knowing it, Ève does Gamliel an immense favor by getting out of his life, because he will be free to link his destiny to that of the lady doctor. Naturally, at the outset the hero feels devastated. Here is another failure added to so many other bitter disappointments that a malevolent fate seems to take pleasure in piling up to prove to him that his life is an exemplary flop. Enclosed in a solitude that he thinks henceforth is permanent, he feels sorry for himself: "And I, I drag myself along like an old tramp looking for a shelter that exists nowhere" (*TD*, 249). But Elie Wiesel has gotten us used to sudden changes in direction in his novels, to miracles on the human plane that burst on the scene without warning. Gamliel falls in love with the forty-year-old doctor, Lili Rosencrantz, who is caring for the elderly Hungarian lady, Zsuzsi Sabo. She turns out to be the ideal companion to accompany him in the autumn of his existence. Lili has a serene beauty that enchants him. She reveals a depth of being that is equal in its way to the mystery that emanated from Esther. Even her sadness adds to the charm of her presence. (Her husband has just left her.) She has the energetic, decisive personality of Colette without the demonic irrationality that was inseparable from the latter. She possesses a lively and sharp intelligence that is every bit worthy of Eve's. She overflows with the generosity and tenderness that characterized the two women whom Gamliel has forever worshipped: his mother and Ilonka. And she adores hearing his stories. Is it surprising, then, that he feels "blessed" when holding her hand? (*TD*, 267).

In fact, Gamliel feels so fulfilled in the doctor's presence that he wonders whether chance has for once acted with imagination and compassion by bringing them together at the bedside of the old dying Hungarian woman. But is Zsuzsi Szabo really the cabaret singer Ilonka? Has she come to die in this New York City hospital to "help him discover the love of that woman and to accept her in his existence?" (*TD*, 291). In his heart of hearts, Gamliel does not believe this, even though he fervently wishes that it were true. It doesn't matter, however. The marvelous Ilonka dominates the final pages of the novel in a spiritual form. Having temporarily assumed the identity of Zsuzsi Szabo in the hero's imagination, she has made possible the coming together of two individuals bruised by life, who were unconsciously searching for one another. Thanks to Ilonka/Zsuzsi, Gamliel and Lili will be able to resume living rather than simply keep going. The redemptive note on which *The Time of the Uprooted* ends makes the novel's conclusion one of the most comforting that the author has ever written. The love Lili Rosencranz bears Gamliel will finally allow the uprooted hero to put down roots in a stable and rich emotional soil.

A Mad Desire to Dance

There exists a passage in the autobiographical narrative, *Little Bibles for Bad Times* by Liliane Atlan, a Franco-Jewish writer who was a contemporary and friend of Elie Wiesel, that could have served as an epigraph for his novel *A Mad Desire to Dance* (2006). In the section of her text titled "The Passersby," Atlan observes that despite the despair with which she feels at times overwhelmed, life contains within itself a kind of grace in the form of elemental energy which compels us to reject nihilism and death:

At times the pain is such that it becomes indestructible.

The story cannot go on.

Yet it does go on, and that is perhaps the greatest miracle of all.[22]

Doriel, Wiesel's tormented hero, illustrates this reflection at the end of the novel by throwing himself without hesitation into a great adventure of love in the twilight of his existence.

With this book, the author makes a stunning comeback on the literary scene. In his two preceding novels *The Judges* and *The Time of the Uprooted*, we noticed a flagging of his inspiration. Here his creativity bounces back in an impressive manner. As in *The Time of the Uprooted*, Wiesel insists on the repercussions of the Holocaust on the consciousness of his hero. But although that event influences directly and indirectly the destiny of Doriel, in this work the novelist places the greatest tragedy of the Jewish people in an entirely different perspective from that of his other heroes. The Shoah appears in *A Mad Desire to Dance* as the unavoidable traumatism of the 20th century as much on the spiritual and intellectual planes as on the moral one, and a traumatism that has left an indelible imprint on the vision that our contemporaries continue to entertain concerning their human condition in the first quarter of our 21st century.

When the story commences, we are at the very beginning of the 2000s. Consequently, the Event is already situated in a relatively remote past. The characters no longer dwell on its multiple horrors. But even though they are brief, their evocations of it remain heartrending. When they refer to that most nightmarish of epochs, it remains for them an incurable wound with which they have managed to live. Twenty years following the Second World War Samek Ternover, Doriel's billionaire benefactor, can establish a certain distance vis-à-vis the excruciatingly painful experience he had lived in Nazi-occupied Poland. In several sharp, succinct phrases he describes

---

[22] Liliane Atlan, *Petites Bibles pour mauvais temps*, Paris : L'Harmattan, 2001, 39.

for the hero the systematic degradation to which the concentration camp detainees were subjected. The human being who was meant to aspire to infinity was brutally plunged into non-being: "The individual became unrecognizable, stripped of everything, beyond anything. For us, the city shrank to a street, the street to a building, the building to a room, the room to a cattle car; one's fortune was reduced to a bundle of clothing, the bundle to a bowl, and happiness to a miserable and sole potato. And man with an incommensurable potential was nothing more than a mere number, and the number became ashes."[23]

Thus, the Holocaust touches off a meditation on the madness that lies in wait permanently for the human being, on the abyss of cruelty and chaos into which he risks falling, and, by contrast, on the fragile nature of the happiness he pursues tirelessly.

This meditation is organized around the hero, Doriel. When we meet him at the beginning of the novel, he is an extremely mature man in his early sixties. He seeks out the help of a psychiatrist, Thérèse Goldschmidt, to cure him of the pathologic anguish that bears down on him to the point of asphyxiating him spiritually. Whenever he is upset by a word, a phrase, a recollection or a sudden association of ideas, the hero starts dredging up secrets that had been repressed for a long time. During the sessions that last several years, however, he persists in hiding his essential hangups. Doriel describes his visits at Dr. Goldschmidt's office in the first person, shares with the reader his reflections on the spiritual malaise that is undermining him, refers to himself sometimes in the third person, and speaks occasionally to his deceased parents as though to find in them the comfort and tenderness that are sorely lacking in his life. It is only at the end of the novel that Doriel confirms what we have suspected for a while: he is composing his text several years after having stopped his treatment with the psychiatrist, and at the moment when, fulfilled at last in a love marriage with a woman much younger than him, he awaits the birth of his first child. It is for them, therefore, as well as for his parents, that he intends the book he has almost finished. But *A Mad Desire to Dance* has another side to it. It evokes the drama that Thérèse Goldschmidt lives through in her relationship with a patient who both fascinates and disturbs her. She jots down her reactions in her own diary. As we will discover, these two narratives are necessary for us to fully understand the torment that

---

[23] Elie Wiesel, *Un désir fou de danser*, Paris : Éditions du Seuil, 2006, 299; referred to henceforth as *DF*.

is overwhelming the protagonist and the puzzled reaction he sets off in supposedly "normal" people.

Doriel Waldman upsets his therapist because he presents himself too often to her as an adversary to be confronted rather than a patient to be cared for. He desperately seeks out her help but fiercely and unrelentingly opposes her attempts to uncover the shameful key motive that will no doubt lead to the source of his illness. By turns moving and hostile, sincere and a wildly inventive storyteller, anguished and fantastically playful, the hero does not allow his secrets to be captured by the Freudian methods of analysis that Dr. Goldschmidt applies. Moreover, she senses within him a dimension of excruciatingly painful spirituality that remains impermeable to her probing. Indeed, Doriel is not only an individual who suffers atrociously but seems to embody the pessimistic consciousness of our present epoch which wonders whether the human species will be condemned sooner or later by its omnivorous selfishness. Being of the Jewish faith, the hero knows what the role of every man and woman should be during their existence on earth: "To help the Creator make His creation more welcoming and His creatures more righteous, more charitable" (*DF*, 307). Unfortunately, fear, anguish, doubt and guilt make of his existence a kind of torture chamber that prevents him from seeking a reason to live in this lofty ideal.

All these emotions as well as their spiritual and moral repercussions create in Doriel a form of madness of a pathological intensity. Doriel acknowledges this at the very beginning of his narrative. Speaking of the redeeming love that his young wife has brought him, he asks himself the following questions: "Has she saved me from the mute death that resignation to solitude implies? Of madness in its terminal phase, too, I emphasize the word "terminal," the way one talks about a cancer when it is incurable?" (*DF*, 11). The illness afflicting the hero seems all the more singular since he did not go through the hell of the concentration camps. As a child in Poland under the Nazi occupation, he certainly was familiar with hunger, fear and humiliation. But other coreligionists like his former Talmudic master, Reb Yohanan and the latter's wife, Rivka, suffered much more in their flesh and spirit. They had been part of the last convoy to Auschwitz. They had survived "the daily horrors and the selection at Birkenau" (*DF*, 135). Once liberated, they did not plummet into an irremediable despair. If Doriel has allowed himself to be subjugated by his ill-being, it is because other factors have come into play to aggravate it: a hyper-sharp sensitivity, a memory that seems to overflow from all sides and an imagination that borders on delirium.

At the time he speaks of it to his psychiatrist, the madness of which he is a prisoner submerges him to the point that he is convinced, as he tells her, that he has become the victim of a *dibbouk*. According to Jewish legend, a *dibbouk* is an identity thief. It is the damned soul, wandering and exiled, of a person already dead who seeks to capture that of a live human being. Once that damned soul has taken possession of the other, the individual thus subjugated is certain that he has lost his self-mastery. Instead of deciding freely how he will act, he undergoes the influence of someone else who is organically linked to him without, however, being him. As Doriel explains to his incredulous therapist, the *dibbouk* manifests itself as a protean and imperious being: "When he invades a person, the dibbouk is omnipresent, cunning, but not always diabolical, since he suffers... Agile, unpredictable, determined and devoid of scruples, he drags me off like a prisoner laden with chains; his salvation depends on mine, but at the same time mine is conditioned by his" (*TD*,30). Thus, to paraphrase the poet Arthur Rimbaud's famous statement, Doriel is convinced that his "I" has become an "other." He feels the presence in himself of a being who is nourished by his flesh and blood while having an independent life of his own. Hence his tendency to oscillate between frenetic activity and apathy; hence the intestinal warfare that takes place in his consciousness. Hence his belief that he must find a way of getting out of the labyrinth where he is trapped with his *dibbouk* so that he can regain his self-possession. This is the substance of a long conversation he has with the venerable poet, Reb Yitzhok, whom Doriel has sought out, almost in despair, to find a remedy for his spiritual and moral sickness. The luminous wisdom of the master will, perhaps, help him reconquer his identity: " I expect from you, I told him, in a hesitating tone, that you will guide me towards the path that will bring me back to myself" (*DF*, 291). Although Doriel believes literally in the existence of the *dibbouk*, the non-believer can legitimately interpret it as the metaphor for a grave deterioration of mental health that brings on a dysfunctional behavior bordering on nihilism.

And yet the anguish that has been bearing down on the sexagenarian since his childhood did not always get the better of him. Before the unleashing of the Second World War, Doriel, as a little child, blossomed forth in an atmosphere of salutary religious spirituality. Conscious in his way of the Jewish notion that the eternity of the God of Israel reveals itself in every instant of earthly life, he would welcome the Sabbath with joy. In fact, even after reaching adulthood, this memory of celebrations on the seventh day continued illuminating the shadows of his ill-being and softened them with its sweetness: "The child in me remembers with nostalgia: I would hum while walking from the prayer house with my father, and when I became bigger, both of us would sing the *Shalom aléi-hem, malakhéi hasharét*, "Peace to you, serving angels, angels of peace," and my child's heart would burst with happiness" (*DF*, 119). Even during the war little Doriel enjoyed moments of genuine emotional and spiritual plenitude. About fifty years later, the adult he has become describes for his therapist a *seder*, or meal shared by the family during *Pessah*, or Passover, in which he participated. The joy that reigned at that time between the members of his family, the looks of tenderness his parents exchanged have remained so real for him that he feels, when recalling that evening, the need to pray: 'And I who have not prayed for eternities, I feel a prayer gushing from my heart that suddenly desires to reach the celestial throne, but it expires as it flies upwards" (*DF*, 123).

If this prayer "expires as it flies upwards," it is because the war with its trail of horrors and its far-reaching consequences have shaken if not destroyed his confidence in human nature. An impressionable child, he witnesses directly and indirectly antisemitic acts of barbaric cruelty. His big sister Dina, so intelligent, dynamic and intrepid, is mowed down by a Nazi bullet the day she goes out of her hiding place to enjoy the sun's splendor after having been denounced by a spy paid off by the German conquerors. His little brother Joseph, so frail and vulnerable, is shoved with other children deprived of their parents into a cattle car and shipped off towards an atrocious death in one of Hitler's murder factories. Luckier than those two, Doriel hides with his father in a barn in the country but lives constantly in fear of being betrayed by a venal neighbor and ferreted out by the police. To go unnoticed, they are obliged to scrutinize their slightest gestures and words.

Young Doriel is traumatized in another manner, however, and this traumatism increases in importance as he matures. Thanks to a very subtle and perspicacious mind, he figures out the consequences of the Holocaust's engulfing insanity. He becomes in his way its echo chamber. This dreadful episode of racial extermination, including the killing of one and a half million babies, reveals, according to him, the barbarity of mankind and, what is infinitely more angonizing for someone who wants to believe, the apparent impassibility of God. He describes himself as a dreamer "who sees the light coming from another age" (*DF*, 58). But this light that is supposed to symbolize a lofty civilization founded on the respect of the human person is converted into annihilating energy without the Creator deigning to intervene to stop the massacre of His creatures: "And suddenly [the light] is transformed into fire, it is the fire, the fire that an insane woman sees in the train that is taking her, along with her starving children, and their silent grandparents, towards the realm where all of life topples over into death; she sees gigantic flames biting the sky that, set ablaze, opens up like a tomb where are extinguished the sparks of souls considered to be immortal. So, the mad dreamer begins to sob with his whole body and thinks that if he sheds enough tears, who knows, they will perhaps extinguish the fire; and God Himself, in a spurt of remorse or gratitude, will say thank you to him" (*DF*, 59).

Another disastrous consequence of the war: torturing doubts about the relationship that existed between his father and mother. Like every child who adores his parents, little Doriel tended to idealize them. After a tumultuous session at the psychiatrist's, the adult he has become solemnly affirms to himself that his parents had a deep love for one another. Nevertheless, Dr. Goldschmidt's persistent questions open a fissure that gets wider and wider. Doriel is forced to bring up to the surface events that he would have wanted to repress forever. Of course, he always knew these events had taken place, but the pain resulting from them remains so tenacious that he is afraid, a half-century later, to reflect on them. When his therapist succeeds in reactivating these memories of a distant past, she provokes a commotion within the inner landscape of her patient. A veritable seism is unleashed, indeed a tsunami on the emotional and moral levels.

His mother, Léah, had been the impassioned leader of a Polish resistance movement against the Nazi oppressors. Charismatic, the very personification of bravery, she would galvanize her comrades and impel them to go beyond themselves. One of the members of this clandestine movement, Romek, fell desperately in love with her. The latter's sentiments lasted until the end of his life. Did Doriel's mother return this love, if only during the space of a moment? That is the question that assails her son fifty years later, that anguishes and tears him apart. When Thérèse Goldschmidt asks him what he thinks of that man now, fury seizes him to the point that he starts, as she tells him, "to beat his chest all the while stammering incoherent words" (*DF*, 158). The Doriel at the end of the 1990s has never forgiven his mother's comrade-at-arms for having sullied his parents' marriage and, as a result, for having destroyed the marvelous and fragile world they were able to reconstruct after the war: "He is a bastard, a traitor, a scoundrel…I detested him right away, I will detest him till the end of my days... He came over with his hands full of thorns and his heart empty... Guilty of rape, he is not human... One does not steal the mother of a hidden child that a thousand police are hunting down... I repudiate him as a human being the way he repudiated my father... I despise him for the contempt he showed towards my whole family..." (*DF*, 158).

A subsequent session with the doctor confirms this impression that the doubt hovering over Doriel's mind concerning his mother's fidelity, long after the incident that aroused it, has touched off a cataclysm in his soul. The patient uses the term "convulsions" to describe the suffering he endured when he was a boy. Now, the word serves as a detonator to blow up an emotional explosive buried in the depths of his unconscious. The explosion does not occur right away, but once he leaves the psychiatrist's office, the sexagenarian finally remembers the night when, as a child in Poland, he had been racked by convulsions, and that these happened immediately after he had overheard a very tense conversation between his mother and Romek. Doriel relives the drama as though it had unfolded at that very instant: "No doubt [Romek] is asking her a question, because Maman replies right away by shaking her head: "No, it is over." The man insists and Maman repeats: "I told you: it is over. You should not try to break up a family, and certainly not mine." Again, he perseveres. And Maman, in a reproachful tone, replies: "The past is the past; if you persist, you will simply make it ugly." With his head bowed like a guilty person, the man whispers: "Once, just once, that is all I ask you." Maman is getting ready to say something, but Father has already returned" (*DF*, 265-266). It is significant that the young Doriel and the sexagenarian he has become don't strive to exploit the margin of indetermination surrounding the words of this dialogue to minimize the impact of their replies. After all, his mother's words: "No, it is over," and "The past is the past," could have alluded to purely platonic sentiments. The relationship that she had with Romek could have been limited to a simple affectionate camaraderie. And in the latter's entreaty: "Once, just once," Doriel could have seen the despair of an unsuccessful lover.

Unfortunately, a half-century after hearing this exchange of words, Doriel persists in seeing in it the possibility of a temptation his mother would have perhaps not resisted if the circumstances had been propitious. Hence the distress that overcomes him fifty years later when he remembers the scene, and the dark pessimism that tyrannizes him. He has not, then, remained a bachelor and chaste because he had not yet found the woman of his dreams. He has not, then, rejected marriage because he did not want to bring children into a world too cruel to deserve them. Perhaps he enclosed himself in a desperate solitude because he did not believe that redemptive love could exist. One can understand why young Doriel did not cry during his parents' funeral after they were killed in a car accident just as they were preparing to emigrate with him to Israel. They had, for him, incarnated conjugal harmony and loyalty. Their death dealt him such a devastating blow that the sorrow he felt put him beyond tears.

Towards the end of the novel Doriel brings up one last time in the doctor's presence the question of the relationship between his mother and her unhappy admirer. The therapy sessions have by now ended. The psychiatrist has given up. She acknowledges she is unable to help her patient since she is unsuccessful in tracking down the cause of his somber despair. Now that their relationship has changed, the hero invites his therapist to listen to a story that he is going to tell her. It is about his encounter thirty-five years before with Romek's brother, the billionaire Samek Ternover. The latter confirms to the young man Doriel was in the 1960s that his brother had, indeed, been madly in love with Léah. Sensing that death was approaching, he begged his brother Samek to try to find the woman he had loved without hope and transmit a final message to her. After many failed attempts to respect his deceased brother's wishes, Samek was able to discover Doriel, the son of the beloved woman, in New York City. Neither Samek nor Romek had heirs. Romek had no desire to bring children into the world because he was still in mourning for his great, unrequited passion. Samek didn't want children either, having survived the nightmare of the death camps. He did not believe that humanity deserved to receive the ones he could bring into the world. Thus, they designated Doriel as their sole heir.

As soon as the reader discovers the source of the hero's financial wealth, he can measure the depth of the guilt complex that afflicts him. Despite the extraordinary generosity of the two brothers, Doriel has never been able to forgive Romek for the all-consuming passion that the latter felt for his mother despite Léah's resolve to remain faithful to her husband. What intensifies this guilt complex is his acceptance of the Ternover fortune. Granted, he does not wallow in insolent luxury. He uses it to rescue the needy; he is involved in many charitable projects. But he has nevertheless become a billionaire thanks to a man he continues hating, and Doriel still hates Romek—we cannot overemphasize this—because he keeps torturing himself by the possibility that Léah could have loved her comrade-at-arms "not all the time," as he says, "not even for a week, but for one night, one hour" (*DF*, 310). Thus, it is not at all surprising that on hearing this bizarre story from Samek Ternover himself, Doriel has the impression that his head "is no longer functioning, [that] it is freezing up and [that] it is going to explode from one instant to the next" (*DF*, 310).

In other circumstances, the Jewish religion could and should have brought him comfort and some measure of appeasement. Is it not centered on man's earthly existence? Does it not propose an exalting ideal to follow? Let us recall that for Judaism it is necessary for each man and woman to conduct themselves as though their acts had cosmic repercussions. According to the faith of Moses each human being has an infinitely precious value. Does not the Talmud affirm that when one saves one single life, one saves at the same time the whole universe? Unfortunately, Doriel is far too shaken by the catastrophe of the Holocaust to renew his commitment towards the God of Israel. Without confessing this explicitly, it would take very little for the hero to give the Creator of the universe a failing grade. On several occasions during the novel, he expresses terrible doubts about the validity of the Creator's decisions and about His conduct towards His creatures that border on blasphemy.

One day in the Hassidic neighborhood of Brooklyn, Doriel, still a young man, encounters an erudite homeless man who boasts about teaching wisdom. Although the hero is horrified by the words this singular personage is uttering, he does not think of contradicting him because he himself is already assaulted by all kinds of harrowing questions. Now the screwball dares to propose a sacrilegious interpretation of the divine nature. The Master of the universe, he maintains, has irremediably messed up His creation. He is henceforth the prisoner of the bad decisions he has made and needs to be freed from them as much as man does. To Doriel's panic-stricken reactions, the hobo replies in a disillusioned manner. Let us listen to them:

-But then, I cried out.

-Then what?

- ,,,.then, what is our quest for God worth, what do we do with our thirst for God, with our faith in an all- powerful and merciful God?

The beggar gazed at me while shaking his head in commiseration:

-One day, my dear fellow, you will understand... (*DF*, 22-23).

Many years later, he finds himself in a clinic after a failed suicide attempt. Doriel overhears the words spoken by his roommate who is out of his mind, words that reflect the hero's own anxiety concerning the designs of the God of Israel. When Doriel questions him the next day about it, that man accuses the Lord of Creation of having chosen the Jews for all time as his favorite victims. As proof, the roommate points to all the tragedies that have crashed down on them from the time of their exodus from ancient Egypt till Auschwitz. To allow such barbarous acts to be committed against a people that was no more guilty than others, God's judgement had to be skewed, and the "strange man" as Doriel calls him, is on the verge of saying it. He stops at the last second, but the implications of his thinking are no less blasphemous: "One knows that for a man born blind, God is blind, but what about a man born crazy: is his god crazy, too...? May God forgive me..." (*DF*, 289). If one accepts that man's reasoning—and Doriel does not oppose it—could one not go even further to explain the evil that reigns over our earth for so many thousands of years? At another moment Doriel dares ask the following question: Is man not the failure of God's creation, since He has allowed one and a half million innocent Jewish children to die?

Another reason explains the doubts that the hero entertains concerning the God to whom he so yearns to address fervent prayers. After the death of his parents, he is taken into custody by his uncle Avrohom, a sincerely good and generous man, but a Hassidic fundamentalist who brings him up in New York City in a rather stifling religious climate. Doriel admires the Hassidic sect but cannot adhere unreservedly to its form of Judaism. He certainly remains sensitive all his life to the intemporal dimension of the Jewish faith as the Hassidim practice it. What counts for them is the Word revealed by the Almighty. Divine law must always take precedence over the exigencies of temporal existence even if it contradicts reason. Divine law demands obedience to a moral code that preaches piety, compassion and generosity, "sublime words," Doriel points out, "drawn from the trashcans of history, as Marx and Lenin, the most famous doctors of society in revolution, would say" (*DF*, 121). The hero also considers very moving " the absurd hope" of the Hassidim regarding the coming of the Messiah at the end of time that will establish forever the reign of fraternal peace and justice.

Nevertheless, the rigidity of this sect exasperates him in the end because the Hassidim tend to turn their backs on reality in favor of an eschatology that no doubt exists only in their imagination. His exasperation reaches its climax as concerns their hateful intransigence towards the state of Israel. Some of them live there, receive the protection of that country, have the right to practice their form of religion, but instead of showing their gratitude to the Hebrew state, they never stop praying for its annihilation. According to them, Israel and all the secular Jews who believe in it deserve death because they are violating the immutable law of the Lord by refusing to await the coming of the Messiah. It matters little to the Hassidim that the young nation is the only place in the world that accepts unconditionally all Jews fleeing persecution. It matters little to them that the existence of such a country before the unleashing of the Second World War would undoubtedly have saved their European coreligionists from the murderous fury of the Nazis. Even before leaving France for America under his uncle's tutelage, he witnessed a violent verbal confrontation in Marseille between the latter and the head of Zionist recruiters who would have wanted to take Doriel to Israel in conformity with his deceased parents' wishes. From this exchange emerge the pragmatism of non-religious Jews towards which Doriel will be more and more inclined and the fanaticism of the Hassidim that he will tolerate less and less:

> The Zionist leader, a big redhead, must have thought he was speaking at the United Nations: "After what our people went through, at a time when the survivors of the worst of catastrophes no longer know where to go to find a bit of respite, a bit of rest, you are going to tear this child from his great family?" And Avrohom shot back: "And God in all this, the God of Israel, are you forgetting Him?" The redhead: "You dare invoke God? Here? Now? But where was He when we needed His goodness, His justice, His power?" Avrohom: "He was with us. Like us, He suffered! Like us, He had his fill of a murderous secular humanity!" The redhead: "But you are joking! A God prisoner of child murderers! And you still believe it?" (*DF*, 163)

Thus, Doriel rejects this intransigence. But another reason explains his increasing disaffection with the Hassidic milieu: their puritanism in sexual matters. In the name of an absolute of moral purity, the young men of the sect cope with their sex drives either by repressing them or by pretending they don't exist. As for contact with women, it is forbidden to know them in the biblical sense before marriage. It is even forbidden to enjoy the slightest physical intimacy with a member of the opposite sex. This repression results in a guilt complex and a mutilation of the being on the emotional level. Granted, Doriel tends to be distrustful of women for metaphysical motives as well: a somber pessimism impels him to avoid marriage for fear of bringing into the world children who, according to him, will be condemned to unhappiness. But had he not been so programed by his milieu to be so wary of his libido, perhaps its elemental gushing thrust could have triumphed over his ill-being and helped save him. Moreover, as he confesses to Dr. Goldschmidt, he has always been attracted to feminine charm and beauty. In the revelations he makes to the doctor, there is unquestionably more than just a bit of poetic fabrication, because Doriel has a most fertile imagination. But his propensity to enrich reality nevertheless reflects the desire to live a great adventure of passion.

As for the women who have aroused him during his life, however different their characters, they had this in common: they were all fascinating. There was Rina, a kind of unleashed earth mother who believed she was the reincarnation of Lilith. She seemed the metaphor for the black magic that erotic attraction contains. After Rina came Nora, a young, enterprising divorcee. She caused a commotion within him but gave up on him when having to deal with his fear of sexuality that seemed to hem him in as though he was in a straitjacket. Ruth succeeded Nora, the daughter of his uncle, by turns teasing, sweet and ardently sensual. Did she really encourage him to transgress the law with her despite her being already engaged or was it just a fantasy that he would have loved to act out? Afterward, he encountered Maya in Israel. Her beauty, energy and courage excited him. She, too, had suffered from the consequences of the Holocaust but refused to wallow like him in a sadness for which there was no consolation. Then Ayala appeared, a lovely young woman both deeply serious and serene, whom he met briefly on an aircraft bringing him back from Paris to New York. Would she have really given up her fiancé for him? Doriel would never know since Ayala disappeared as quickly as she had come into his life.

Non-fulfillment thus characterizes his existence, especially in the domains of love and religious faith. If he had been endowed with more willpower and been able to commit himself to a project with a transcendent significance, he could have perhaps freed himself from his demons. Indeed, during one of his sojourns in Israel he meets two men who, precisely, have managed to confer a new meaning on their lives by taking big risks to reconstruct themselves. They represent other possibilities of existence that Doriel could have explored if he had had the courage to do so. The first, Tamir, revolted against a Jewish religious milieu at least as rigid as the one in which the hero felt imprisoned. The Israeli man's father was even more intransigent than Uncle Avrohom in Brooklyn. The latter, at least, could feel pity for the young Hebrew state to which so many enemies were unrelentingly opposed during the Six Day War as well as the Kippur one. The *Rosh Yeshiva* or school Principal as Tamir's father was called even prayed for the destruction of Israel although he had been living there permanently. Before going by his present name, the young Israeli man was called Béinish. He was the most brilliant student, the most fervent on the religious level, the most idealistic in the school, the one who was cited as a model for the others. Everyone agreed that he was destined to become an illustrious scholar and rabbi. One day he became friends with a soldier in the Israeli army and finally understood the perils that the state had to confront, the very state that his father and the other Hassidim wanted to see destroyed. The attitude of those people now seemed to him highly immoral. As though he had undergone a metamorphosis, Béinish broke with his religious milieu and his family, left his wife and his in-laws with whom he had been staying, and entered the secret service of his country. To emphasise this total break with his past and his assumption of a new identity, he now called himself Tamir.

Tamir is the one who introduces Doriel to Laurent, for whom the former feels an immediate and intense empathy. Doriel recognizes in him "a spiritually ill person" (*DF*, 241). Laurent still bears the traces of the demons with which he has wrestled but his season in hell has made him an infinitely stronger person. He had enlisted in the French Resistance movement during the Second World War. Totally committed to the struggle against Nazi oppression, intrepid to the point of foolhardiness, he had slain a German officer who was about to arrest him. In retaliation, the Germans assassinated a group of hostages. Laurent went through a period of agonizing remorse until he encountered by chance in a restaurant the daughter of one of the prisoners killed in his place. The tears he shed at that moment liberated him from his guilt complex and allowed him to make a fresh start in life. Like Tamir, he joined the Israeli secret service and enjoyed the certainty of accomplishing indispensable work. When Doriel makes his acquaintance, he compares the exciting life of his new friend to the rather lackluster one he has been dragging around since he became an adult. When speaking of Laurent to Dr. Goldschmidt, he expresses his regrets this way:

-On listening to him, I was saying to myself that I was born too late.

-Is that all?

-No. I also said to myself that he had had the good luck to be able to make over his existence. To give it a meaning. To make happy those who loved him. When I compare myself to him, I feel useless. I have done nothing, built nothing, obtained nothing. The important events have not affected me, the sublime ideals have not attracted me. Compared to his history, mine seems insipid, puerile and rather vain. (*DF*, 242)

The exceptionally dramatic adventures that Laurent has lived were, perhaps, a kind of Pascal-like diversion that enabled him to anesthetize his existential anguish. Nevertheless, it is evident that dangerous action prevented him from drowning in his ill-being. And Doriel wonders, in the doctor's presence, whether he would have allowed himself to be dominated by his secret demons had he embarked on a life of adventure just like his friend.

Doriel will never find the answer to this question. Tamir strove to persuade him to join the Israeli secret service as a spy in an Arab country, a career in which he would have finally found the satisfaction of accomplishing something of great significance. Doriel refused the invitation for a rather subjective reason. He felt that Tamir had not shown enough confidence in him: "Despite my curiosity, he never really explained to me why he had abandoned his wife, poor Reisesle. That did not please me" (*DF*, 259). Later, Doriel will learn that the person chosen for this espionage mission "was arrested. Tortured. Hanged" (*DF*, 259). Yet another reason for his already heavy guilt complex to bear down upon him even more since that man was killed in his stead.

Powerless to exorcize on his own his guilt complex and despair, Doriel finally has recourse to psychiatry. But from the moment he enters Dr. Thérèse Goldschmidt's office, a painful drama irrupts that will leave an imprint on them both. The problem, of course, is Doriel himself, and he knows it. He sincerely wants the doctor to succeed in rescuing him. By his own confession, however, he sabotages the therapist's work by refusing to go with her all the way into the labyrinth of his solitude where he has allowed himself to be walled up alive. He acknowledges his responsibility on various occasions for the failure of his treatment. What he says when their sessions are over sums up his thinking: "Today, as I am concluding my story, I admit that the failure is indeed my fault and not Thérèse's: she did her work scrupulously, but I did everything to put obstacles in her path. She had fulfilled her commitment, not me (*DF*, 291).

What is he afraid of? Let us recall that he had succumbed once before to the temptation of suicide. Given the despair that is tearing him apart and dragging him to the very limits of nihilism, he no doubt remains fearful of embarking on that inner journey again and this time going all the way. He would perhaps awaken once more the hideous beasts inside of him who are now asleep. Once fully aroused, they would perhaps be capable of pushing him to the brink. In that case, nothing, absolutely nothing and no one would be able to stop this suicidal urge. He evokes this thought one day when he opens his heart in her presence about the car accident where his parents lost their lives and, consequently, the feeling of regret that continues to haunt him: "I should never have left them. I should have hung on to my mother's hand, to my father's arm. Not let them die without me. I know I'm wrong, that it wasn't my fault. I was too small, and they were too determined. I know that the Angel of Death always triumphs over the living, past and future. But here you are making a mistake, Doctor: knowledge does not help man find the essential answer, nor peace without pretentions. There is a level where the love of God and self-knowledge are useless" (*DF*, 200).

Doriel's tragedy is compounded by the fact that he has absolutely no faith in language. The most diverse and contradictory notions clash in his mind to the point where he no longer succeeds in keeping them in order, and the language that is supposed to help him accomplish this task reflects, in turn, the chaos that submerges him. Instead of celebrating the triumph of clarity and reason, language seems to bear witness to the victory of insanity: "unwholesome and malevolent fusion of notions, terms, tableaus: what meaning can be uncovered in a sentence that is, of necessity, devoid of one? And the arrangement of words that gets incessantly modified? It happens that a coma changes place: it runs, it runs between the words, catching it is impossible. Is the coma crazy, too?" (*DF*, 219). In those conditions, it would have been impossible for the doctor to cure him. Thérèse Goldschmidt is a Freudian psychiatrist. She believes that the psyche functions according to knots of elemental urges that often have a sexual basis. When the complex network composed of these knots gets short-circuited, all one has to do is plumb the subconscious depths of the patient to track down the repressed motive that has created the problem without his being aware of it. Once the sick person becomes conscious of its presence, he can harness all his energy to combat it with the help of the therapist. During their sessions, the doctor had tried to zero in tirelessly on the "gaps," the "slips," in [his] ideas, memories and words" (*DF*, 117), even at the risk of provoking her patient and pushing him more than once to the brink of fury.

The psychiatrist's dilemma lies in the fact that the illness devouring her patient remains impervious to the methods she uses. She fails because Doriel's sickness is situated in a domain to which she does not have access: metaphysics. Pragmatic, indifferent towards religion, solidly rooted in her purely terrestrial existence, convinced that problems of a psychic nature can be resolved through reason, Thérèse is powerless to join Doriel at the centre of his labyrinth where he asks agonizing and insoluble questions about the very meaning of his existence. She cannot confront the omnivorous minotaur of spiritual doubt which she would have so wanted to help him slay because she can barely even imagine it. Moreover, when she attempts to accompany him on this voyage into the murky shadows of his soul, she has the impression of being out of her depth and losing her way just like him. This is why she tells Doriel that she will put an end to their sessions: "I don't lack courage, but faith is not my business. A lamentable situation. I am suffering because of it. I no longer have confidence in my judgement. We are no longer making progress. Your compartmentalized zones remain obscure; no light, no warmth penetrate there" (*DF*, 293). Every time Doriel seemed to be giving her a key, he would change the lock. But there is worse. Her patient draws Thérèse into such dangerous regions for her mental balance that she wonders whether he has become her *dibbouk*. She had identified to such an extent with her patient's sickness that she was nearly affected by it. As she admits to him, "God is my witness that I have tried everything, I even risked everything. My husband realized this before me and that brought us as a couple to the verge of disaster" (*DF*, 293).

Sent back to his demons by the doctor for whom he ended up feeling a genuine empathy, Doriel seems condemned more than ever to solitude. It is then that a miracle occurs in the etymological sense in the novel's final pages: redemption through love. Cynical minds would maintain that Elie Wiesel has made a beautiful young woman, Liatt, take on the role of the *deus ex machina* because he was anxious to proclaim the victory of hope over despair. But one could reply that life is marvelous to the extent that the renewal of a human being can come about through a purely fortuitous encounter. This is what happens to Doriel at his favorite pastry shop on Madison Avenue. He discovers Liatt there, the woman of his dreams. And he believes they are predestined to love one another because her smile is that of a frightened child, the very same one he had during the burial of his parents.[24].

At first glance, their meeting would appear to be leading straight towards catastrophe. Liatt, a server at that New York pastry shop, has already accumulated, at thirty-six, numerous relationships among which several had been rather stormy. By contrast, Doriel, who is old enough to be her father, has never lived through an adventure of passion. Despite these significant differences, they are really made for one another. Liatt has an imaginative and playful side as well as a touch of craziness. She understands the humor full of fantasy that Doriel shows whenever he enters the café. She senses right away that the sexagenarian's words, which others would interpret as the ravings of a madman, represent his attempt to exorcize the nightmare of life through insanity. When he asks for a shirt and a tie to accompany his croissant and his hot chocolate, she answers him without being in the least disconcerted: "I'm sorry, I no longer have any shirts or ties. But I can propose black gloves, you'll see, they are beautiful and will suit you perfectly" (DF, 312). Liatt is also a risk-taker and enjoys adventures. Like a bolt from the blue, Doriel invites her to leave her job definitively and follow him. She accepts the invitation and leaves behind her job and customers.

But the sexagenarian interests her and soon will captivate her for reasons that are far more serious. She discovers in him the same vulnerability that characterizes her. In addition, thanks to her intuitive depth, she feels that this man in the twilight of his life carries within him treasures of tenderness that he yearns to lavish on the woman he loves. When Liatt asks him: "What are we doing here?" his reply does not fail to move her deeply: "So you want to know what we are doing here. I could answer you quite simply that we are both striving to transform an apparently fortuitous encounter into a story that could easily, with a bit of luck, be placed under the sign of destiny which, really, has more imagination than us" (DF, 318). Convinced by the love that Doriel declares to her, she will accept most will-

---

[24] An elderly lady whom Doriel encounters in the cemetery where he has gone to meditate at his uncle's grave confirms that, when she had seen him for the first time at his parents' funeral, he had that same smile of a frightened child. That smile, she said, broke her heart. See DF, 329-330.

ingly a union with him that represents "an act of defiance against logic and nature" (*DF*, 327). For his part, the sexagenarian realizes that he is going to embark on the most exciting adventure of his whole existence. When the young woman tells him her name, Liatt, which means in Hebrew "You belong to me," he invents a new one for himself that reflects his sentiment of gratitude: Od, which means in that language, "I give thanks."

Thus, at the end of his spiritual trajectory strewn with doubts, sorrows and torments, Doriel finds completeness. His adventure illustrates the passage in the Talmud that Elie Wiesel has inscribed as an epigraph for his novel. It concerns four men who penetrated the orchard of knowledge. The first looked at it and lost his life. The second looked at it and lost his reason. The third looked at it and lost his faith. The fourth looked at it and left the orchard in peace. Now Doriel has been, by turns, these four men. His despair nearly killed the possibility for him to love and be loved. His *dibbouk* nearly locked him up for good in his solitude with the loss of intellectual landmarks that isolation from others implies. His metaphysical anguish was on the point of making him lose confidence in life, therefore in the God in whom he so yearned to believe. Finally, the discovery of love on the threshold of old age brough him the splendid blossoming forth that he no longer expected. It is not at all surprising, then, that like the traveler who has just reached the summit of a mountain and "glimpses the abyss through the clouds," Doriel experiences "a mad desire to dance" (*DF*, 330). Despite the frightening bout of dizziness that overcomes him when thinking about the fragility of his destiny and the dangers involved in the risk he is taking, he absolutely insists on celebrating life which has probably become for him synonymous with God. And this life deserves to be glorified and remains all the more precious because its nature is ephemeral.

The Sondenberg Case

Truly, Elie Wiesel does not cease astonishing us. Two years after publishing a masterpiece, *A Mad Desire to Dance*, he offers us, in 2008, and at the age of eighty, another novel with impressive moral and spiritual breadth, *The Sonderberg Case*. There are striking parallelisms between these two works. Like Doriel in *A Mad Desire to Dance*, the hero of this new novel, Yedidyah, feels disoriented to the point of flirting with nihilism before magnificently regaining self-mastery towards the end of his trajectory. Again, like Doriel, Yedidyah lives under the curse of the Holocaust. For both, it implies an unerasable blot on our human condition and a tragedy that will bring shame to the human species till the end of time. The Shoah draws behind it for Yedidyah as well as for Doriel a whole trail of agonizing questions for which there are no satisfying answers. Yet, while running along parallel lines, their destinies are not in the least identical. Doriel's parents had been able to escape Hitler's fury. Yedidyah's were its victims. In addition, Yedidyah encounters during his career the grandson of a man who could have been their killer. That encounter allows the author to orchestrate splendidly once again the theme with tragic resonances of the individual's responsibility towards his fellow man.

At first glance, Yedidyah does not appear predestined for suffering, despite his doctor's warning at the beginning of the novel that his physical health will perhaps be threatened. One would think he is a fulfilled man. He has a captivating and loyal spouse, Alika, with whom he sustains a relationship as satisfying on the intellectual and emotional levels as it is exciting from the sexual point of view. Naturally, they have their fights from time to time and their verbal confrontations can be fierce. But this is perfectly normal, since the closest of couples go at one another now and then. He is the father of twin sons whom he adores, and their existence represents a blessing for him. He is surrounded by parents, grandparents, uncles and aunts whom he cherishes. He is happy, too, in his professional life. Yedidyah is a journalist and the drama critic of a highly respected daily newspaper in New York City and enjoys the esteem of his colleagues.

Until he reaches the fifty-year mark—we must guess his age because Wiesel never gives precise details about it—he feels neither traumatized nor even bruised by the Holocaust. At least he doesn't think he is. Granted, this tragedy of the Jewish people remains in the individual and collective consciousness of his family members. It hovers over them like a sinister shadow. During joyous celebrations like weddings, Yedidyah's extended family never fails to remember all those who were not fortunate enough to survive that infernal hurricane of history. But the memory of the Shoah remains rather remote. Inasmuch as life must go on, his people prefer not to approach the subject directly. In fact, most of the time they pretend that the event never existed. As the hero explains:

> War? A taboo, forbidden memories. Directly or indirectly, it had struck all our families. Even on my mother's side: so many uncles, aunts, cousins and next of kin had disappeared. Obscurely, we understood that they all were part of our collective memory [...]

181

But what did I know about the concrete experience of that time? Denunciations? Life in the ghetto? Hunger, Crowded living conditions? "Actions" that preceded deportations? The hunting down of children? Constant fear of being separated overnight from loved ones? Sealed trains going towards the unknown? Suffering that had no name? If my father alluded to these exceptionally, one had the impression he was talking about events related in medieval manuscripts or even more ancient ones.[25]

The horrors of the Second World War will finally bear down on the hero's personality. When that occurs, certain traits of his character that he had managed until then to dominate will become exacerbated and will drive him to the edge of despair. Well before the moment at which a long-hidden secret touches off a cataclysm within Yedidyah, he reveals tendencies towards nervousness and indeed anxiety. He feels instinctively he is suffering from a loss that he can't put his finger on. He sometimes has the impression of living in seclusion. Kathy, a rather enticing colleague in her thirties and eager to accumulate masculine trophies, notices this with her usual perspicacity. She has no desire to seduce him; according to her, he is not her type. All the more reason for him to become conscious of the grave problems she has uncovered in him. This is how she scolds him:

> We've known each other for a long time now, my boy […] I've been watching you, observing you. You intrigue me. You live in a world of your own; entrance forbidden to strangers. Agitated, nervous, a tormented soul: you're never satisfied, never happy. Why do you remain so closed, stubborn, insensitive to the warmth and beauty of the world? Why do you refuse simple pleasures? Why do you push aside what is offered to you? Why do you hang on to your solitude? One would say that you see a danger, an enemy in every woman. And a betrayal in every instant of joy. Why? I would like to understand. (*CS*, 140-141)

Yedidyah can find nothing to reply to this ruthless analysis.

But Kathy is not the only woman to criticize him. His wife, Alika, doesn't beat around the bush either. She reproaches him for not loving her as much as he did in the past. She resents his moments of absent-minded-

---

[25] Elie Wiesel, *Le Cas Sonderberg*, Paris : Grasset, 2008, 86-87; henceforth referred to as *CS*.

ness that are happening more and more frequently. She is almost jealous of his work as a journalist that is taking over his life. She accuses him of no longer sharing with her their common love of the theatre as he did at the beginning of their relationship. This problem in their marriage has occurred because Yedidyah has been fascinated for some time by a totally new form of drama for him: an earth-shaking trial. A court of justice does indeed resemble a stage show. When a verdict must be pronounced concerning a presumed murderer, one is present at a play of which the episodes and dénouement are unpredictable. As for the lawyers, they conduct themselves like outstanding actors. Paul Adler, Yedidyah's boss, is the one who has exhorted him to cover the case of a sensational murder that has drawn the attention of New York City. He is convinced that Yedidyah, as a drama critic, will know how to convey to the newspaper's readers the theatrical side of the trial far better than journalists trained in this line of work. And he is right.

This is how the hero meets a German university student, Werner Sonderberg, who is accused of having killed his uncle, Hans Dunkelman, in the Adirondak mountains in the north-west part of New York State. This encounter will have significant repercussions on his existence many years later. But even during the trial the young man's presence disturbs him deeply. In the first place, the presumed murderer appears distant, detached, indeed indifferent towards the tragedy of which he remains, nevertheless, the principal actor. Then, he seems even to have blinded himself to the disastrous consequences for his future of this act of murder that he is accused of committing. When the judge asks him the crucial question, "Guilty or not guilty?" Sonderberg replies: "Guilty and not guilty" (*CS*, 106). Obviously, the court is stupefied by such an answer. But Yedidyah is trying to go beyond this stupor. He is convinced that a terrible drama is unfolding in the accused man's conscience without being able to put his finger on it. He shares his impressions with Paul Adler during a conversation:

Here is someone who is fighting and I don't know against whom or against what.

-Against the system?

-Possibly.

-Against fear?

183

-Perhaps.

-If he is guilty, he risks capital punishment and at the minimum perpetual reclusion. Isn't that a good enough reason to be afraid?

-Yes. But there is something else, I feel it. Attribute this to this intuition that the theatre teaches us to cultivate (*CS*, 119).

It is only much later that Yedidyah will understand the deep meaning of the young German's ambiguous declaration. Werner Sonderberg himself will enlighten the mystery for the journalist; he will reveal to the latter the terrible anguish that was tetanizing him spiritually on the day he pronounced the bizarre phrase, "guilty and not guilty." Fortunately for the accused, the doctor who was assigned the job of examining Hans Dunkelman's body provided the court with the irrefutable evidence that Sonderberg could not have committed the murder, since he had left the place before his uncle died.

Werner Sonderberg reappears in the hero's life well after the trial and, as we will see, at the most opportune moment for the latter. When Yedidyah sees the young man again, he is going through a crisis that leaves him almost felled. His parents finally have the courage to tell him the truth that they had carefully hidden up till then: he is not their biological child. He is the child of Holocaust victims. They adopted him when he was four years old. Completely shaken, the journalist is convinced that he no longer has an identity. The agonizing doubts he constantly entertained about himself before being struck dumb by this revelation now seem fully justified. During his periods of introspection, he tended to brood for no apparent reason. "I feel fragile, fractured. Nailed," he declared in a moment of profound discouragement. A story came back to his mind about a young girl who loved everyone, including parents, cousins and friends while detesting herself, and who jumped out of the window to put an end to her life. This is the deplorable state into which he sinks on discovering that his parents are false parents and that his real parents, who were deported to a death camp, were reduced to ashes without burial.

How can he save himself? How can he tear himself away from a distress that seems to him irremediable? His wife, Alika, tries in vain to reason with him. She reminds him that his adoptive parents have always loved him like a child of their own flesh and blood. Yedidyah does not deny this, but he still notices a void within him that he will never be able to fill. In desperation he consults a psychiatrist who specializes in hypnosis.

He hopes in this way to move backwards towards the memories of his early childhood buried under the traumatisms of the war and of his more recent experiences, to resurrect that part of his existence indispensable for the reconstruction of his identity, and to put an end to his psychological mutilation. Thanks to the therapist's techniques, Yedidyah seems to retrieve unsettling images of his past. He sees again the pretty little town where he had lived as a very young child. He sees himself hidden in a cellar with his parents and older brother. His parents lavish their tenderness on him to calm his anguish. His brother shows him affection by playing with him. Then his memory draws him into a place filled with bad-tempered, hate-ridden people. It is almost necessary to become invisible in order not to provoke them. Above all one must not complain about suffering.

As a result of these hypnosis sessions, Yedidyah starts to speak with his dead family, no doubt to calm the sorrow of having lost them so early. The imaginary dialogues he entertains with them are all the more moving since they underscore the impossibility of reconstructing the past and the necessity of going back to real life. In the conversation he has with his mother one perceives implicitly his awareness that his early childhood cannot be recovered—despite his heartrending desire to preserve it—and that he must, to survive, move forward. Otherwise, he will be in danger of enclosing himself in a living death:

-Did you hug me often?

-All the time.

-While speaking to me?

-While whispering in your ear words of love.

-In silence also?

-Also.

-Hug me, Mama.

-I don't have the right to do it.

-But you love me, you have just told me so.

185

-I love you, my child.

-Then hug me once, just once.

-No.

-Why not?

-Because I want you to remain alive. (*CD*, 207-208)

He imagines this conversation during a very agitated night. His wife is convinced he is having a bad dream and that he is delirious. But from this nightmare will later emerge a renewed will to live.

As a Jew, Yedidyah could have looked for succor and comfort in the God of Israel. After all, he was brought up in a rather conservative Jewish milieu. His family, especially his father and grandfather are imbued with the intense spirituality of a faith going back thousands of years. But for the hero, God seems singularly absent and ambivalent if not incomprehensible. From the outset Yedidyah is assailed by grave doubts about the so-called goodness and justice of the Creator. He quotes the Talmud according to which after completing His creation, the Lord of the universe was unemployed. Consequently, he decided to get busy arranging marriages. But, as Yedidyah wonders, could he also have had fun provoking divorces and drawing man into crime? (*CD*, 45). Connected to this idea of a lack of responsibility on God's part towards His creatures is the conception of History as an interminable chain of bloody events that He did nothing to stop. According to the protagonist's grandfather, "History itself will be judged" (*CD*, 57). But if, as his grandson answers him, "Creation were nothing but a big and long trial" (*CS*, 57), should not the Author of it be judged as well? When Yedidyah asks him this most disquieting question, the grandfather does not react. An unshakeable believer, he refuses to question the goodness of the God of Israel.

But Yedidyah, for his part, cannot stop doing this. According to him, God manifests shocking irresponsibility by engendering a human species so riddled with contradictions, "so complicated, unpredictable and hung-up, that it seems, as a result, congenitally blighted" (*CD*, 242). Hence the countless misfortunes that have struck earth from time immemorial. Hence the impossibility of knowing if the Master of the universe created man to be His partner in a forever unfinished enterprise of moral perfectibility or if He has simply abandoned him to his deplorable fate. The totally unjust death of his older brother in an extermination camp would then be an illustration of this second hypothesis.[26] In accents of rare eloquence that recall the doubts of the disbeliever in Blaise Pascal's *Les Pensées* (Thoughts), who longs to believe but is incapable of achieving that goal, Yedidyah expresses in his diary this heartbreaking questioning: "Could it be that man is condemned to advance towards death because he is the victim or the orphan of God or because he is His partner?" (*CS*, 242). In this atmosphere of uncertainty, it is inevitable that Yedidyah deplores once again the absence of a transcendent dimension that might confer rock-solid certitudes on his existence: *Why am I here rather than elsewhere? Why am I me, whereas I could not be, or I could be someone else?* (*CS*, 243). In the face of such strong doubts, an Alfred de Vigny or an Albert Camus would have turned away from God with a glacial politeness or would have given up investigating a rather futile subject. They would have washed their hands of it.

But Yedidyah remains too imbued with Jewish spirituality to give up his search. At the end of the narrative, the words of the Sages of Judaism come to his rescue. God is no longer envisaged as the incomprehensible Master of creation but is exalted for his compassion and justice. In fact, He becomes the extrapolation to the infinite of these two virtues. According to the hero, man is forced to carry on alone on this earth as best he can, "but he knows that, if one is to believe the Sages, when a Righteous person dies, God weeps and makes the heavens weep. And their cries reverberate in the immensity of the oceans" (*CS*, 247). The God of Israel serves, thus, as a model of moral perfection to be emulated. Herein lies His supreme significance.

For reflections of this perfection to take on tangible forms in our earthly existence, the Righteous are necessary. Fortunately, at every epoch, even the most tormented and bloody, these exceptional individuals have existed. It is the presence of such people, upright, generous and resolved to live according to their noble principles that finally restores Yedidyah's faith in life. These are the ones who ensure, in their respective ways, the redemption of an unhappy humanity. First, there are his adoptive parents,

---

[26] Concerningf the death of Yedidyah's older brother and of the disappearance of his birth certificate when a Russian bomb demolished the archival wing of the municipal building in Davarovsk, his brother's birthplace, the narrative gives us the hero's thoughts: "Was it possible? Even for God? Did he sometimes give life in order to erase it right away? Why? Yedidyah had no answer. But he discovered one thing. That it was possible" (*CS*, 187-188).

grandfather and uncle who have lavished their love on him unconditionally. Ever since his childhood they have represented for him the great founding principles of Jewish ethics: generosity, justice and compassion. It is very significant that when Yedidyah wonders how he will be able to console Werner Sonderberg and alleviate the latter's distress, he begins by talking to him about his adoptive grandfather.

Another individual of eminent nobility who leaves an indelible impression on him is the servant of his biological parents in Hungary, the sweet and humble Maria. Before Yedidyah's family was deported, that woman with the sublime heart persuaded them to entrust him to her care. She passed him off as her own illegitimate child. To make her lie appear more plausible, she invented a story of a terrifying rape of which she had been the victim. Her own family received her with her so-called "baby." Maria's father and mother treated her in the most ignoble manner, convinced they were dealing with their daughter's bastard, but at least they did not denounce Yedidyah to the Nazis, and he was thus able to escape the nightmarish fate meted out to his family. After the war, Maria brought the child to a Jewish agency that found a New York City family for him in which he grew up. Once an adult, Yedidyah succeeded in finding his benefactress in his native village. According to Maria's nephew, the disappearance of the baby whom she had protected so courageously during the Nazi regime had made her sick. She withdrew to the barn behind the house to "sleep" and "shed tears in silence" (*CF*, 184). When the very mature man Yedidyah has become sees her again after so many years, she is already a withered old woman, almost senile, locked up in an almost impenetrable mutism. Yedidyah is not sure she has understood the very sweet and affectionate words he pronounces in her presence. He is angry with himself for having come too late with gifts for her. But he feels for her an infinite gratitude mixed with immense sorrow when he thinks of all this uncommonly fine woman had to endure to save his life: "Here was a courageous, honest and honorable woman, who honors humanity, and she was treated as an object worth less than nothing! How does one live in a world where values are perverted to this degree? And where human sentiments are so devalued? And yet, fortunately, this Maria Petrescu exists: if Christians no longer frighten Jews, it is thanks to her. But what suffering she must have endured! Heartbreaking and magnificent heroine" (*CS*, 181-182).

After Maria, another Righteous Gentile comes into the hero's life: Werner Sonderbrg. The two had not seen each other since the time of the trial. Why is the German so anxious to meet the journalist now? He explains frankly the reason for his visit. He admired the reports that Yedidyah had written about him. He appreciated the efforts the hero had expended to be equitable: "Your accounts were never cut and dried, he declares, You hesitated, you had doubts... That seemed to me, how shall I say it, morally interesting" (*CS*, 215). Having so much esteem for the former columnists of his trial, he confides to him a secret he has never divulged to anyone: the uncle he was accused of having killed was not his uncle but his grandfather. A particularly odious grandfather because he remained an impenitent Nazi until his final breath, proud of the acts of cruelty he had committed against his helpless victims, and an unconditional worshipper of Hitler. A grandfather who had escaped the Allies' justice after the war and had concealed himself behind a false identity. Werner and the old man had a fight over the subject of hatred. The grandfather took pride in still hating the presumed enemies of Hitler's Germany whereas his grandson wished to combat hatred so that humanity would not be condemned to sustain toxic relationships indefinitely. The grandson, completely disgusted, finally repudiated the old man and returned quickly to New York City. As for the Nazi grandfather, he killed himself in a fall on the mountain or committed suicide after having gotten drunk.

The reader willingly forgives Werner Sonderberg for his inability to go beyond the hatred he felt for Hans Dunkelman and fanatics of all kinds, and Yedidyah's grandfather clears Werner morally as well. The grandfather, generally so compassionate, and he, too, a survivor of the death camps, had maintained before his grandson that his hatred of Nazi Germany would be eternal even though he knew that, according to the Talmud, God alone has the right to hate. Let us listen to the old man's reaction to the narrative of Vassili Grossman where the great Russian author relates the sadism of a German officer who ordered a butcher, Mazor, to show him his professional skill by slitting the throats of his neighbor's three little children: "But I, I tell you: Mazor is not guilty. These Germans are. And I curse them. I will curse them till the day I die. I will curse them while weeping and holding back my tears. I will curse them during the day and I will curse them at night. I will curse them in the name of the dead and in the name of the living. I will curse them for Mazor and Vassili Grossman... (*CS*, 88-89). Moreover, does not Werner's repulsion in the face of his grandfather's self-satisfied barbarity testify to his nobility? But the grandson of the Nazi killer would not let himself be convinced by such arguments because he remains so tormented by the history of his country and his family.

Viewed in this light, one realizes that the relationship between Yedidyah and Werner is based on a kind of inverted symmetry. The journalist is searching for an identity buried in the depths of his memory. The former accused man would like to extirpate his own. The first yearns to retrieve the identity of his early childhood to put an end to his psychological mutilation. The second would like to acquire another one as a way of re-starting his life. On listening to the German talk about the guilt complex that is piercing him, the Jewish journalist realizes that all things considered, he is much less to be pitied than his interlocutor. Werner Sonderberg will never be able to escape the curse that his grandfather inflicted on him. Yedidyah, at least, has nothing to reproach himself for on that score. He will not spend his life trying to exorcize an infernal past.

And yet—to use one of Elie Wiesel's favorite phrases—the fury that explodes in Werner Sonderberg's heart when he tells Yedidyah about the incredibly violent confrontation he had with his grandfather proves to us that the German does possess an identity he can be proud of: that of a Righteous person who fights tirelessly against the ugly brute concealed in the depths of our human condition. And for him, this fight is centered on his rejection of Nazi fanaticism. Just like terrorism reveals itself often as a perversion of religious faith, Nazism represents for Sonderberg a perversion of patriotic loyalty. During their altercation in the Adirondacks, Hans describes for his nauseated grandson the motives that impelled him to espouse the Nazi cause. Germany had been humiliated by the western world after the First World War. The country was stagnating in misery. The powerful financial interests supported, according to him, by the Jews, were responsible for the misfortunes of the German people. Only Hitler could restore their lost pride. Naturally, the desire to help regenerate one's country is laudable in theory but for Werner's grandfather obsessed with the Führer, that passion quickly transformed itself into something totally repugnant. Hans, like all of Hitler's unconditional admirers, invoked German nationalism to give free rein to his latent sadism without feeling monstrous about it. The Nazi ideology founded on the fallacy of racial superiority and looking for scape goats, legitimized the emergence of primitive brutality among its partisans. Even worse: it glorified this brutality. Thus, it invited its followers to dehumanize themselves. This is why the grandfather could enumerate with a diabolical delectation all the acts of turpitude in which he participated as an officer of the German army. A half-century after having piled up so many crimes, he continued boasting about them: "Kamenets-Podolsk and the Hungarian Jews. Kiev and the Ukrainian

Jews. Vilno and the Lithuanian Jews. Barbed wire as far as the eye can see. The huge common graves. I saw that. Heads smashed. Infants beaten, jeered at, trampled, used as targets. I saw that. The undressing sessions. The stupor of women pushed into the gas chambers. Mute old men with the faces of smashed stones. I saw that. What did I feel? Nothing. I didn't feel anything. The gun I carried, I was that gun" (*CS*, 227-228).

Obviously, Hans' boasting simply touches off in Werner a fit of anger and disgust. With stunning lucidity, he understands that his grandfather has irremediably sullied himself by his barbaric conduct. The old man's life represents shame for his country and for all humanity. To deny the humanity of other human beings by trampling on them as though they were pieces of filth, is to deny one's own. It means reducing this humanity to zero. The old Nazi is too blinded by his perverted nationalism, too poisoned by his vile ideology to see himself as he is. But his grandson does not fail to make him comprehend this. Hitler's officer wanted to inflict an exemplary punishment on innocent Jews. He, now, is the one to endure this punishment. Without his being aware of it, his cruelty has come back to hit him like a boomerang:

> According to a Jewish saying life is a wheel that never stops turning. Look at yours: what you did to the Jews, you are living right now. You wanted to isolate them, you are the one isolated; you hunted them down, it is happening to you; you did not allow them the slightest chance to live without anguish, and anguish will no longer leave you...And you will know the destiny of your Master... His gigantic Nazi empire began to shrink: the continent was reduced to a country, the country to a city, the city to a street, the street to a bunker—and he as well, the Führer, was consumed by flames. (*CS*, 232-233)

Werner Sonderberg repudiates his grandfather all the more easily since he holds the latter responsible for the death of another righteous person, his own father. Indeed, Werner's father could not stand the behavior of Hitler's henchman. His overwhelming disgust became a cancer that finally killed him. Certainly, Jonas, one of Yedidyah's colleagues, would be opposed to Werner's hardness toward his old Nazi grandfather because, in his opinion, one should never set oneself up as someone else's judge. But one could answer him that however ruthless it may be, Werner's judgement reflects the determination to never again allow such infamous acts to be tolerated.

Thus, the sacred fury that explodes within Werner Sonderberg provides the most eloquent proof that man has at his disposal sufficient freedom to choose between Good and Evil. He can either scale the summits or tumble down into the abyss. After Maria Petrescu, the young German, Werner Sonderberg, shows his Jewish interlocutor the path to follow. Their acts constitute a most salutary reminder. Henceforth the journalist finds himself at an existential crossroad where he has two options left. He can let himself be engulfed in a sterile despair or, on the contrary, renew his commitment towards his fellow man and, as a result, celebrate life with all its disconcerting complexities, ambiguities and contradictions. Inspired by the example of the Righteous he has known, and supported by the Jewish spirituality that has nourished him since his childhood, Yedidyah accepts this second option.

Several days before his death, his grandfather bequeaths to him a precious legacy by offering him advice that represents the distillation of the wisdom of a whole existence: "Certainly, my little one, life is a beginning. But everything in life is a new beginning. As long as you live, you are immortal because you are open to life and the living. A warm presence, a call to action, to hope, even to smile in the face of misfortune, a reason to believe, to believe despite failures and betrayals, to believe in the humanity of the other, this is called friendship. (*CS*, 246-247). In these sublime words one can perceive a message that the great Franco-Jewish philosopher, Emmanuel Lévinas, would not disavow. In his masterly book, *Autrement qu'être ou au-delà de l'essence* (Otherwise than Being or Beyond Essence), he establishes a distinction between the *dire* (the saying) and the *dit* (the said). The first designated the form in which a thought is expressed or structured, a totally flexible form always open to new nuances and new precision. It strives to coincide with the fluid movement of life. The second is contained in that thought itself. As soon as it is formulated, it remains fixed. Its form is forever subjugated. Lévinas prefers by far the saying to the said in relationships with the Other for the simple reason that the first guarantees openness and continuous availability between two individuals. It is not difficult to guess that Yedidyah's venerable grandfather, just like Lévinas, gives the primacy to the saying. One can talk all one wants about artistic truth apropos of roles in a play, and the drama critic in Yedidyah never fails to admire that quality. But an individual's personality overflows the role or roles in which we tend to enclose him/her. The drama of life is infinitely more complex than the drama we can watch in the theatre. Hence the grandfather's exhortation to his grandson. He recommends that

Yedidyah welcome others on their own terms in a surge of generosity and affection, and that he live as though every one of his acts had cosmic repercussions. In this way he will be able to acquire immortality within the heart of each instant of his existence. And sustaining such warm and respectful relationships with others is the best definition of friendship.

In this context of a renewed and strengthened will to live we can understand the complex structure the author conceived for his novel. At the beginning of the book, we learn that the hero, an already very mature man, is ill and that his illness may even be very grave. Then we follow his spiritual and professional itinerary, by turns moving forward in the present or going backwards to different periods of his past, until the narrative comes full circle by bringing us back to the moment when he receives his medical diagnosis. By describing for us the voyage Yedidyah has taken until his appointment at the doctor's office where he receives the bad news, Wiesel intends to reassure us about his hero's state of mind. At the end of the novel, the hero is much stronger than he was as a young man. After his identity crisis he finally achieves what was sorely lacking in him during his youth and maturity: spiritual serenity. The sickness that is lying in wait for him right now will perhaps be mortal. At least he will know how to face it courageously, because he desires ardently to pursue his earthly adventure and, as a result, give life an enthusiastic vote of confidence.

Hostage

Throughout his long career as an author and defender of human rights, Elie Wiesel has raised his voice against the scandal of undeserved suffering. Thus, it was inevitable that he would devote a novel to the kind of innocent victim who, to the shame of our contemporary era, seems to have multiplied: the hostage, used cynically by so-called "revolutionaries," be they religious or political, as leverage for blackmail. This book, titled simply *Hostage*, was published in 2010. The novelist depicts not only the dispossession of the self that is implied by sequestration but also the prisoner's tenacious resolve to fight with all his mental, spiritual and physical strength against a form of degradation that resembles the one inflicted on the detainees in the death camps.

Several events shook up the author and compelled him to compose this work. There was the capture of the young French man Ilan Halimi, in 2005, by a gang of vicious thugs. They tortured him to death to obtain a ransom from his family. Then an Israeli soldier, Gilad Shalit, was taken hostage by members of Hamas within the territory of the Hebrew state. He was held captive for years in a secret hideout and his abductors never allowed the Red Cross to visit him. But the incident that left the most terrifying imprint on Elie Wiesel unfolded in San Francisco three years before he wrote this novel. As he explained to the French news magazine *Le Point*, a negator of the Shoah had prepared a detailed plan to kidnap him: "He wanted to force me to declare that the Holocaust had not taken place."[27]

The novel is centered on a forty-year-old Jew from Brooklyn, Shaltiel Feigenberg, kidnapped in broad daylight in 1975 by a small group of the far left committed to the Palestinian cause. The American security forces collaborate with those of the state of Israel to liberate him. What saves the hero from death, however, is his ability to sow doubt in the mind of one of the terrorists, the Italian Luigi, on the soundness of the latter's revolutionary ideal, and to arouse within him a surge of compassion.

It would have been such a pleasure for us to acknowledge in *Hostage* another masterpiece worthy of the two preceding novels, *A Mad Desire to Dance* and *The Sondenberg Case*. A triple success for a novelist who was 83 years old at the time would have been a remarkable achievement. In my opinion, *Hostage* is clearly superior to *The Judges* and *The Time of the Uprooted*, but not quite on the level of the other two. If *Hostage* had been the first of Elie Wiesel's novels that I was reading, I would have welcomed it with unreserved admiration, because it is an exciting detective story that also contains spiritual, moral and intellectual density. But as I have already remarked, the reader cannot resist comparing each new text of a great writer with those that have preceded it, which is a way of honoring his talent. In this light, one must state that *Hostage* reveals certain weaknesses as well as elements that I would call vintage Wiesel.

The weaknesses are of a structural order. They consist of episodes which, without being unnecessary, are not linked organically enough to the novel's framework. The first describes the life of Shaltiel as a young boy during the Nazi occupation in Galicia. Granted, I understand the reasons why the novelist inserted it there. When the hero who has become a hostage resurrects through his memory his childhood in a Europe terrorized by Hitler's fury, those recollections confer on his captivity in the United States many years later a dimension of poignant irony. Is it fair that an innocent man who had suffered so much thirty-five years earlier during the Holocaust should be once again the victim of ruthless fanatics? But

---

[27] *Le Point*, section "Culture," 09/09/2010, in electronic version.

these recollections of such a sorrowful past could have been incorporated more deftly into Shaltiel's interior monologues. As Wiesel has constructed them, they tend to draw us away from the terrifying drama that the hero is living through, a drama that could degenerate into tragedy at any moment.

The author also emphasizes the games of chess that, highly gifted in this area, Shaltiel played almost daily with a very influential German officer, Fridrich von Waldenshohn. The German's passion for this game and the sincere admiration he has for the Jewish boy's talent saved the latter from the nightmare of deportation. It is possible that the novelist wanted to establish a parallelism between the situation of young Shaltiel who played with the officer to protect himself from death and the mature man he has become who exploits all his intellectual resources to induce his Italian abductor to call into question his revolutionary zeal. But I am convinced this idea would have been much more effective if Shaltiel himself had remembered these hours spent fighting for his survival as an adversary of von Waldenshohn while he was striving to use all his cunning with the terrorists to avoid being assassinated.

I would put forward the same judgment on the whole substantial episode devoted to Shaltiel's older brother, Pavel. The latter, an ardent idealist conquered by the dream of a social paradise during Stalin's reign of terror, becomes disillusioned when he realizes that behind the façade of brotherhood in the USSR looms the most criminal of tyrannies. Later, completely detoxified on the ideological level, he embraces again the Jewish faith of his youth. We have already gone down this path in the splendid *The Testament*. The big difference between the two, however, is that in the earlier novel the hero's spiritual evolution constitutes its vital centre. In *Hostage* Pavel's intense drama remains on the periphery of his brother, Shaltiel's story. Here again, I think I know what the writer intended to show us: the communist vision of a fraternal society dissipates like a mirage in the face of the shadowy forces of human nature that it could not foresee and subdue. This collapse of an ideal in the USSR is contrasted with the hideous caricature that radical left-wing terrorists make of it in New York City when they abduct Shaltiel. But the novelist could have led us to understand this comparison in a much more subtle and concise manner during one of the sequestered hero's interior monologues. Indeed, at the risk of incurring the accusation of heresy, I would maintain that the novel would have gained enormously in dramatic power if it had concentrated almost exclusively on Shaltiel's captivity and the moral triumph he achieves over his kidnappers.

Despite these weaknesses, the rest of the novel is so strong that it makes us almost forget them. A large part of this strength rests on the character of Shaltiel himself, surely one of the most winsome that Wiesel ever imagined. The hero, an extremely gifted man on the intellectual level, with a very generous heart and a delightfully whimsical imagination, is a professional storyteller. He especially enjoys telling stories to children and elderly people. The young people enchant him with their ability to feel wonder. The senior citizens melt his heart with their tears that he endeavors to convert into smiles. His spiritual teacher, One-Eyed Paritus whom we have already met in *The Judges*, a perpetual traveler in search of the elusive Messiah, inculcated upon him the primordial importance and veneration of words. During their sojourn in India, this most unusual of personalities had given him precious advice: "Celebrate words instead of scorning them, raise them to the level of prayer so that high above, the Judge of men will give them the feel of serenity."[28] Shaltiel will never forget this. Thanks to the precision, rigor and eloquence of his language, he orchestrates magnificently, during his sequestration, in his interior monologues and dialogues with his captors, a certain number of the author's essential themes. By analyzing them, we will gain a better understanding of the hero's personality.

A hostage in the hands of terrorists determined to wrest from him a declaration favorable to their cause is vulnerable because of his body. The goal of his captors is to turn it into a torture chamber. They attempt to inflict on him physical sufferings so intense that his mind will no longer function with lucidity. They hope, consequently, to suffocate it and reduce their captive to a rag, a condition just about identical to the kind that detainees in the Nazi death camps had to endure. The author describes in the following terms the torment to which Shaltiel is subjected:

> Shaltiel discovers his worst enemy: it is not his memory overflowing with events, poems and faces, nor his exacerbated sensibility, it is his body. Yes, his whole body, failing. From his head to his ears. The Arab torturer uses it perversely to weaken his resistance and destabilize his mind. Deprived of food and sleep, his eyelids weigh down on him with the heaviness of lead. His tongue sticks to his palate. His lips, torn. His head bursts. His lungs also. And

---

[28] Elie Wiesel, *Otage*, Paris: Grasset, 2010, 34; henceforth referred to as *O*.

his shoulders, his hands, his fingers are shot through with new kinds of pain. Breathing is an ordeal. (*O*, 174).

If Shaltiel had not succeeded later on in swaying Luigi, then in arousing his compassion, it is quite possible that he would have succumbed to this ordeal. Perhaps his mind would have finally yielded.

It is Shaltiel's memory that give him the strength to resist his torturers. This faculty has always had a primordial importance for Elie Wiesel. We need simply recall his novel *The Forgotten*. The hero, Elhanan Rosenbaum dreads the progressive disintegration of whole sections of his knowledge, which would lead inevitably to the shrinking of his personality since we are the total of what we have learned and lived. Shaltiel puts up, then, a fierce resistance to his abductors by drawing from his memory key moments of his existence. Among the numerous recollections that allow the storyteller to transfigure the sordid reality of his sequestration and revitalize his mind are his descriptions of the peace that would prevail during the Sabbath within his family in New York. Here is one of the most beautiful:

> When they returned home on Friday night, his father was radiant: he no longer had any health or money worries. The three candles on the table, one for each member of the family, the wine for the kiddush, the two braided breads prepared with as much skill as love by Malka, the mother-in-law: Shaltiel lived all week exclusively for those moments. It mattered little that the meal was poor: it brought all three of them together around the same table; sometimes with his cousin Arele, all savouring the little they had, united by a love that made his heart tremble: what more could they desire? (*O*, 25).

Rushing also to his rescue when he needs them are the images of his wife, Blanca, so tender, understanding and loyal, friends whom he cherishes like Nathanaël, the first pupil at the school who accepted him as a comrade, and Jonathan whose deep empathy he aroused through his talent as a storyteller, One-Eyed Paritus, his majestic spiritual teacher, and his parents who always lavished their love on him unconditionally. All these memories bring him comfort and courage in his desperate attempt not to sink into a moral and spiritual black hole. Moreover, he realizes this at a moment when he tries to assess his state as a hostage: "His mind functions, his memory, too: Shaltiel is reassured. But, in his situation, is this an advantage? Would it not be better to mix up everything, indeed, to erase everything? No. Anything but chaos or amnesia" (*O*, 145).

But in addition to the resources of his memory, what enables the storyteller to stand his ground in the face of his torturers is his intellectual integrity and his moral uprightness, qualities that are an integral part of a spiritual entity which, for lack of a better term, Elie Wiesel calls the soul. At the beginning of his sequestration, the hero wonders whether he will manage to face the increasingly brutal physical pressure that his Arab captor, Ahmed is imposing on him. He remembers Lenin's companions and distinguished Russian generals who had broken down under torture during Stalin's reign of terror. He also remembers the words of the great Jewish sage, Maimonides, according to whom to pay the ransom of an innocent hostage is an act of virtue. But despite this temptation to declare himself vanquished to make his physical pain stop, despite the permission given to him by such a great moral authority and his normal fear of death, one would say that a force unknown to him beforehand is impelling him to continue putting up an iron-clad resistance.

In the first place, Shaltiel is sustained by his conviction that torture constitutes a monstrous outrage committed against human dignity because it consists in wresting from the victim confessions in which he does not believe. Torture has as its goal the smothering of the mind under the physical pain it inflicts. This is the meaning of his reaction to the howls of hatred coming from his Arab captor: "Saltiel nods his head, his nose bloody: yes, he loves the people of Israel, but no, he has never threatened Palestinians…Where does his courage come from? Because he is innocent? He is not a hero, but… but what? He doesn't know. He only knows, between two fainting spells, that the Arab is torturing him and that torturers are never right." (*O*, 175). But there is another reason, even more essential, that explains his unbreakable will to resist. The two terrorists are intent on making him condemn Israel, the Jews of the diaspora that support it enthusiastically, and the United States that is the most faithful ally of the Hebrew state. To deny everything he stands for would represent for the storyteller a kind of spiritual self-assassination. Of course, he would recover his freedom, and his physical agony would cease right away, but he would never again be able to live with himself. Or if he continued living, it would be with a dead soul. His life in the physical sense would constitute a living death because, having repudiated his most precious values and, as a result, trampled on his integrity, he would no longer have any essential reason to exist. In such a situation, physical annihilation would be preferable. This is the meaning of his retorts to Ahmed's questions and insults. According to Shaltiel, the torturer is condemned to defeat:

-But you are a Jew?

-Yes, I am a Jew.

-And an American?

Yes, I am an American Jew.

-Linked to the Zionists and to Israel?

-Yes. Linked is the right word. Linked through my soul.

-Why through your soul?

-To tell you that you can strike my body, wound it and even crush it, but my soul remains free, beyond your reach. You will never imprison it. (O, 273)

In comparison to this nobility, terrorism as it is embodied by Ahmed and Luigi seems repugnant, Of the two, Ahmed especially is the one who fills one with horror. As a novelist who strives to be equitable, Elie Wiesel is anxious to make us understand the reasons that could have led the fanatical Arab to practice cruelty systematically to the point of dehumanizing himself. He and his family stagnated in refugee camps; they were more than uprooted; they were devoid of a nationality, social and political dregs that no country wanted. Several members of his family were killed in confrontations with the state of Israel. Here are legitimate motives for his anger. But to leap from genuine grievances to a melodramatization of history and a belief that all Jews are responsible for the misery of Palestinian refugees is completely reprehensible, yet Ahmed makes this leap quickly. With his rigid if not simplistic mind, Ahmed has allowed himself to be poisoned by his hatred of Jews to the point that not only does his hatred possess him, it devours him. And scaling the heights of madness, he invokes Islam in a perverted form to justify his need to kill and destroy. This terrorist is even more the prisoner of his antisemitism than Shaltiel is his hostage. If he no longer had any hatred to vomit out, he would no longer have any reason to live. Here is how the novelist describes him: "According to him, the Jewish infidels would survive only to be chastised by Allah and oppressed by his devoted servants. They were surely the cause of all the evil that bears down on the world. Transgression incarnated, impurity personified, this is what they are. The vermin of the earth, the cancer of society, the enemies of peace, the negation of happiness, it is them again. (*O*, 69-70)

Fortunately for Shaltiel, the other abductor, Luigi is not corrupted by this visceral fanaticism. His kind appears in an intellectual form, which means that the Italian is a philosopher despite himself. As the storyteller observes, for a thinker reality cannot be reduced to a melodrama where the actors of history belong either to the camp of Good or to the camp of Evil. History is composed of a whole gamut of nuances, and the thinker knows this. This knowledge will perhaps prevent him from being a killer: "Shaltiel senses that he has less to fear from the Italian than from the Arab. He must surely question himself about the objective necessity of this adventure. He must have read Pindar and Nietzsche, Hölderlin and Wittgenstein. A philosopher does not become an executioner, he is incapable of being one" (*O*, 153). The storyteller is going to exploit his brilliant intuition to the limits. During several conversations with Luigi, he will succeed in undermining the foundations of the Italian's terrorist ideology. He will do so by demonstrating to his captor that his extreme left-wing engagement is based on a superstructure of illusions, and that his true personality resides elsewhere.

But before being able to go ahead with this project, Shaltiel must listen attentively to the Italian's description of the road he travelled to become a terrorist. He was born in a well-to-do family, and his father was a Mussolini fascist and proud of it. In other words, the latter espoused an ideology that exalted brute force, the submission of the individual to the state, contempt for the weak and the belief in a superior race. Luigi's adherence to the radical left represented, then, the revolt of a son nauseated by his father's personality and values. The Italian abductor's dilemma stems from the fact that by wanting to exorcize the spirit of a father he considers obnoxious he latches on to a ruthless idealism that leads more or less to the same result: contempt for and destruction of human life. Luigi can assert as much as he likes before Shaltiel that he is neither antisemitic nor cruel. His ideology drags him down in that direction because of his engagement in favor of Palestinian terrorists.

Luigi execrates human nature for its acts of oppression, its generalized corruption, its cowardly compromises, its hypocrisy and lies to such an extent that he is ready to set fire to the world to purge it of all its evil. He will adhere, consequently, to any terrorist organization that strives to revolutionize history through violence. Hence his career as an ideological hitchhiker. Before committing himself to the Palestinian cause, he sympathized with the Baader-Meinhoff gang in Germany and the Red Brigades in Italy. Assassinating innocent people to annihilate Evil does not frighten him in the least, because, as he explains to his Jewish interlocutor, innocence does not serve any purpose in ameliorating an intrinsically rotten human condition. He dares even refer to the Holocaust to support this monstrous idea. When he tries that, the storyteller attacks Luigi with a kind of saintly indignation. Throwing caution to the winds, indifferent now to his own personal safety, seething with fury, he accuses his captor point blank of being a piece of scum who plays at being a revolutionary to blow up his ego sky high. His diatribe deserves to be quoted in its entirety:

How dare you! You are using Jewish suffering to increase it! Have you not, then, understood anything? You reproach History for its blunders, and you damn it for its ignominious acts! You, an anarchist? A nihilist? You are nothing but a miserable adventurer greedy for power! You attribute your so-called revolutionary motives to my people's tragedy, whereas, by means of the Jew that I am, you are ready to contribute to it! It is not enough for you that your father is guilty, that he nourished the hatred that made him important, powerful and tyrannical, you still want to resemble him! Come on, shake yourself, get rid of your mental aberrations! Wake up from your supposedly intellectual wild imaginings! (*O*, 297).

And, as the coup de grace to clobber Luigi, Shaltiel shows him a photo of his father bearing on his wrist the number of the death camp where he had been a prisoner.

The next day, Shaltiel finishes his undermining work. Knowing that the Italian is fond of stories, he relates one that contains an allegory. A blind king does not recover his eyesight until he sheds tears for the first time. The pain he has just experienced allows him to finally understand the sorrows of his subjects and to feel compassion for them. Beforehand his kingdom had been nothing more than an abstraction for him. Now it is a place filled with human beings in need of consolation. The Monarch finally realizes that each one of his subjects is an individual who contains in himself an infinitely precious universe. As soon as he grasps this truth, he becomes a genuine father for his people. Being very perspicacious, Luigi does not fail to uncover the moral of his story. A deeply human conception of existence will replace his abstract and inhuman view of history. It will manifest itself by a surge of compassion. He will finally untie the ropes that had bound Shaltiel's wrists and ankles and will let him escape, while telling him: "All this, I'm doing it for your father" (*O*, 390). Luigi knows that his unselfish decision will carry with it very dangerous consequences for him, but one would say that a categorical imperative rising from the depths of his being compels him to perform this act.

Thus, in his way, and no doubt without his being aware of it, Luigi incarnates the Messiah for the first time in his life. Before making this redeeming gesture, he seemed to vacillate. Shaltiel had succeeded in undermining his ideological foundation, but would that have been sufficient for him to perform an act that was in flagrant contradiction to everything he thought he believed in? The storyteller can sense this radical change in Luigi even before it occurs. He expresses this in the form of a question: "Could it be, then, that every human being feels attracted to what is good while at the same time is drawn by curiosity to what is evil? A trace of Cain like any other, in parallel to and sometimes in conflict with that of Abel?" (*O*, 388). Backed up against the wall by Shaltiel's eloquence and passion, Luigi rids himself of his obnoxious ideology, of his false historic persona and finally allows his heart to speak. By choosing to be the liberator of his hostage, his former abductor brings him a second gift, as precious as his freedom. Thanks to Luigi's gesture, Shaltiel will be able to create an inheritor with his wife Blanca. Having had a brush with death, Shaltiel has a dazzling intuition. He realizes that to renew the love he bore his wife in the past and to draw them closer to one another in the future, they will have to produce children. This act will be the best possible homage they can offer to life. Now that he is a free man, he will be able to do so. This is not one of the least important of the gifts that Luigi offers Shaltiel before disappearing.

BY WAY OF CONCLUSION
THE MESSIAH IS ALL OF US

L uigi's gesture, as noble as it is unexpected, as well as the vote of confidence that Doriel, Yedidyah, Gamliel and Claudia give to life, illustrate, each one in his or her way, their conviction that human relationships represent the supreme value. Shaltiel believes this fervently, too, because he strove despite his physical suffering to humanize his Italian captor. Now, wishing to link one's existence to that of another individual means assuming an immense responsibility towards him/her. The one that Malkiel accepts in *The Forgotten* is of a different nature but implies the same certitude that we do not live exclusively for ourselves. The transfusion of memory that Malkiel effects from his father's mind to his own testifies to his resolve to accomplish for Elhanan Rosenbaum this messianic mission. Unable to revitalize the latter's mind, his son, Malkiel, will guarantee his father a posthumous existence by creating a family with Tamar and by inserting all of his future children within the immemorial history of the Jewish people. The same holds true for many other heroes in Elie Wiesel's novels. Obviously, the first two in *Dawn* and *Day* go the wrong way. But the others, whether they be Michael in *The Town Beyond the Wall*, Gavriel in *The Gates of the Forest*, David in *A Beggar in Jerusalem*, Paltiel Kossover in *The Testament*, the old vagabond in *The Oath*, the anonymous protagonist in *The Fifth Son* or Raphaël in *Twilight*, all accept, often in sorrowful or even tragic circumstances, to fully assume their responsibilities as Jews by coming to their fellow man's rescue. Without always proclaiming this explicitly, they affirm by their conduct that the Messiah is all of us.

The whole of the writer's oeuvre orchestrates this theme. We discover a particularly moving manifestation of it in his books with a religious orientation devoted to the great personages of Judaism, real or legendary, from the biblical prophets and the venerable sages of the Talmud to the Hassidic rabbis of the 18th century. The author of the two volumes titled *Hassidic Celebrations*, always had a special predilection for the Hassidim. One can understand this. The spiritual leaders of so many Jewish communities threatened by persecutions in that period in Europe brought their coreligionists courage and comfort by propagating a new interpretation of the Jewish faith. For them it is a fraternal celebration in a spirit of love and joy. It suffices that each one of us welcomes the other with kindness for the Savior to appear in the relationship. Since we all possess "strange powers" according to the Hassidim, it behooves us to deploy them in favor of our sisters and brothers to "modify the course of History" and shorten the road leading us from the exile to the kingdom.

In addition to persuading their coreligionists that they are indispensable for the coming of the Messiah, the Hassidic masters found several other ways of enhancing their worth in their own eyes. They affirm that their fellow Jews are integral components of Israel's eternal memory. The Becht, one of the most illustrious rabbis in central Europe in the 18th century, reminded his flock that there existed an organic solidarity between them and their ancestors of biblical times: "All that they have done, they have done for us and in our name; and all that we undertake is for them and in their name that we undertake it."[29] The spiritual guides also emphasize the immediate accessibility of God for His children. Since He is, He reveals himself in "every being, in every quiver and every fragment of being" (*CH*, 20). Being One, He remains the same for all His creatures who aspire towards Him, whatever may be the paths they take in trying to approach Him.

This accessibility of God explains the singular relationships that can develop between Him and His creatures. Certain Hassidic masters like Rabbi Levi-Yitzhak of Berditchev entertain with the Creator a friendship where aggressiveness, pugnacity and love are indissolubly connected. Once, the Rabbi reproached God in very vehement terms for His disloyalty towards the people with whom He had concluded a sacred alliance: "Remember: on Mount Sinai You were walking around with your Torah

---

[29] Elie Wiesel, *Célébration hassidique* II, Paris : Éditions du Seuil, 1981, 14; henceforth referred to as *CH*.

like a merchant who can't manage to get rid of his rotten apples. You proposed Your commandments to all the nations who turned away, all of them, with contempt. Israel was the only one who declared itself ready to accept them, to accept You. Where is its reward?" (*CH*, 53). Another time, the Rabbi uttered this devastating statement: "Know that if Your reign does not bring grace, charity, we will conclude that You are seated on a throne of imposture." (*CH*, 55).

We see the same aggressiveness, the same boldness in Elie Wiesel and certain of his protagonists. But they come to terms with the God of Israel's impenetrable silence by transforming it. Instead of reigning over the cosmos like a presence exterior to humanity and independent from it, the novelist and certain of his heroes internalize God. The God of Israel becomes essentially anthropomorphic. He reveals His presence as the irrepressible spiritual force within the heart of our human condition. A force that compels us to transcend ourselves in an incessant and untiring war waged against the brute coiled up in the obscure depths of our being. Or, to use another image, God, for the author of *A Mad Desire to Dance*, is a kind of hyper-powerful spiritual hydro-electric station that we carry within ourselves, to which we can connect to fully develop our loftiest aspirations. The energy that we draw from this source allows us to become heroes without striking up romantic and ostentatious poses. Thus, God manifests Himself in the fraternal relationships that men and women sustain with one another. We are not far from the central concept of the philosophy of another great Jewish thinker, Emmanuel Lévinas. The latter believed that the approach of the Other in his unfathomable mystery and the vulnerability of his face awakens in the subject the intuition of the infinite. Consequently, the human condition represents a paradox. We are finite vehicles carrying a spiritual content that is infinitely greater than our ability to conceive it. For Lévinas, the trace of the infinite appears in the ethical relationship and remains inseparable from it. Elie Wiesel would not disavow this idea.

It seems to me that Elie Wiesel himself authorizes this interpretation. In November 1998 I had the pleasure and the honor of conversing with the author about the book that I was going to devote to his novels. During a very lively and friendly conversation, I asked him the following question: "Elie, if you had not maintained on many occasions in your various writings that you believe in God, I would have sworn that for you God was nothing more than the extrapolation to the infinite of the most noble aspirations in man." And his enthusiastic response was: "But that's exactly it!"

Now, to carry the image of God within oneself implies immense responsibilities. And the author has always done his utmost to remain worthy of his own demanding moral standards. As I mentioned in the Preface, convinced like many of his own characters that it was necessary to come to the rescue of men and women plunged in affliction, Elie Wiesel went to Nicaragua to support the persecuted Indian tribes. He bore witness in favor of the Jewish "Refuseniks" in the former USSR, just as he became the spokesman for the victims in Cambodia of the genocidal enterprise of the monstrous Pol Pot.

After the Second World War the winner of the Nobel Prize for Peace had entertained the hope that the human species would never again plummet into the abyss of cruelty and madness to which armed conflicts inevitably lead. Of course, this was an illusory hope. And yet, despite his lucidity concerning human nature, the novelist, just like many of his protagonists, has always refused to give up. He has always rejected despair even when overwhelming evidence provided by history seemed to justify such an attitude. He was convinced that some individuals, at least, would always be able to draw from their reservoir of spiritual energy that one can call God, enough strength to transcend, in certain circumstances, their fragile beings and conduct themselves as Messiahs towards their fellow man and woman. Being conscious of the presence of God within man, Elie Wiesel always preferred to light a candle rather than curse the darkness.

SELECTED BIBLIOGRAPHY

WORKS BY ELIE WIESEL

La Nuit. Préface by François Mauriac. Paris : Éditions de Minuit, 1958; reprinted. 1995. A new version (parallel to the American reedition) takes into account the issue of the original Yiddish manuscript. It is obvious that this original text was considerably revised in 1958 by Raymond Lindon's publishing house.

L'Aube. Paris : Éditions du Seuil, 1960; reprinted coll. Points, 1995.

Le Jour. Paris : Éditions du Seuil, 1961; reprinted. 1996.

La Ville de la chance. Paris : Éditions du Seuil, 1962; reprinted. 1968.

Les Portes de la forêt. Paris : Éditions du Seuil, 1964; reprinted coll. Points, 1985.

Les Juifs du silence. Paris : Éditions du Seuil, 1966; reprinted 1986.

Zalmen ou la folie de Dieu. Paris : Éditions du Seuil, 1968.

Le Mendiant de Jérusalem. Paris : Éditions du Seuil, 1968; reprinted coll. Points, 1983.

Entre deux soleils. Paris : Les Éditions du Seuil, 1970; reprinted 1986.

Célébration hassidique : portraits et légendes. Paris : Éditions du Seuil, 1972; reprinted coll. Points, 1986.

Le Serment de Kolvilàg. Paris : Les Éditions du Seuil, 1973; reprinted 1986.

Célébration biblique : portraits et légendes Paris : Les Éditions du Seuil, 1975; reprinted coll. Points, 1991.

Un Juif, aujourd'hui. Paris : Les Éditions du Seuil, 1977; reprinted 1986.

Le Procès de Shamgorod, tel qu'il se déroula le 25 février 1649. Paris: Les Éditions du Seuil, 1979.

Le Testament d'un poète juif assassiné. Paris : Les Éditions du Seuil, 1980.

Contre la mélancolie : Célébration hassidique II. Paris : Les Éditions du Seuil, 1981.

Paroles d'étrangers. Paris : Les Éditions du Seuil, 1982.

Le Cinquième fils. Paris : Éditions Grasset et Fasquelle, 1983; reprinted 1987.

Signes d'exode. Paris : Éditions Grasset et Fasquelle/coll. Figures, 1985.

Discours d'Oslo. Paris : Éditions Grasset et Fasquelle, 1987.

Le Crépuscule, au loin. Paris : Éditions Grasset et Fasquelle, 1987; reprinted. coll. Livres de Poche, 1988.

L'Oublié. Paris : Éditions du Seuil, 1989; reprinted coll. Points, 1991.

Silences et mémoire d'hommes. Paris :Les Éditions du Seuil, 1989.

Célébration talmudique : portraits et légendes. Paris : Les Éditions du Seuil, 1991.

Tous les fleuves vont à la mer : Mémoires 1. Paris : Les Éditions du Seuil, 1994.

Et la mer n'est pas remplie : Mémoires 2. Paris : Les Éditions du Seuil, 1996.

Célébration prophétique : portraits et légendes. Paris : Éditions du Seuil, 1998.

Les Juges. Paris : Les Éditions du Seuil, 1999.

Le Temps des déracinés. Paris : Les Éditions du Seuil, 2003.

Un désir fou de danser. Paris : Les Éditions du Seuil, 2006.

Le Cas Sonderberg. Paris : Grasset, 2008.

Otage. Paris : Grasset, 2010.

Cœur Ouvert. Paris : Flammarion, 2011.

STUDIES ON ELIE WIESEL'S OEUVRE

Berenbaum, Michael. *The Vision of the Void: Theological Reflections on the Works of Elie Wiesel*. Middletown, Connecticut: Wesleyan University Press, 1979.

Brown, Robert McAfee. *Elie Wiesel: Messenger to All Humanity*. Notre Dame: University of Notre Dame Press, 1983.

Engel, Vincent. *Fou de Dieu ou Dieu des Fous : l'œuvre tragique d'Élie Wiesel*. Brussels : De Boeck-Wesmael, 1989.

Estess, Ted L. *Elie Wiesel*. New York : Unger, 1980.

Fine, Ellen S. *Legacy of Night: The Literary Universe of Elie Wiesel*. Albany: State University of New York Press, 1982.

Friedemann, Joë. *Le Rire dans l'univers tragique d'Elie Wiesel*. Paris : Nizet, 1981.

Saint-Chéron, Philippe-Michaël de. *Elie Wiesel, pèlerin de la mémoire*. Paris : Plon, 1994.

Sibelman, Simon P. *Silence in the novels of Elie Wiesel*. New York: St. Martin's Press, 1995.

Walker, Graham B., Jr. *Elie Wiesel: A Challenge to Theology*. London: McFarland, 1988.

ARTICLES ON ELIE WIESEL

Davis, Colin. "Understanding the Concentration Camps: Elie Wiesel's *La Nuit* and Jorge Semprun's *Quel Beau Dimanche!*". *Australian Journal of French Studies* 28 (1991) : 291-303.

Fine, Ellen. « Dialogue with Elie Wiesel". *Centerpoint: A Journal of Interdisciplinary Studies* (Autumn, 1980): 19-25.

Friedman, Maurice. "Elie Wiesel's Messianism of the Unredeemed". *Judaism* 38 (1989): 310-319.

Friedman, Maurice. "Elie Wiesel: The Job of Auschwitz". *The Hidden Human Image*. New York: Dell, 1974, 106-34.

Garber, Frederick. "The Art of Elie Wiesel". *Judaism*22 (1973): 301-08.

Idinopulous, Thomas A. "The Holocaust in the Stories of Elie Wiesel". *Soundings* 60 (1972): 200-215.

Leviant, Curt. "Elie Wiesel: A Soul on Fire". *Saturday Review* 31 (January 1970):25-28.

Lovsky, F. "Elie Wiesel, compagnon des morts d'Israël ». *Foi et Vie* 68 (1968) : 36-58.

Nehr, André. « Le Silence et l'être : Elie Wiesel ». *L'Exil de la parole : du silence biblique au silence d'Auschwitz*. Paris : Éditions du Seuil, 1970, 228-45.

Rosmarin, Léonard. « Marxisme et messianisme dans *Le Testament d'un poète juif assassiné* d'Élie Wiesel ». *Dalhousie French Studies* 64 (Autumn 2003) : 25-32.

Rosmarin, Léonard. « Et Dieu dans tout cela? Réflexions sur l'œuvre d'Elie Wiesel ». *Hekateia* 2 (2003) :165-84.

Rubenstein, Richard. « Job and Auschwitz ». *Union Seminary Quarterly Review,* vol. XXV, no. 4 (Summer 1970): 420-30.

Sherwin, Byron. "Elie Wiesel and Jewish Theology". *Judaism*18 (1969): 39-52.

Sibelman, Simon P. "The Dialogue of Peniel: Elie Wiesel's *Les Portes de la forêt* and Genesis 32 :23-33 ». *The French Review* 61 (1988): 747-57.

Simon, Pierre-Henri. "*Le Mendiant de Jérusalem* ». *Le Monde* (November 23, 1968).

INDEX

211